MW01009727

THE WORLD'S BEST NATIONAL PARKS IN 500 WALKS

Hiking routes and rambles through nature's most enticing environments

MARY CAPERTON MORTON

Foreword by Heather Anderson

THUNDER BAY
P · R · E · S · S
San Diego, California

Thunder Bay Press
An imprint of Printers Row Publishing Group
9717 Pacific Heights Blvd, San Diego, CA 92121
www.thunderbaybooks.com • mail@thunderbaybooks.com

Printers Row Publishing Group is a division of Readerlink Distribution Services, LLC. Thunder Bay Press is a registered trademark of Readerlink Distribution Services, LLC.

Correspondence regarding the content of this book should be sent to Thunder Bay Press, Editorial Department, at the above address. Author, illustration, and rights inquiries should be addressed to The Bright Press at the address below.

This book was conceived, designed, and produced by
The Bright Press, an imprint of The Quarto Group
1 Triptych Place, London
SE1 9SH
United Kingdom
T (0)20 7700 6700

www.quarto.com

Thunder Bay Press
Publisher: Peter Norton
Associate Publisher: Ana Parker
Art Director: Charles McStravick
Acquisitions Editor: Kathryn Chipinka Dalby
Editor: Dan Mansfield

The Bright Press
Publisher: James Evans
Editorial Director: Isheeta Mustafi
Managing Editor: Jacqui Sayers
Art Director: James Lawrence
Designer: Tony Seddon
Cover design: Emily Nazer
Picture Researcher: Charlotte Rivers
Project Editor: Rica Dearman
Senior Editor: Caroline Elliker

Library of Congress Control Number: 2021940243

ISBN: 978-1-64517-628-2

Printed in Malaysia

28 27 26 25 24 3 4 5 6 7

RIGHT An ancient Roman-era footpath runs through Turkey's Köprülü Canyon.

CONTENTS

FOREWORD
4

INTRODUCTION
5

CHAPTER ONE
NORTH AMERICA
8

CHAPTER TWO
SOUTH AMERICA
122

CHAPTER THREE
EUROPE
150

CHAPTER FOUR
AFRICA AND THE MIDDLE EAST
262

CHAPTER FIVE
ASIA
304

CHAPTER SIX
AUSTRALASIA
354

INDEX
394

IMAGE CREDITS
400

FOREWORD

I visited my first national park when I was a teenager: Sleeping Bear Dunes. The significance of the national park was not something I understood then, but a few years later, within Grand Canyon National Park, I sensed the enormity of the wildness on Earth. I began to see what would be lost without the protection of those park boundaries.

By the time I became a park ranger at Glacier National Park, I fully understood the importance of preservation and the vast array of landscapes that national parks around the world protected. I began hiking as a hobby, but it quickly became an obsession and eventually a life purpose, which has taken me on myriad treks often within national parks—dozens of which are included in *The World's Best National Parks in 500 Walks*. I've completed long-distance treks measuring thousands of miles and I've set records for time on some of these. I have been named a National Geographic Adventurer of the Year and authored several books about my experiences.

Mary Caperton Morton pulls together a tremendous range of walks, from the national parks of the American West and the volcanic heart of Africa to the great walks of New Zealand—treks certain to inspire exploration and a chance to forge connections which lead to concern for preservation.

As David Brower perfectly stated: "The wild places are where we began. When they end, so do we."

Heather Anderson

INTRODUCTION

Every morning, the sun rises on a slumbering supervolcano in northwest Wyoming, illuminating rainbow-hued geothermal pools and gushing geysers, as vast herds of bison and elk graze in wildflower meadows, circled by packs of wolves and lone grizzly bears. This unique landscape and its abundant wildlife still exist thanks to an act passed on March 1, 1872, that crowned Yellowstone National Park as the world's first national park.

Nearly 150 years later, "America's best idea" to protect and celebrate natural landscapes has gone global and more than 4,000 national parks and preserves can be found across every continent. Millions of people visit these parks each year to revel in the spectacular grandeur of Mother Nature.

The World's Best National Parks in 500 Walks is the perfect inspiration for every explorer, from the armchair traveler to the veteran hiker, with full-color photos and vivid descriptions of some of the world's most spectacular hiking trails. The book begins in North America, and then moves across the western hemisphere to Central and South America before skipping across the Atlantic Ocean to Europe and Africa, then Asia and Australasia. National parks on island territories are grouped geographically, rather than politically, since you're more likely to visit the Canary Islands on a trip to Africa than a trip to Spain. →

LEFT Backpacking in Yellowstone National Park, one of North America's premier wilderness areas.

The 500 hikes are spread out among 336 national parks. Some parks are represented by multiple hikes of varying intensities, ranging from short, scenic strolls to multiday backpacking trips. Which hikes you choose and how far you go will depend on your level of fitness and experience. There are route descriptions for all hikes and the longer entries include basic maps—but be sure to obtain more detailed maps before setting off.

Check with a park ranger about current trail conditions, local rules and customs, and whether you need a permit or a guide. It's important to honor the seven principles of Leave No Trace ethics to minimize your impact on the landscape. Also, educate yourself about the indigenous history of the area before your hike. Some parks are centered on sacred homelands and the indigenous stewards of the land were often forcibly removed to make way for tourists and development—only very recently is this dark history being acknowledged. Some parks are partnering with local tribes to restore their rights and access to their homelands, but a lot of work remains to repair tribal relationships. Many modern trails follow ancient footpaths, and honoring this history is an important part of respecting the landscape.

I started hiking in college, when I adopted a young, hyperactive border collie mix and realized that both of us greatly benefited from daily walks. Over the next fifteen years, those walks evolved into hikes, backpacking trips, and mountaineering expeditions. I've hiked most of the North American trails in this book and a few of the international hikes as well. I average twenty-five trail miles a week or a hundred miles a month. At this rate, I'll walk enough miles to circle the globe before I turn forty.

LEFT AND RIGHT The Vanoise Massif mountain range in the Western Alps of southeastern France.

On every hike, I bring a backpack with the ten essentials: navigation (map, GPS, compass), first-aid kit, sun protection, shelter (tarp or emergency blanket), knife, headlamp, fire starter, extra food, water and water filter, and extra warm and waterproof clothing. The deeper you get into the backcountry, the more self-sufficient you need to be. I've taken courses on wilderness survival and wilderness medicine (I am a certified Wilderness First Responder)—and I always carry a satellite communication device for emergencies.

Be prepared—but don't be intimidated. Hiking is simply walking and every mountain is climbed one step at a time. In many thousands of trail miles, I've never been seriously injured, lost, or threatened. My experience on a search-and-rescue team in Montana taught me that the most important safety net is to tell somebody you trust where you're going and when you'll be back.

Whether you're looking for an easy stroll on a boardwalk to peer into the turquoise geothermal depths of Yellowstone's Abyss Pool or to embark on a multiday trek through prime grizzly bear habitat, *The World's Best National Parks in 500 Walks* is sure to inspire you to lace up your hiking boots and see more of the world—and maybe even circle the globe—on your own two feet.

Mary Caperton Morton

On top of Cloud's Rest, a side trip off the John Muir Trail in Yosemite National Park.

AKA The Blonde Coyote

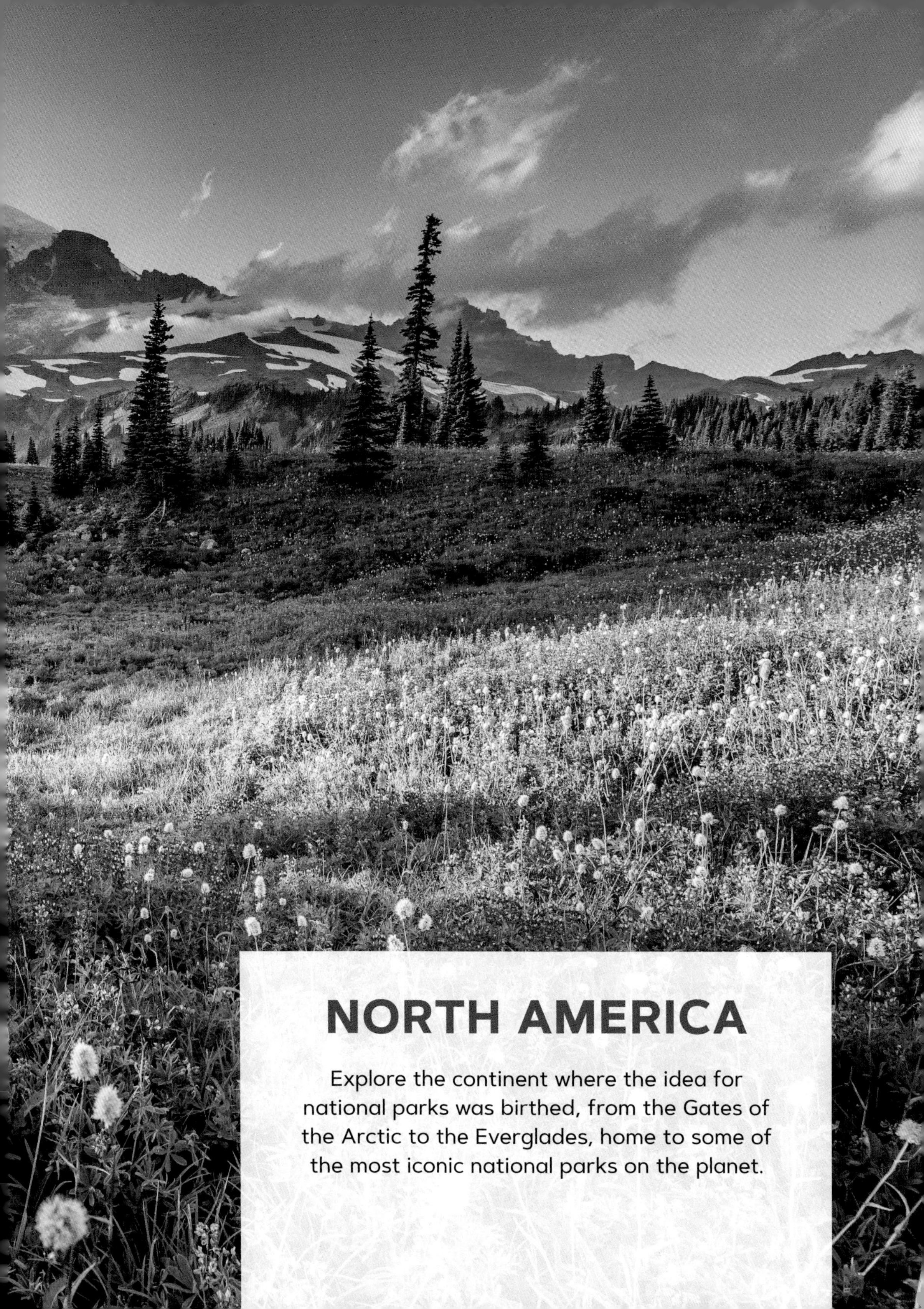

NORTH AMERICA

Explore the continent where the idea for national parks was birthed, from the Gates of the Arctic to the Everglades, home to some of the most iconic national parks on the planet.

1

King's Throne Peak Trail

KLUANE NATIONAL PARK AND RESERVE

YUKON

Kluane National Park and Reserve is all about the peaks and includes the country's highest point: 19,550-foot Mount Logan. It's best left to high-altitude mountaineers, but mere mortals can instead tackle the King's Throne. The trail starts at Kathleen Lake and gains over 4,500 feet of elevation on its 4-mile route to the summit at 6,530 feet. Halfway up you'll reach a rocky amphitheater that is the seat of the King's Throne—a good stopping point with excellent views.

2

Rainforest Figure Eight

PACIFIC RIM NATIONAL PARK AND RESERVE

BRITISH COLUMBIA

When you visit this national park on the coast of Vancouver Island, pack your rain gear, as the area gets drenched by over 100 inches of rain a year. But if you are properly prepared, wet weather is no reason to avoid the park. On this easy 2-mile double loop, raised boardwalks keep your feet out of the mud, while informational signs tell you about the area's plants and animals. The most enchanting plants are some of the smallest: lichens and mosses festoon the forest, decorating nearly every branch.

3

West Coast Trail

PACIFIC RIM NATIONAL PARK RESERVE

BRITISH COLUMBIA

Experienced backpackers up for a classic British Columbian adventure should consider tackling the West Coast Trail, a weeklong 47-mile coastal trek between Port Renfrew and Bamfield. The challenging route alternates between rocky beaches and rainforests, requiring multiple river crossings and ladder climbs as it follows an abandoned lighthouse telegraph line. Permits are available between May and September.

4

Iceline Trail

YOHO NATIONAL PARK

BRITISH COLUMBIA

This stunning loop trail starts with the magnificent Takakkaw Falls—named for an expression of awe in Cree. It spills out of the meltwater from the Daly Glacier and falls for more than 1,200 feet to the valley floor, making it the second-highest waterfall in Canada. The trail then climbs up to the Iceline Shelf, overlooking the Yoho and Little Yoho Valleys and surrounding glacier-dotted peaks. For most of the 13-mile loop, you'll hear Takakkaw thundering across the valley.

LEFT Spectacular views of Mount Logan and Kathleen Lake await on the King's Throne Peak Trail.

ABOVE The dog-friendly Iceline Trail offers scenic vistas of glaciers and valleys.

5

Walcott Quarry

YOHO NATIONAL PARK

BRITISH COLUMBIA

Visit a famous fossil location, set on a ridge between Wapta Mountain and Mount Field.

DISTANCE
12.5 miles, elevation gain 2,700 feet

START
Yoho National Park Visitor Center in the town of Field

DIFFICULTY
Moderate

SEASON
Tours offered July to September

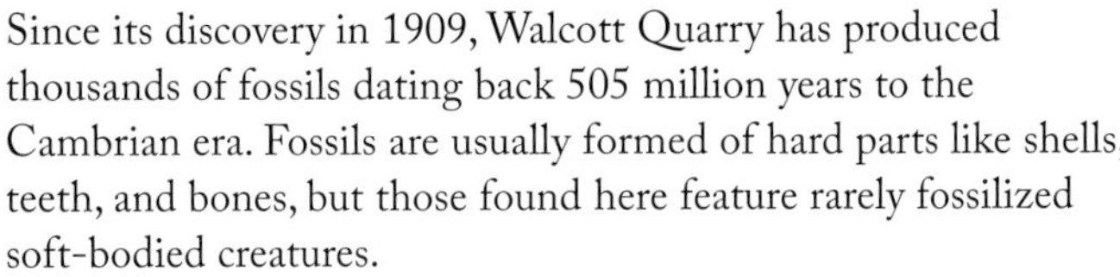

Since its discovery in 1909, Walcott Quarry has produced thousands of fossils dating back 505 million years to the Cambrian era. Fossils are usually formed of hard parts like shells, teeth, and bones, but those found here feature rarely fossilized soft-bodied creatures.

To visit Walcott Quarry, you must go with an interpretive guide through Parks Canada or the Burgess Shale Geoscience Foundation. The hike is rigorous but spectacular, with views of Yoho Lake, Emerald Lake, Hidden Lake, and the dramatically glaciated Presidential Mountains.

You'll be able to sift through the broken layers of shale at the quarry to look for fossils. Just don't pocket any! More than 15,000 specimens collected at this site are stored in the archives at the Smithsonian, but there are still many more to find.

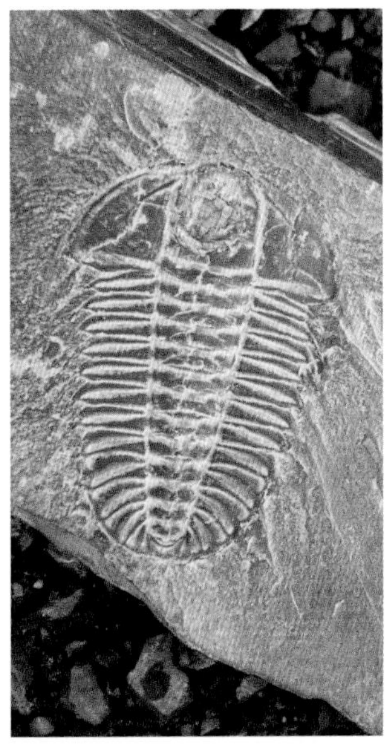

LEFT A trilobite fossil found at Walcott Quarry.

ABOVE RIGHT The view from Burgess Pass when visiting Walcott Quarry.

BELOW RIGHT Searching for fossils at Walcott.

Astotin Lakeview Trail

ELK ISLAND NATIONAL PARK

ALBERTA

Wapiti may be the stars of Elk Island, but herds of bison, moose, mule deer, and white-tailed deer all converge to make up the densest population of hoofed mammals in Canada. Black bears, lynx, and wolves are also seen here, along with more than 250 bird species that either live in or migrate through the park. See how many species you can spot on this partially paved 2.5-mile loop on Astotin Lake's shoreline.

7

Skyline Trail

JASPER NATIONAL PARK

ALBERTA

Marvel at panoramic views on one of the highest and most scenic treks in the Canadian Rockies.

- **DISTANCE**
  27 miles
- **START**
  Maligne Lake or Signal Mountain trailheads
- **DIFFICULTY**
  Moderate
- **SEASON**
  July to September; wildflowers peak in August

The well-maintained, well-graded Skyline Trail runs along the crest of the mountains for 27 miles between Maligne Lake and Signal Mountain. Most of the route soars above the treeline, providing outstanding views of the surrounding mountains and the park's famous Icefields Parkway.

Most people complete the trek in two to four days, hopscotching between designated camping areas along the route. Campsites come with bear lockers to store your food, running water, and outhouses. The trail can be hiked in either direction, but the elevation gain is more moderate if you start from the Maligne Lake trailhead and hike north.

8

Valley of the Five Lakes Loop

JASPER NATIONAL PARK

ALBERTA

The Canadian Rockies are famous for their vividly blue lakes and waterways, caused by the erosive power of glaciers that grind rocks into fine powder. Suspended in water, this fine dust reflects sunlight, generating striking shades of blue and green. This easy 3-mile loop takes you past five lakes, all in slightly different shades of aquamarine due to their varying depths.

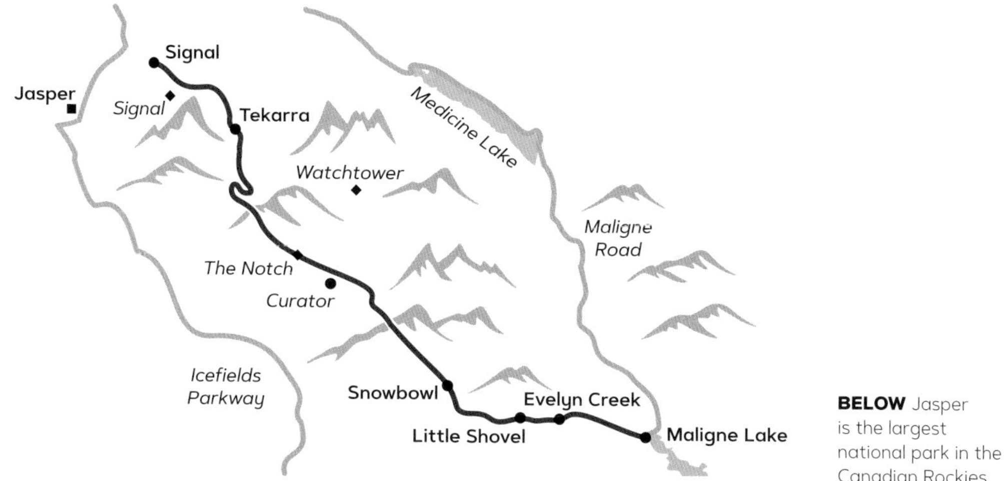

BELOW Jasper is the largest national park in the Canadian Rockies.

ABOVE You'll need skis, snowshoes, and/or ice-traction devices to hike along Lake Louise in winter.

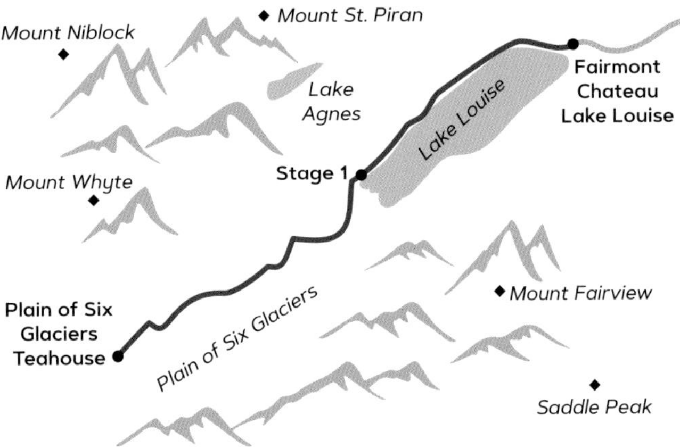

9

Lake Louise Lakefront Trail

BANFF NATIONAL PARK

ALBERTA

Cast your eyes upon a turquoise lake against a striking backdrop of snowcapped peaks.

DISTANCE
6.8 miles round trip to teahouse, elevation gain 1,215 feet

START
Fairmont Chateau Lake Louise

DIFFICULTY
Easy and partially wheelchair accessible around lake, moderate to teahouse

SEASON
Year-round; the teahouse is open June to October

An easy, partially paved trail starts at the grand Fairmont Chateau Lake Louise on the east end of the long, narrow lake and follows the northern shore. You can continue hiking to the west end of the lake on the Plain of Six Glaciers, which leads to the Plain of Six Glaciers Teahouse—a backcountry refuge that has served fine loose-leaf teas to hikers since 1924.

Lake Louise is also a ski resort and is accessible year-round; the area receives prodigious amounts of snow in the winter.

10

Tunnel Mountain Trail

BANFF NATIONAL PARK

ALBERTA

This 2.8-mile out-and-back hike starts in downtown Banff. Well-graded switchbacks make easy work of the almost 900-foot elevation gain, ending at an overlook of picturesque Banff and the surrounding mountains. You can hike this trail in winter, but you may need ice-traction devices on your boots. Fun fact: Tunnel Mountain has no tunnel. The Canadian Pacific Railway found a cheaper way around the mountain, but the name stuck.

11

Salt Pan Lake Trail

WOOD BUFFALO NATIONAL PARK

ALBERTA

Wood Buffalo National Park is the largest national park in Canada and the second-largest national park in the world—it's bigger than Switzerland! The park protects the world's largest herd of wood buffalo, a northern subspecies of the American bison. The 4.5-mile Salt Pan Lake Trail follows a gentle slope to the top of an escarpment, providing excellent views of the Northern Boreal Plains. You may spot buffaloes, wolves, moose, or whooping cranes.

12

Bear's Hump Trail

WATERTON LAKES NATIONAL PARK

ALBERTA

This national park sits just over the U.S.–Canada border from Glacier National Park. Together, the two parks form the Waterton–Glacier International Peace Park. No glaciers remain in Waterton, but you can see their handiwork in ice-carved features like glacial troughs, hanging valleys, and cirques. To get a bird's-eye view of these, hike up the Bear's Hump, a short but steep trail that leaves from the Waterton Lakes Visitor Center. The trail switchbacks up the flank of Mount Crandell to a craggy outcrop that indigenous people thought resembled the muscled hump on a grizzly bear's back.

RIGHT Take in the incredible glacial features on the Bear's Hump Trail.

13

Continental Divide Trail

WATERTON LAKES NATIONAL PARK

ALBERTA

Set out on this epic trail that stretches between Canada and the U.S.–Mexican border.

DISTANCE
3,100 miles, usually completed in sections or in six months

START
Waterton Park, Alberta

FINISH
Crazy Cook Monument, Big Hatchet Mountains, New Mexico

DIFFICULTY
Hard due to remote, mountainous terrain and challenging logistics

SEASON
March to October

Thousands of people hike the entire Pacific Crest Trail (PCT) and Appalachian Trail (AT) each year, but fewer than 200 people complete all of the Continental Divide Trail (CDT). That's due to the route's high, remote, and unforgiving terrain.

The CDT runs south from Waterton Lakes National Park for 3,100 miles. Most backpackers who aim to hike the whole trail in one season start at the southern end in the early spring.

The route is challenging not only because of the relentlessly mountainous terrain, but also the logistics—unlike the PCT and AT, where hikers can resupply in towns along the way, the CDT is more remote, with fewer road crossings. Weather is also a factor, as the southern desert sections are hot and dry; the Colorado Rockies have daily thunder and lightning storms; and the Wyoming and Montana sections can dole out freak summer snowstorms as winter looms.

So, why hike the CDT? Because it's one of the highest, wildest, longest, and most beautiful hikes on the planet.

RIGHT The colorful Red Rock Canyon in Waterton Lakes National Park.

Georgian Bay Marr Lake Trail

BRUCE PENINSULA NATIONAL PARK

ONTARIO

The Bruce Peninsula juts out into Lake Huron, partially enclosing Georgian Bay. The bones of this pointed finger are composed of limestone from the Niagara Escarpment, an ancient coral reef laid down more than 400 million years ago in tropical seas. This easy 3-mile loop features Georgian Bay, where you can explore some of the escarpment, including the Grotto—one of the park's most photographed features.

Beausoleil Island Trail

GEORGIAN BAY ISLANDS NATIONAL PARK

ONTARIO

Georgian Bay Islands is the largest freshwater archipelago in the world, with more than 30,000 islands scattered throughout this bay in Lake Huron. The national park protects sixty-three of these islands, including the largest, Beausoleil Island. You can hike right around the island on this 8-mile loop. You might spot black bears, bobcats, coyotes, porcupines, and timber wolves.

16

Gaspé Point Trail

FORILLON NATIONAL PARK

QUÉBEC

The Gaspé Peninsula sticks out where the Saint Lawrence River meets the Gulf of Saint Lawrence. This setting comprises deep forests, salt marshes, sand dunes, and sea cliffs, all in one small finger of land. Traverse through all of these microcosms on the 5-mile out-and-back trail to Gaspé Point, a dramatic headland with incredible views of the surrounding sea cliffs.

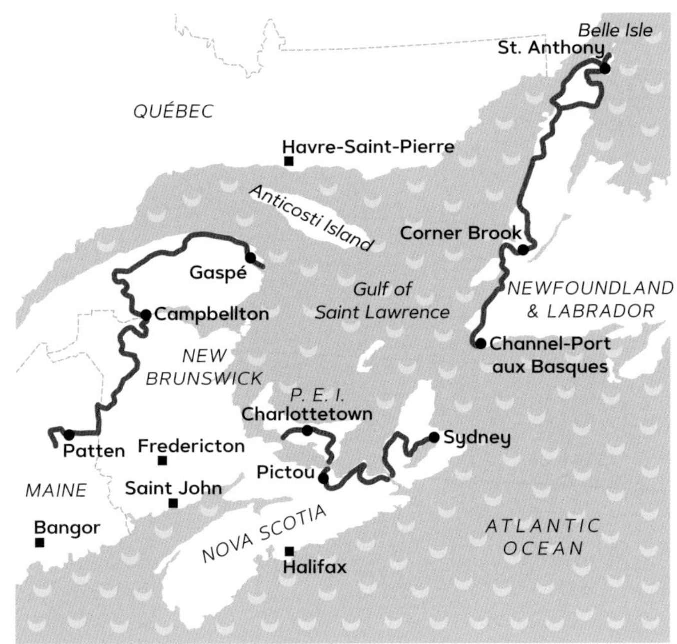

17

International Appalachian Trail

FORILLON NATIONAL PARK

QUÉBEC

Walk part of the International Appalachian Trail on the Canadian extension of the famous route.

DISTANCE
2,190 miles, usually completed in sections

START
Baxter State Park, Maine (at terminus of AT)

DIFFICULTY
Hard due to remote trail, travel logistics, and route finding

SEASON
June to September

Gaspé Point serves as a jump-off point for the Canadian extension of the International Appalachian Trail. From here, you board a ferry to Prince Edward Island, Nova Scotia, and then to Newfoundland, where the trail runs to the northernmost tip, Cape Bauld. Another ferry crossing of the Strait of Belle Isle delivers you to the official northern terminus of the trail and the North American Appalachian Mountain chain at Belle Isle.

In geologic terms, the Appalachian Mountains don't end in North America—and neither does the trail. Parts of the Appalachians formed during collisions that created the supercontinent Pangaea around 250 million years ago—long before the Atlantic Ocean opened and separated North America from Europe. These ancient wayward Appalachians can be found in western Europe and northern Africa, and in 2010 the International Appalachian Trail was expanded to include sections in Greenland, Iceland, Scotland, the UK, and Spain.

ABOVE The International Appalachian Trail is a continuation of the Georgia-to-Maine trail.

LEFT Percé Rock sits in the Gulf of Saint Lawrence on the tip of the Gaspé Peninsula.

18

Fundy Footpath

FUNDY NATIONAL PARK

NEW BRUNSWICK

Don't get caught out by the tides on this hike that passes some of the most extreme tidal changes in the world.

DISTANCE
30 miles, usually completed in four to six days

START
Fundy National Park headquarters in Alma, New Brunswick

DIFFICULTY
Hard due to rugged terrain and tidal changes

SEASON
April to October

The Bay of Fundy is sandwiched between New Brunswick and Nova Scotia in northeastern Canada. Fundy Footpath hugs the coast from Alma to St. Martins, giving you unparalleled views of the famous 52-foot tidal changes. The high tides are a product of the bay's high northern latitude, narrow shape, and quirks of the underlying seafloor. In one twelve-hour tidal cycle, 100 billion tons of water flows in and out of the bay.

Fundy Footpath is a 30-mile trail that goes up and down almost constantly, racking up over 9,000 feet of elevation gain. The Fundy Hiking Trail Association recommends taking five days to complete the route, starting in Alma so that you complete the most strenuous sections first. Time your hike with the tides, as some sections are impassable and extremely dangerous at high tide.

19

Coastal Trail

FUNDY NATIONAL PARK

NEW BRUNSWICK

To see the highest tides in the world, head out for an all-day hike on the Coastal Trail, a 12.5-mile out-and-back route that provides panoramic views. Every six hours, the water level in the bay vacillates by more than 50 feet, exposing vast swaths of the seafloor at low tide.

ABOVE Large areas of the seafloor are visible at low tide in Fundy National Park.

20

Merrymakedge Beach

KEJIMKUJIK NATIONAL PARK

NOVA SCOTIA

Kejimkujik National Park protects an ancient canoe route that linked the Bay of Fundy to the Atlantic Ocean across the interior of the peninsula via a series of lakes and rivers. Kejimkujik means "little fairies" in the native Mi'kmaw language; these fairies play a prominent role in Mi'kmaw legends.

On the eastern shore of Lake Kejimkujik, the Mi'kmaw people carved petroglyphs (rock carvings) into outcroppings of slate. These are highly protected and can only be visited by guided tours through Parks Canada.

You can visit the lake on a trail that starts at Jakes Landing for an easy 3.7-mile round-trip hike. You may spot pileated woodpeckers and hear the haunting call of the common loon.

21

Acadian Trail

CAPE BRETON HIGHLANDS NATIONAL PARK

NOVA SCOTIA

Experience Cape Breton Highlands National Park in all its glory on the Acadian Trail. This 5.5-mile loop has it all: hiked clockwise, the first half climbs 1,200 feet to overlook the rugged coastline, the Chéticamp River Valley, and the park's highland interior. The second half descends along a cascading creek through mossy woods. Hike in groups and make noise, as black bears, coyotes, and moose are common here.

22

Green Gardens Trail

GROS MORNE NATIONAL PARK

NEWFOUNDLAND

The beginning of the Green Gardens Trail is anything but green—the route passes through a barren landscape known as the Tablelands, where mildly toxic rocks support little plant life, giving this area a desertlike quality. The route then descends 1,300 feet through boreal forests and flowering meadows to a beach of volcanic rocks. Explore the sea stacks and sea caves, but beware of rising tides. Return the way you came for a 7-mile round-trip hike.

You'll encounter rolling open alpine scrubland on the Long Range Traverse in Gros Morne National Park.

23

Long Range Traverse

GROS MORNE NATIONAL PARK

NEWFOUNDLAND

Gros Morne National Park takes its French name from the second-highest peak on the island—the "peak that stands alone." You can tag this high point on the 22-mile Long Range Traverse. You'll first ride a ferry across the Western Brook Pond freshwater fjord, and then bushwhack up a steep ravine past the curiously named Pissing Mare Falls. Once you reach the plateau above, you'll spend a few days traversing open alpine scrubland up and over 2,648-foot Gros Morne Mountain.

24

Terra Nova Coastal Trail

TERRA NOVA NATIONAL PARK

NEWFOUNDLAND

In this easternmost national park in Canada, a series of rocky fingers juts out into Bonavista Bay, creating a wildly intricate coastline of cliffs, exposed headwalls, and sheltered inlets and coves. This 2.8-mile trail follows Newman Sound, meandering through boreal forests and the intertidal zone to Pissamere Falls. Keep your eyes peeled for sea life, shore birds, and moose.

25

Koyukuk River Route

GATES OF THE ARCTIC NATIONAL PARK AND PRESERVE

ALASKA

Hike through a remote and untamed landscape, devoid of any roads or designated trails.

DISTANCE
102 miles, completed in sections or over two to three weeks

START
Bettles, Alaska; access by charter plane

DIFFICULTY
Hard due to logistics, route finding, and challenging terrain

SEASON
July to August; bring bug spray and a head net

Gates of the Arctic National Park and Preserve is no place to start a hiking career. However, for experienced trekkers, the mighty North Fork of the Koyukuk River provides a spectacular route through this immense wilderness. From its headwaters on the Arctic Continental Divide, the river runs south for more than 100 miles through the heart of the Central Brooks Range, bisecting the Frigid Crags and Boreal Mountain that form the "Gates of the Arctic."

To hike the North Fork of the Koyukuk, you'll need to arrange a charter plane to drop you off and pick you up. In this rolling tundra terrain, even hardened hikers will average only about six miles a day, so you'll need to either pick a manageable section, carry two to three weeks' worth of food, or arrange for airplane supply drops along the way. Be careful with your food—bears are common here.

26

Savage Alpine Trail

DENALI NATIONAL PARK AND PRESERVE

ALASKA

Look for brown bears as you follow the Savage River's wide watercourse and gravel bars upstream.

- **DISTANCE**
  4 miles one way with park service shuttle, elevation gain 1,400 feet
- **START**
  Savage River Campground
- **DIFFICULTY**
  Moderate
- **SEASON**
  May to October; fall colors peak in September

This hike begins at the Savage River Campground and gradually climbs uphill, where you may be rewarded with views of Denali. But don't bank on seeing the mountain—only about a third of visitors to the park get to see it because of frequent cloud cover. You're more likely to spot a brown bear, wolf, moose, or mountain goat.

In the late summer and early fall, the trails around the Savage River are sometimes closed due to foraging bears, as they fatten up for winter. Check the trail's status at the visitor center or with a ranger and hike in a group, make noise, and carry bear spray—and know how to deploy it. Give any animal you see plenty of space—remember, you are a visitor in its home.

27

Horseshoe Lake Trail

DENALI NATIONAL PARK AND PRESERVE

ALASKA

Denali National Park and Preserve has something for everybody, including casual strollers and wildlife watchers. This 2-mile loop around Horseshoe Lake won't take more than an hour or two—unless you stop to watch the resident beavers, who are often seen gnawing down trees to add to their submerged stick palaces.

28

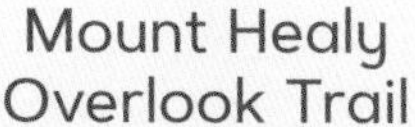

Mount Healy Overlook Trail

DENALI NATIONAL PARK AND PRESERVE
ALASKA

At 20,310 feet, Denali is the tallest peak in North America—but it's not the only mountain in the park. This short but steep trail climbs partway up Mount Healy. Starting at the visitor center, there are a couple of viewpoints on the way up to the 3-mile mark, where the official trail ends. You can continue another 1.5 miles to reach the summit at 5,716 feet above sea level for breathtaking views.

LEFT A caribou crosses the Savage River, a classic example of a glacially carved braided river.

29

Brooks Falls

KATMAI NATIONAL PARK AND PRESERVE

ALASKA

In wildlife documentaries, the footage is iconic: huge salmon leap up a waterfall only to be caught in the jaws of a massive brown bear. During the salmon run, you can hike to Brooks Falls on an easy 3-mile out-and-back trail. On a busy day, two dozen bears may be safely watched from three wooden viewing platforms. The most talented fisherbears catch as many as thirty salmon a day! Always be bear aware: hike in groups, make noise, carry bear spray, and be respectful of the animals' space.

30

Valley of Ten Thousand Smokes

KATMAI NATIONAL PARK

ALASKA

Hike through a landscape that is so Moon-like, NASA astronauts have trained there.

DISTANCE
36 miles one way with park service shuttle, elevation gain 1,500 feet, completed in three to five days

START
Valley of Ten Thousand Smokes

DIFFICULTY
Hard due to remote terrain, route finding, river crossings, and bear activity

SEASON
June to September; snowshoes may be needed over the pass in early summer

ABOVE LEFT A brown bear in Brooks Falls in Katmai National Park and Preserve catches a salmon.

LEFT The Katmai caldera formed during the Novarupta eruption.

On June 6, 1912, a once lush, green river valley was transformed by the eruption of the Novarupta volcano. It spewed more ash than any other volcano in the twentieth century—more than thirty times that of the 1980 Mount Saint Helens eruption. More than a century later, the valley remains an otherworldly moonscape devoid of vegetation, filled with deep ash piles. The valley is surrounded by monumental snowcapped mountains festooned with glaciers.

The park service offers an easy, ranger-led hike across the valley floor, or experienced adventurers can trek 36 miles from the Valley of Ten Thousand Smokes, across Katmai Pass, to the Pacific Ocean at Katmai Bay. As this is a well-known brown bear seasonal migration route, keep food in bear-proof containers provided by the park service.

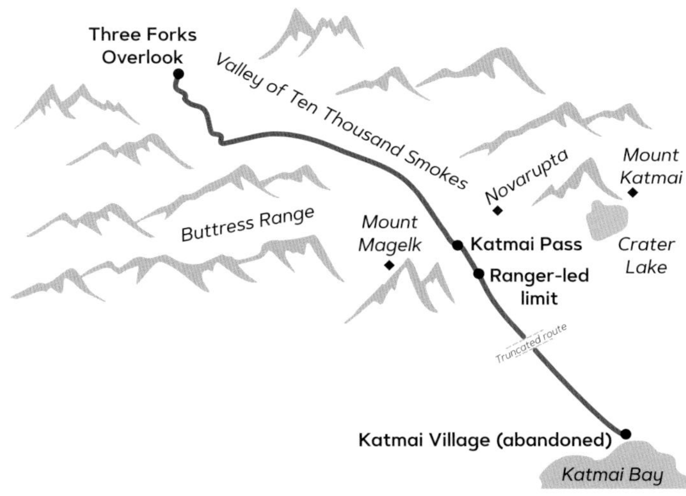

31

Harding Ice Field Trail

KENAI FJORDS NATIONAL PARK

ALASKA

The Harding Ice Field sprawls over 700 square miles, giving rise to thirty-eight individual glaciers. To lay eyes on the largest ice field in Alaska, head up this trail. The well-maintained, but relentlessly steep, route gains 3,800 feet in a little over 4 miles, topping out at a viewpoint of ice glistening as far as the eye can see.

32

Seven Pass Route

WRANGELL–SAINT ELIAS NATIONAL PARK AND PRESERVE

ALASKA

Treat yourself to a weeklong trek in North America's largest national park on the Seven Pass Route. To tackle the 40-mile backpack through the Chugach Mountains alone, you'll need to be comfortable with both river and glacier crossings, as well as camping in bear country. Alternatively, let a guide lead the way on this ultra-classic, ultra-scenic route.

33

Bartlett Cove to Point Gustavus Beach Trail

GLACIER BAY NATIONAL PARK AND PRESERVE

ALASKA

Rivers of ice spill into the Gulf of Alaska in Glacier Bay National Park and Preserve. For a pleasant beach stroll rich in wildlife, including humpback whales, sea otters, and bald eagles, follow the shoreline south from the Bartlett Cove docks for up to 6 miles to Point Gustavus.

34

Observatory Trail to Mauna Loa

HAWAIʻI VOLCANOES NATIONAL PARK

HAWAIʻI

Summit the largest active volcano on Earth, located on Hawaiʻi's Big Island.

DISTANCE
13 miles out and back to summit, elevation gain 2,700 feet

START
Mauna Loa Observatory

DIFFICULTY
Hard due to rugged lava rock terrain

SEASON
Hawaiʻi's dry season runs from April to October

RIGHT The Observatory Trail to Mauna Loa offers spectacular views across the island.

If more than half of Mauna Loa wasn't underwater, it would be higher than Mount Everest (29,029 feet), as it rises 30,085 feet from the seafloor to the summit.

Conquering Mauna Loa is a big hike; the shortest route starts at the Mauna Loa Observatory. The trail is marked by a series of stacked black volcanic rocks called ahu. You'll hike up through many layers of cooled lava, alternating between fields of smooth textured pāhoehoe and jagged ʻaʻā lava. You'll also pass the remains of collapsed lava tubes, where hot lava once flowed through corridors of rock, and frozen lava fountains called spatter cones.

Once you reach the summit crater, Mokuʻāweoweo, you'll find the only bathroom facilities along the route—an open-air pit toilet sitting above a seemingly bottomless lava fissure. Day hikers can continue to the true summit at 13,667 feet above sea level, while overnight hikers with reservations can head to the Mauna Loa Cabin, on the edge of the crater.

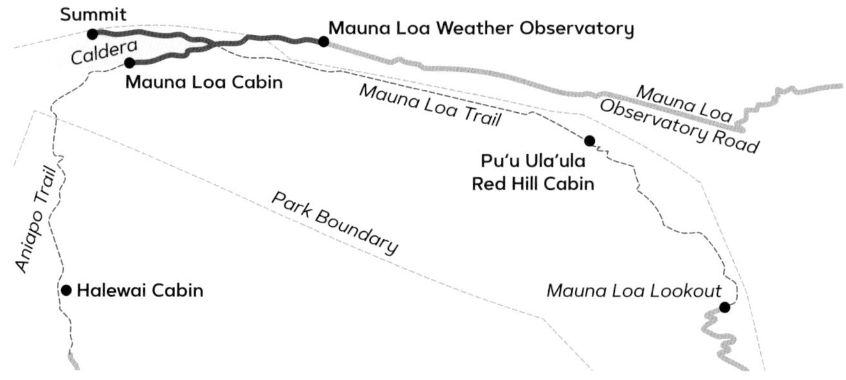

35

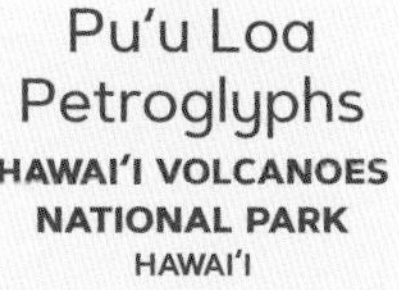

Pu'u Loa Petroglyphs

HAWAI'I VOLCANOES NATIONAL PARK

HAWAI'I

Native Hawaiians have been living atop one of the world's most active volcanoes for many generations, and reverence for the Hawaiian volcano deity Pele dominates many aspects of traditional island culture. To see a record of prehistoric life in Hawai'i, take an easy 1.5-mile stroll to a gallery of more than 23,000 petroglyphs, called ki'i pōhaku, carved into volcanic rock on the southern flank of Kīlauea—one of the volcanoes in the park. An elevated boardwalk winds through the site. Do not touch the rock art or walk on the rocks; they are both very fragile.

36

Pipiwai Trail

HALEAKALĀ NATIONAL PARK

HAWAI'I

The adventure to Waimoku Falls actually starts on the drive to the trailhead: snaking around 620 curves, the Hāna Highway is a winding scenic coastal drive. The Pipiwai Trail travels through lush tropical rainforest and then a dense bamboo forest, past several waterfalls, before ending at Waimoku Falls. The 4-mile out-and-back trail is often muddy and slippery, so trade your island-life flip-flops for hiking boots.

37

Hoh River Trail to Blue Glacier

OLYMPIC NATIONAL PARK

WASHINGTON

Rainforests and glaciers seem unlikely neighbors, but you can visit both in one epic 37-mile backpacking trip in Olympic National Park. Following the Hoh River, you may spot Roosevelt elk—the largest elk species in North America. In the fall you might hear the whistles of the bulls' bugling rutting call.

After about 15 miles of rainforest you'll reach a steep landslide that must be down-climbed using a rope and a ladder. In another couple of miles you'll get your first glimpse of the Blue Glacier. The best views are in another mile atop the Lateral Moraine—a pile of rocks pushed to the side by the moving ice. You'll see the entire length of the glacier from its origins on Mount Olympus to the waterfall plunging from its outlet.

38

Blue Lake Trail

NORTH CASCADES NATIONAL PARK

WASHINGTON

To fully experience the wonders of Blue Lake, you'll need to bring a fishing rod on this 4.5-mile round-trip trek. Wild native cutthroat trout, named for the distinctive red slash on the lower jaw, are numerous in this gin-clear lake. Visit in July and August when wildflowers are abundant.

39

Cascade Pass Trail

NORTH CASCADES NATIONAL PARK

WASHINGTON

Cascade Pass Trail is a steep but spectacular introduction to the high-alpine country of the North Cascades. Climbing steadily up a series of switchbacks, the trail quickly gains 1,780 feet of elevation. After the first few miles, the pass offers sweeping views of the valley, the often snowy granite peaks, and their glaciers. Turn around here to keep this a day hike, but there are numerous options for prepared backpackers and mountaineers from Cascade Pass.

40

Panorama Point

MOUNT RAINIER NATIONAL PARK

WASHINGTON

Enjoy a panoramic view of Mount Rainier, as well as neighboring stratovolcanoes Mount Adams, Mount Saint Helens, and Mount Hood, from this viewpoint on the south side of Rainier. Stratovolcanoes are volcanoes that are usually steep-sided cylindrical cones made up of layers of lava flows and volcanic ash. Bring binoculars on this 5.4-mile loop to get a better look at the Nisqually Glacier. You may also spot determined mountaineers in the distance, zigzagging up the snowfields to the summit.

LEFT The Hoh River Trail passes through old-growth rainforest sprinkled with bright green moss.

41

Wonderland Trail

MOUNT RAINIER NATIONAL PARK

WASHINGTON

Circle Mount Rainier on a trail that racks up enough elevation to climb to the summit—twice.

DISTANCE
93-mile loop, elevation gain 22,000 feet, usually completed in eight to fourteen days

START
Multiple starting points

DIFFICULTY
Hard due to elevation gain and rugged terrain

SEASON
July to September

RIGHT You'll pass through deep forest and subalpine meadows on the Wonderland Trail.

Log some quality time with Mount Rainier, without tackling its 14,411-foot summit, on this 93-mile loop. While the Wonderland Trail is far less fraught than a summit climb—less than half of summit attempts are successful, and storms, rockfall, and avalanches kill climbers every season—it's not necessarily easy: the trail gains and loses elevation almost constantly, racking up over 20,000 feet of climbing.

The loop encircles the mountain and can be hiked in either direction; whichever way, you'll get a crick in your neck from admiring the stunning views of the mountain's many faces. Water is plentiful along most of the route, supplied by streams fed by the stratovolcano's many glaciers.

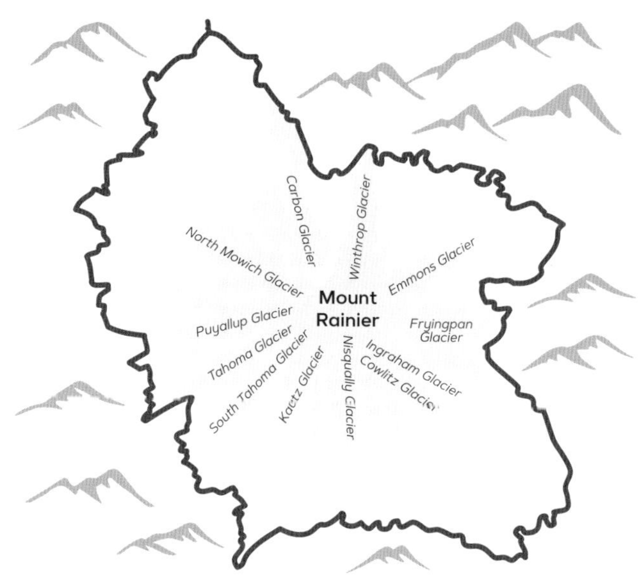

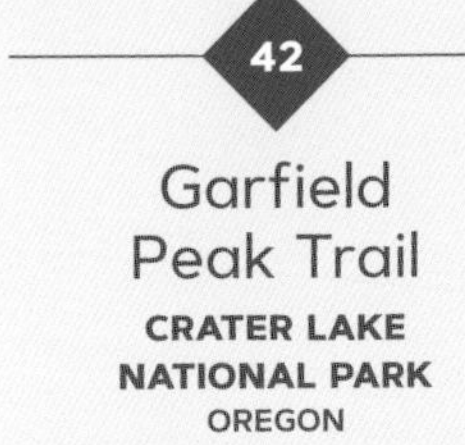

Garfield Peak Trail

CRATER LAKE NATIONAL PARK
OREGON

For a bird's-eye view of Crater Lake, head up to Garfield Peak. The 8,060-foot summit offers panoramic views of the lake, Phantom Ship and Wizard Island, and the crater rim, as well as the surrounding peaks of the Cascades. In July and August the meadows along the trail bloom with lupine, paintbrush, and wild arnica. This 3.4-mile out-and-back trail can also be hiked in winter on skis or snowshoes, but winter storms can drop legendary amounts of snow and reduce visibility to zero.

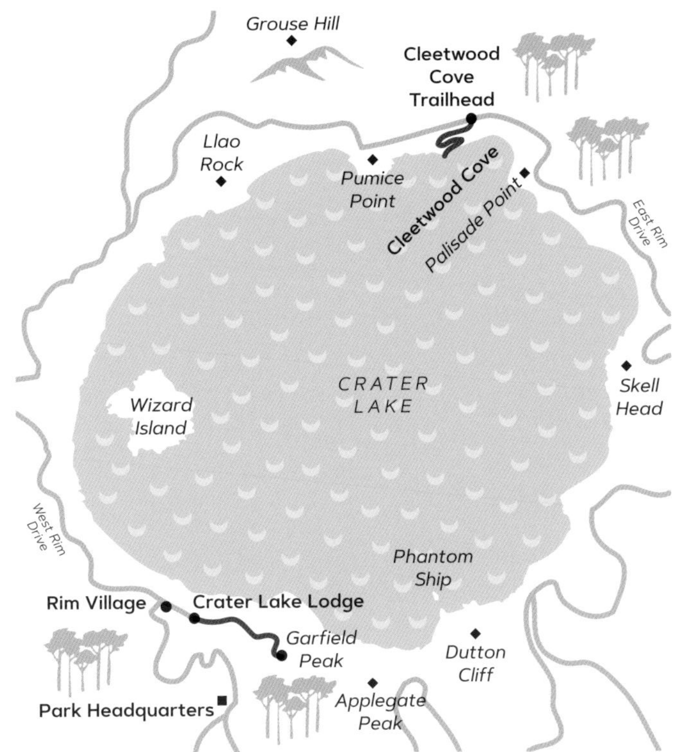

43

Cleetwood Cove Trail

CRATER LAKE NATIONAL PARK

OREGON

Follow a trail to one of the clearest lakes on Earth, on what is the only legal route to the water.

DISTANCE
2.2 miles out and back, elevation gain 700 feet

START
Cleetwood Cove Trailhead on East Rim Drive

DIFFICULTY
Moderate

SEASON
Mid-June to October

LEFT Crater Lake, with Phantom Ship visible in the foreground to the right.

RIGHT The lack of sediment and pollution in the water makes Crater Lake crystal clear.

The catastrophic eruption of the Mount Mazama volcano some 7,700 years ago was forty times more powerful than the 1980 eruption of Mount Saint Helens. Afterward, the mountain collapsed in on itself, opening a yawning crater. Over the next few hundred years, the 6-mile-wide crater filled with rainwater and snowmelt, eventually creating a lake.

Crater Lake has long been revered by the indigenous Klamath Tribe. Artifacts have been found under the extensive ash layer from the eruption, indicating that people must have lived in the area and witnessed the event, which features prominently in tribal mythology. Klamath warriors used to run down the steep crater walls to the water. Modern-day hikers can test their own mettle on the Cleetwood Cove Trail, a 1.1-mile, 700-foot drop on steep switchbacks.

44

Lady Bird Johnson Grove Trail

REDWOOD NATIONAL PARK

CALIFORNIA

Stroll beneath the world's tallest trees, under a canopy of redwoods that tower above the forest floor.

DISTANCE
1.5-mile loop, minimal elevation gain

START
Lady Bird Johnson trailhead, near Thomas H. Kuchel Visitor Center

DIFFICULTY
Easy

SEASON
Year-round

RIGHT These redwoods can grow to over 300 feet tall.

FAR RIGHT Lady Bird Johnson Grove Trail is one of the most popular walks in Redwood National Park.

This regal grove of redwoods was dedicated in honor of the former First Lady of the United States, Lady Bird Johnson, wife of President Lyndon B. Johnson, in 1969 for her conservation work. The easy 1.5-mile loop winds past dozens of striking specimens, each explained via an informational pamphlet available at the trailhead.

To truly appreciate the magic of a redwood forest, hope for foggy weather; not only does fog make the towering forest look otherworldly, it's also the secret of the redwoods' success. The mammoth trees grow only in a narrow band along the California coast to take advantage of the fog that accumulates there. The trees are able to take up water from the fog and keep growing through the state's rain-free summers. Since this upland grove sits at a higher elevation of 1,200 feet, it tends to be foggy more often, making for a hauntingly beautiful hike.

Redwood Creek Trail

REDWOOD NATIONAL PARK
CALIFORNIA

For a peaceful redwoods experience, head out on this easy 15.5-mile out-and-back hike. Somewhere along the way, hidden on a steep hillside next to a side creek, towers "Hyperion"—the tallest known tree on Earth at 379 feet tall. Discovered in 2006, its exact location is kept secret to protect the behemoth, which is thought to be 600–800 years old. At the end of the trail you can find the 368-foot Libby Tree, in Tall Trees Grove. This hike makes for a perfect overnight backpacking trip with plentiful campsites along Redwood Creek.

46

Bumpass Hell Trail

LASSEN VOLCANIC NATIONAL PARK

CALIFORNIA

A place named Bumpass Hell sounds like a place to avoid, but this is one of the best geothermal hikes in North America outside of Yellowstone. The funny-sounding moniker was actually inspired by an unfortunate accident, when a pioneer explorer named Kendall Bumpass fell into a boiling mud pot and eventually lost a leg to the resulting burn. The park service has since built a wide, smooth trail and boardwalk to guide visitors safely on this 2.7-mile out-and-back hike.

47

Lassen Peak Trail

LASSEN VOLCANIC NATIONAL PARK

CALIFORNIA

Lassen Peak erupted in 1915, spreading ash more than 200 miles. This national park was created in part to preserve the region for long-term scientific study of how ecosystems recover after major volcanic events.

For an aerial view of the landscape, hike to the rocky top of Lassen Peak on this moderate day hike. The trail gains 2,000 feet in just over 2.5 miles to the summit of one of the planet's largest lava domes.

48

Condor Gulch Trail to High Peaks Trail Loop

PINNACLES NATIONAL PARK

CALIFORNIA

Rock climbers and bird-watchers alike flock to Pinnacles National Park, drawn by the unique geology and one of the West's most famous birds. After going extinct in the wild in 1987, the California condor was bred in captivity and released in a few prime habitats in the western United States, including Pinnacles. It's not a pretty bird—the largest flying scavenger in North America looks like an overgrown vulture with drab plumage and a featherless head. Keep your eyes on the sky on this classic 5.5-mile loop. Condors are often spotted from the High Peaks section of the trail in the early morning and early evening.

LEFT The Lassen Volcanic Park Highway is closed in winter due to deep snow.

BELOW The California condor has an astonishing 9-foot wingspan.

49

Clouds Rest

YOSEMITE NATIONAL PARK

CALIFORNIA

Take in views of valleys, canyons, lakes, and peaks in every direction on this quiet hike.

DISTANCE
13 miles from Tioga Road, elevation gain 3,000 feet

START
Tenaya Lake on Tioga Road

DIFFICULTY
Hard due to distance, elevation gain, and narrow ridgeline; acrophobics beware!

SEASON
June to October

ABOVE RIGHT Views across Yosemite National Park from the Clouds Rest route.

BELOW RIGHT The narrow knife-edge section might put some people off this hike.

This isn't the busiest or highest viewpoint in the park, but it might be the most dramatic. Bring binoculars to spy on those hiking up the cable route on Half Dome, the most famous nontechnical summit in Yosemite.

With such breathtaking views, why isn't Clouds Rest as crowded as Half Dome? A 13-mile round day hike from Tioga Road keeps most people away, and then there's the knife edge—a narrow section of ridgeline with sheer cliffs on the north side and a formidable drop-off to the south. Fortunately, the rocks underfoot are solid granite and there are plenty of handholds. The knife edge isn't nearly as dangerous as Half Dome's notoriously crowded cable route, but it's enough to deter many people.

You could approach Clouds Rest from Yosemite Valley and avoid the knife edge, but you would have to hike 20 miles and climb over 6,000 feet. Most people tackle this longer route in an overnight or three-day backpacking trip, with a stopover at the Little Yosemite Valley Campground.

50

Lower Yosemite Falls Trail

YOSEMITE NATIONAL PARK

CALIFORNIA

The 1.2-mile loop to see the tallest waterfall in North America can be hiked year-round. But go between December and June when the falls will be flowing—it usually dries up by mid-July. In the winter, when the falls return, the water often turns to snow on the way down and piles in an enormous snow cone at the bottom.

51

Cathedral Lakes Trail

YOSEMITE NATIONAL PARK

CALIFORNIA

This spectacular 8.5-mile round-trip day hike begins at the west end of Tuolumne Meadows and winds up into Yosemite's high country to two of the Sierra Nevada's most picturesque lakes. They share their lofty name with Cathedral Peak, a dramatic, glacially carved summit with two spires that resemble a church's steeples. In 1869 John Muir was the first white man to climb to the top on a steep but nontechnical scramble up the seemingly impenetrable south face.

BELOW A snow cone forms in winter at the base of the 2,425-foot Yosemite Falls.

52

John Muir Trail

YOSEMITE NATIONAL PARK

CALIFORNIA

Running along the crest of the Sierra Nevada mountain range for 211 miles, the John Muir Trail (JMT) is one of the most scenic hikes on Earth. Traditionally, the trail starts at the Happy Isles trailhead in Yosemite Valley and ends on top of Mount Whitney. When hiking the JMT, which runs parallel to the Pacific Crest Trail (PCT) for 170 miles, keep in mind that you're following in footsteps much older than Muir's—the JMT and PCT were built on top of a network of ancient footpaths called Nüümü Poyo, or the People's Trail, that were etched out of the wilderness over thousands of years by the Paiute and other tribes.

53

High Sierra Trail

SEQUOIA AND KINGS CANYON NATIONAL PARKS

CALIFORNIA

If you'd like to tackle a long-distance trail in the Sierra but don't have weeks to hike the John Muir Trail, the High Sierra Trail might be just the ticket. This 72-mile jaunt can be completed in about a week, starting in Kings Canyon, passing through Sequoia National Park, and ending on top of Mount Whitney.

54

Congress Trail

SEQUOIA NATIONAL PARK

CALIFORNIA

See the world's largest tree on this easy 3-mile loop in the Giant Forest of Sequoia National Park. The largest tree is determined not by height but by overall volume. The General Sherman is 275 feet tall, with a diameter of 36 feet at the base, and is estimated to be between 2,300 and 2,700 years old. After visiting the General, continue on the partially paved Congress Trail into the heart of the forest. This trail is accessible year-round, but you may need snowshoes or skis in winter.

55

Mist Falls

KINGS CANYON NATIONAL PARK

CALIFORNIA

Of the three major national parks in the Sierras—Yosemite, Kings Canyon, and Sequoia—Kings Canyon sees the least number of visitors. With only a few roads, the park must be explored on foot.

This 8.7-mile out-and-back hike to Mist Falls is a great introduction to the mighty river canyons that drain the western slope of the Sierras. The trail follows the boulder-strewn South Fork of Kings River up past a series of tumbling cascades to Mist Falls, where water rushes down a granite slab before shooting over a cliff.

11,043
Telescope Peak

56

Telescope Peak Trail

DEATH VALLEY NATIONAL PARK

CALIFORNIA

You won't need a telescope to enjoy the views from the highest point in Death Valley—just a strong set of legs and lungs.

DISTANCE
14 miles out and back, elevation gain 3,300 feet

START
Mahogany Flat Campground

DIFFICULTY
Hard due to elevation gain and altitude

SEASON
October to April; avoid summers in Death Valley, when temperatures soar over 110°F

ABOVE LEFT Incredible views stretch for over 100 miles in every direction from the top of 11,043-foot Telescope Peak.

LEFT The colorful clay and mudstone badlands at Zabriskie Point.

There's no telescope on top of Telescope Peak—the name comes from the jaw-dropping views. Presiding to the west is Mount Whitney, the highest point in the contiguous United States, and to the east, Badwater Basin, the lowest point in North America. From Badwater Basin, at 282 feet below sea level, the terrain rises 11,331 feet to the top of Telescope Peak, one of the most dramatic vertical ascents in North America.

Fortunately, the trail starts much higher, at 8,200 feet. After gaining 1,000 feet, a ridge between Rogers Peak and Telescope provides stunning views down into Panamint Valley and Death Valley.

Air temperature drops by 3.5°F for every 1,000 feet of elevation gained, so when the valley is roasting, the summit may actually be comfortable. Even so, this mountain is best climbed in the fall, before the first winter storms blanket the summit ridge in snow.

57

Zabriskie Point

DEATH VALLEY NATIONAL PARK

CALIFORNIA

Don't let the name scare you—while this is a land of extremes, it's also extremely beautiful. One of the best places to appreciate the array of colors that paint this desert landscape is at Zabriskie Point, where crumbling badlands have eroded into multihued layers. Time your half-mile stroll for sundown and you'll be rewarded with a striking sunset.

58

Badwater Basin Salt Flats Trail

DEATH VALLEY NATIONAL PARK

CALIFORNIA

The lowest point in North America is located in the heart of Death Valley, where a pool of super-salty water sits at 282 feet below sea level, surrounded by white salt flats. It rains about 2 inches a year here, but extreme heat means the evaporation rate is 150 inches a year. As the water evaporates, it leaves behind a crust of salt that has built up over time to cover much of the valley floor. You can hike a few feet or a few miles on this easy out-and-back trail, but beware of heat, dehydration, and disorientation.

59

Cavern Point Loop Trail

CHANNEL ISLANDS NATIONAL PARK

CALIFORNIA

Hike in a mostly undeveloped environment on an island just off the coast of Los Angeles.

- **DISTANCE**
  2-mile loop, elevation gain 300 feet
- **START**
  Cavern Point trailhead, hike clockwise
- **DIFFICULTY**
  Easy
- **SEASON**
  Best September to May to avoid the summer heat

ABOVE LEFT Cavern Point Loop Trail is located on scenic Santa Cruz Island.

LEFT An endangered island fox in the Channel Islands National Park.

The northernmost five of the eight Channel Islands are preserved as part of Channel Islands National Park and have remained relatively undeveloped. The islands' isolation from the mainland has helped shape the evolution of at least 145 unique species found nowhere else on Earth, including a spotted skunk and the Channel Islands fox.

To get to the islands, you'll need to take an hourlong park service boat ride from Ventura Harbor. The 2-mile Cavern Point Loop Trail on Santa Cruz Island has stunning coastal views and opportunities to see some of the islands' unique flora and fauna. You might even spot whales spouting in the Santa Barbara Channel, between the Channel Islands and the mainland.

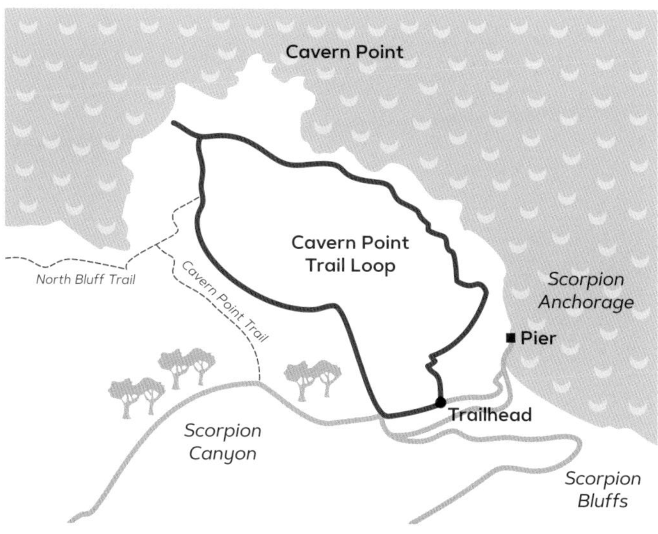

60

Hidden Valley Nature Trail

JOSHUA TREE NATIONAL PARK

CALIFORNIA

Joshua trees look like something out of a Dr. Seuss book. The spiky, spindly *Yucca brevifolia* is a member of the yucca family, found in only a few locations in Southern California, Nevada, and western Arizona. Joshua Tree National Park is one of the most scenic settings for the plant, where it flourishes against a backdrop of jumbled crystalline boulders. This easy mile-long loop is a perfect introduction to the unique ecology of the Mojave and Colorado desert ecosystem.

61

49 Palms Oasis Trail

JOSHUA TREE NATIONAL PARK

CALIFORNIA

No, those waving palm trees aren't a mirage—there's a spring hidden in this canyon in Joshua Tree National Park. On the 3-mile round-trip hike to the oasis you'll pass plenty of Joshua trees, barrel cacti, and other desert flora, but after the sharp and stark desert, the bright green palms surrounding the oasis are especially striking. Bring plenty of water and don't drink at the spring—the watering hole is a crucial water source for desert bighorn sheep and other critters.

LEFT AND BELOW Straddling the Mojave and Colorado deserts, Joshua Tree National Park is a scenic setting for a hike of any length.

62

Bristlecone Pine Glacier Trail

GREAT BASIN NATIONAL PARK

NEVADA

The only glacier in Nevada is nestled on the flank of 13,064-foot Wheeler Peak. This 4.5-mile round-trip trail passes interpretive signs as it runs through a grove of bristlecone pines that are among the oldest trees in the world. In 1964 a graduate student cut down a tree here only to find out it may have been the oldest living organism on Earth, possibly older than 5,000 years! The Wheeler Peak Glacier won't survive much longer; if warming trends continue, the ice will disappear in the next couple of decades.

63

Grand Palace Tour of Lehman Caves

GREAT BASIN NATIONAL PARK

NEVADA

The Lehman Caves are a vast system of intricate limestone caves at the base of Wheeler Peak. To visit them, you'll need to book a ranger-led tour. The Grand Palace Tour is the longer, more comprehensive option, traveling half a mile underground through passages to see rooms like the Gothic Palace, the Music Room, and flowstone formations with evocative names like the Parachute Shield.

64

Trail of the Cedars

GLACIER NATIONAL PARK

MONTANA

Glacier National Park is known for rigorous hiking trails into the backcountry, but you don't need to go far to meet some of the oldest denizens of the park. On the mile-long Trail of the Cedars—one of Glacier's two wheelchair-accessible trails—a raised boardwalk winds past an old-growth grove of 500-year-old red cedar trees. At the halfway point of the loop, you'll cross a footbridge over the dramatic gorge of Avalanche Creek.

LEFT See some of the world's oldest trees on the Bristlecone Pine Glacier Trail.

65

The Highline Trail

GLACIER NATIONAL PARK

MONTANA

This classic day hike has it all: glaciers, grizzlies, and goats! The Highline Trail runs between the Going-to-the-Sun Road and the Continental Divide, providing unparalleled views of the park's high-alpine terrain. It is best done as a 12-mile, one-way shuttle hike, making use of free park service transportation. The crux of the trail is the narrow Garden Wall, with a 100-foot drop on one side. The park usually anchors a handrail along the wall, but it's about 6 feet wide at its narrowest—plenty of room for all but the most affected acrophobics.

66

West Thumb Geyser Basin Trail

YELLOWSTONE NATIONAL PARK

WYOMING

Walk around the springs and geysers of one of the largest supervolcanoes in the world.

DISTANCE
1-mile double loop, minimal elevation gain

START
West Thumb Geyser Basin parking area

DIFFICULTY
Easy; part of the boardwalk is wheelchair accessible

SEASON
May to October

RIGHT Colorful thermal pools abound on the West Thumb Geyser Basin Trail.

The Yellowstone supervolcano (thousands of times more powerful than a regular volcano) was formed by a series of super-eruptions over the past 2.1 million years. An easy stroll on the West Thumb Geyser Basin Trail's double loop is a fascinating introduction to the geothermal wonders of America's first national park. The West Thumb Caldera last erupted 150,000 years ago, helping to shape the west shore of Yellowstone Lake. In geologic timescales, 150,000 years is not that long ago, and hot springs and geothermal vents still seep from the lake bed.

Onshore, against the dramatic backdrop of the lake, you'll pass a multitude of pools colored blue, green, orange, and yellow by microorganisms called thermophiles that thrive in the hot water. Don't dip a toe into one of these pools, as most Yellowstone hot springs are scalding hot!

Stay on the boardwalk at all times, both for your own safety and to preserve the delicate springs and lakeshore, and don't throw anything into the springs.

Mammoth Hot Springs Trail

YELLOWSTONE NATIONAL PARK

WYOMING

For a longer hike that features Yellowstone's most dramatic hot springs, head to the 3.5-mile loop around Mammoth Hot Springs. Here, minerals dissolved in hot water have built a series of pearlescent travertine terraces that change constantly. This part of the park is accessible year-round through the northwestern Gardiner entrance. For a surreal experience, visit the thermal features steaming through the snow in deep winter.

68

Bechler Canyon

YELLOWSTONE NATIONAL PARK

WYOMING

This 31.6-mile trek through the Bechler River Canyon is uniquely Yellowstone—the area is nicknamed "Cascade Corner" for its abundance of rivers and waterfalls. Where else in the world will you find bison-grazed meadows, active geysers, world-class trout fishing, and a soakable hot spring at the base of a roaring waterfall? You can only access this trail in August and September, as river crossings are dangerously high earlier in the summer. Hike in a group, make noise, carry bear spray, and follow all park service food storage regulations.

69

Cascade Canyon Trail

GRAND TETON NATIONAL PARK

WYOMING

Rising directly out of the Jackson Hole valley with few foothills to interrupt the views, the Tetons are one of the most dramatic mountain ranges on Earth. This 7-mile out-and-back hike up Cascade Canyon to aptly named Inspiration Point brings you to the bases of the granite peaks. A park service ferryboat ride across Jenny Lake will cut off 5 miles of hiking round-trip. But walk at least one way around the south shore of the beautiful glacially carved lake, the largest in the Tetons.

70

String Lake Trail

GRAND TETON NATIONAL PARK

WYOMING

For an easy but indelibly scenic stroll in the Tetons, head to String Lake. The first half mile of this trail is wheelchair accessible, leading to a picnic area, and the rest is on packed dirt with occasional roots and rocks. Have plenty of room on your camera's memory card—you won't be able to stop taking pictures of the striking granite spires of the Tetons across the bright blue lake on this 4.4-mile loop.

71

Teton Crest Trail

GRAND TETON NATIONAL PARK

WYOMING

This 40-mile trail passes through the heart of the Tetons. Most tackle it from south to north, passing through the Jedediah Smith Wilderness, Bridger Teton, and Caribou-Targhee national forests and into the national park, rarely dipping below 8,000 feet of elevation. The highlight is the Death Canyon Shelf—a narrow clifftop plateau that erupts with wildflowers in midsummer. Make plenty of noise as bears and moose are common here.

RIGHT The Teton Crest Trail ranks among the most dramatic backpacking trips in the U.S. national park system.

72

Observation Point

ZION NATIONAL PARK

UTAH

Observation Point offers a commanding view straight down Zion Canyon, a deep and narrow multicolored canyon carved into Navajo sandstone by the North Fork of the Virgin River. In August 2019, a large rock avalanche closed the popular Weeping Rock Trail to Observation Point, and instabilities in the rock wall may mean this route is closed indefinitely—but you can hike to Observation Point from the East Mesa Trailhead, a 6.7-mile round trip. This way is actually easier than the original route, as the trailhead is located almost 2,000 feet higher than Weeping Rock.

73

The Narrows

ZION NATIONAL PARK

UTAH

Upstream from Zion Canyon, the Virgin River cuts a deep defile, enclosed by 2,000-foot red sandstone walls. To explore this slot canyon, you'll have to get wet, as the route is the riverbed! Forging upstream with water up to your waist can be cold, even in summer, but it's a beautiful hike.

Rent neoprene socks, canyoneering shoes, and a walking stick in the town of Springdale to help you safely negotiate hiking in the river. You'll want to make it at least 2.5 miles to Wall Street, where the slot canyon narrows to 20 feet. Check weather reports and avoid this hike if rain is forecast due to the dangers of flash floods.

BELOW The Zion Narrows is one of the most iconic hikes in the U.S. national park system.

74

The Subway

ZION NATIONAL PARK

UTAH

After you've hiked the Narrows from the bottom up, now tackle the Subway from the top down. The aptly named Subway is a spectacular pipelike gorge that has been scooped out of the red sandstone walls by the Left Fork of North Creek. This 9.5-mile canyoneering adventure requires technical rappels, down climbing, and swimming across deep pools, so if you're inexperienced, consider hiring a guide.

75

Angel's Landing

ZION NATIONAL PARK

UTAH

Angel's Landing is a hair-raising, albeit popular, hike. The 5-mile out-and-back route starts with twenty-one switchbacks called Walter's Wiggles and then tiptoes along a narrow ridge with sickening drop-offs on both sides to an astounding viewpoint of Zion Canyon.

With no strict permit system to help with crowd control, consider attempting this easily bottlenecked hike early in the morning or, for the truly adventurous, by moonlight.

RIGHT Angel's Landing has chains bolted to the rocks in the most white-knuckle spots.

ABOVE Bryce Canyon has been scooped out of the Paunsaugunt Plateau.

RIGHT Canyonlands National Park is made up of a colorful maze of geologic layers and canyons.

76

Fairyland Loop Trail

BRYCE CANYON NATIONAL PARK

UTAH

Bryce Canyon is not really a canyon; it's more of an amphitheater, and is studded with thousands of hoodoos—towering rock formations that resemble totem poles. The Paiute believe that the pinnacles were people who had been turned to stone, and there are many faces hidden in them.

See how many profiles you can pick out on this 7.8-mile loop in the northern part of the park that snakes among the hoodoos. Summers turn the area into an oven, but snow transforms the landscape into a winter wonderland, so pull some microspikes onto your boots to have traction on the icy sections, or don some skis.

77

Sunset Point to Sunrise Point

BRYCE CANYON NATIONAL PARK

UTAH

This easy 1.1-mile out-and-back stroll along the rim of Bryce Canyon is beautiful at any time of day (or night—the stars are spectacular!). At sunrise and sunset, the slanting angle of the sun adds unforgettable dimensions of shape, color, and shadow to the spectacular scene.

78

Chesler Park Loop Trail

CANYONLANDS NATIONAL PARK

UTAH

Canyonlands National Park is divided into two units: the higher Island in the Sky district overlooks the lower Needles district. This 11-mile loop explores the bizarre rock formations in the depths of the Needles, winding through slot canyons, over slabs of slickrock—smooth, wind-polished rock—through cracks in giant boulders, and past sandstone formations that seem to defy the laws of physics. To stay on trail and avoid getting lost in the literal Maze (a remote and mysterious section of Canyonlands), follow the cairns—small rock stacks that mark the route.

79

Grand View Point Trail

CANYONLANDS NATIONAL PARK

UTAH

An overlook named Grand View Point is sure to deliver the goods, and this 1.8-mile trail in the northern Island in the Sky unit of Canyonlands is as easy as they come. A paved walkway leads to the first overlook, with staggering views south. Markers help point out the La Sal and Abajo mountains, the Needles district, and the confluence of the Green and Colorado Rivers. Beyond the paved sidewalk, a dirt trail continues along the rim to a second, even more astonishing viewpoint way out on the tip of the mesa.

80

Halls Creek Narrows

CAPITOL REEF NATIONAL PARK

UTAH

Hike down into a narrow, shady slot canyon whose perennial stream is a welcome oasis in this harsh desert.

DISTANCE
22.4 miles out and back, elevation gain 2,800 feet, usually completed in three to four days

START
Halls Creek overlook

DIFFICULTY
Hard due to desert terrain and route finding

SEASON
October to May

The southern tail of this long, narrow national park is wedged between the high cliffs of Hall Mesa and the tilted sandstone strata of the Waterpocket Fold. This seldom-visited, quirky, and complex landscape is chock-full of topographical treasures and long-lost relics. Be sure to explore the numerous side canyons off the main Halls Creek drainage, where you'll find ancient ruins, rock art, and bighorn sheep.

Check the weather before going: flash-flood season typically falls between July and September. You don't want to be caught in a slot canyon, where steep walls offer no chance of escape from rising water.

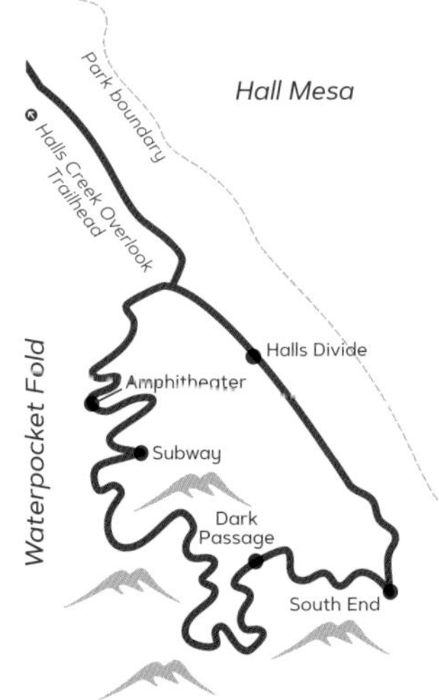

81

Cassidy Arch Trail

CAPITOL REEF NATIONAL PARK

UTAH

Cassidy Arch is named after the Wild West outlaw Butch Cassidy, who once used the area as a hideout. You'll see why on this hike—the rocky, rugged country is perfect for a high-stakes game of hide-and-seek. The 3-mile round-trip trail follows the Grand Wash, a usually dry riverbed, then climbs steeply up the canyon wall. It later crosses bare sandstone slickrock where you'll need to follow cairns to reach an overlook of Cassidy Arch.

RIGHT The spectacular Halls Creek Narrows offers some welcome shade during summer.

82

Devils Garden Loop Trail

ARCHES NATIONAL PARK

UTAH

Explore some of the most spectacular Entrada sandstone arches in the country on this hike.

DISTANCE
7.8-mile loop, elevation gain 1,200 feet

START
Devils Garden trailhead

DIFFICULTY
Moderate

SEASON
September to May

ABOVE RIGHT Delicate Arch resembles a pair of bowlegged cowboy chaps.

RIGHT Double O Arch stands in front of a backdrop of sandstone fins in the Devils Garden.

Entrada sandstone tends to erode into fins along parallel fractures. As water seeps into cracks in these fins, freeze and thaw cycles erode weaker sections of rock, sometimes creating an alcove that may eventually wear a hole. As chunks of rock fall away, the opening widens, in some places creating arches hundreds of feet across.

Less than a mile into the Devils Garden Loop Trail, you'll come across Landscape Arch, the longest arch in North America, with an opening more than 300 feet across. Sections of the arch appear so thin, it's a wonder it's still standing. In the Devils Garden you'll encounter eight more large arches and dozens of smaller arcs, fins, and other unique rock formations.

You can hike the trail either as an out-and-back to Double O Arch, a spectacularly stacked double arch, or as a loop by taking the Primitive Trail. You'll need to follow cairns and do some moderate rock scrambling on this section.

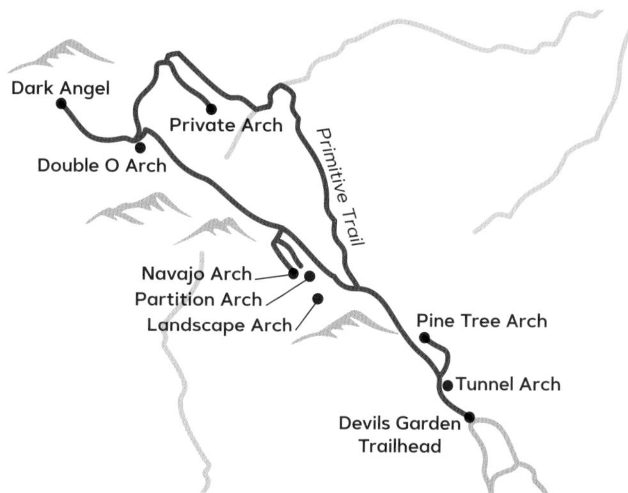

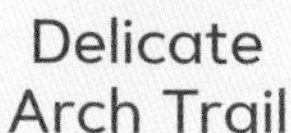

Delicate Arch Trail

ARCHES NATIONAL PARK
UTAH

Immortalized on license plates and on the state's quarter, Delicate Arch might be the most recognizable rock in Utah. A 3-mile out-and-back hike to the iconic arch reveals that it really isn't all that delicate—the roughly 60-foot arch soars above an adjacent basin, the red rocks burning bright against the stark backdrop of the often snowcapped La Sal Mountains.

Rim Trail

GRAND CANYON NATIONAL PARK

ARIZONA

Witness the magnificence of the Grand Canyon without descending down into it.

- **DISTANCE**
  13-mile shuttle hike, elevation gain 600 feet
- **START**
  Any shuttle stop on the South Rim
- **DIFFICULTY**
  Easy; some sections are paved and wheelchair accessible
- **SEASON**
  Year-round

ABOVE RIGHT You'll be mesmerized by epic views on the Rim Trail.

RIGHT Unlike the North Rim, the South Rim is open year-round.

The Grand Canyon Rim Trail runs along the South Rim of the canyon for 13 miles from the South Kaibab Trailhead to Hermit's Rest. The park offers a free shuttle bus with fourteen stops along this trail, so you can choose a hike of any length.

One of the most scenic and informative sections of this route is the Trail of Time, a 3-mile section between the Yavapai Geology Museum and Maricopa Point. Information stations here cover the geology, ecology, and history of the canyon.

A series of bronze markers set into the path help you understand the vast expanse of geologic time, with just over 3 feet equaling one million years. The Grand Canyon was carved in only six paces, while quite a few more steps are needed to travel back in time to the 1.8-billion-year-old layers in the bottom of the canyon—some of the oldest rocks on Earth.

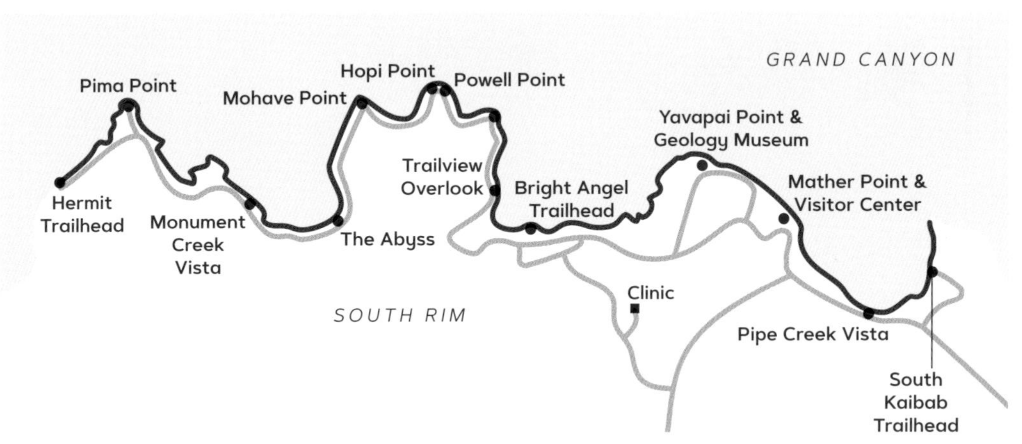

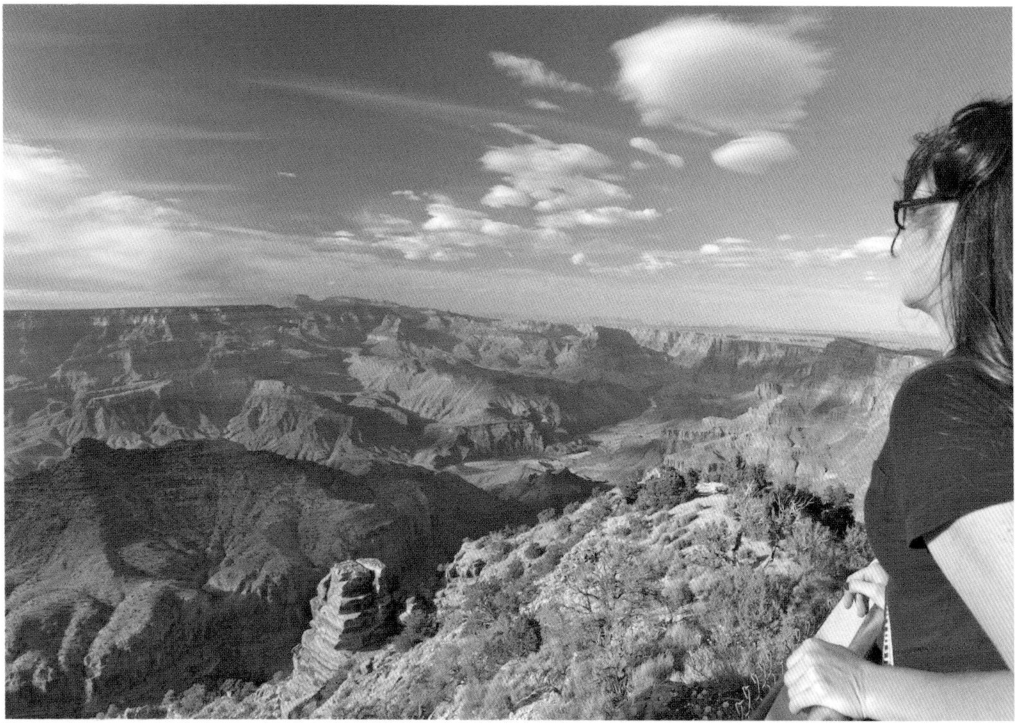

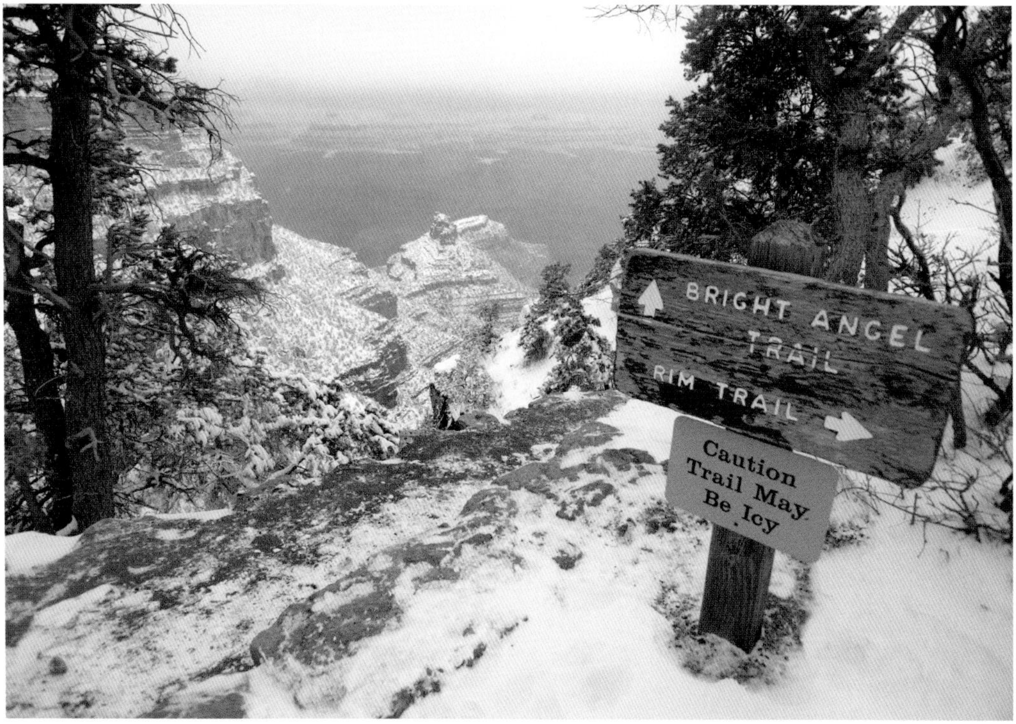
BRIGHT ANGEL TRAIL
RIM TRAIL
Caution Trail May Be Icy

85

Boucher Trail to Hermit Trail Loop

GRAND CANYON NATIONAL PARK

ARIZONA

In the late 1890s, a miner named Louis Boucher lived in the Grand Canyon near Hermit Creek, and blazed his own routes into and out of the canyon. Follow in his footsteps on this wild 20-mile loop that requires route finding, scrambling through rock bands, and long traverses around deep side canyons. Descend on the Hermit Trail and ascend the 5,800 feet back up to the rim on the Boucher Trail to make a counterclockwise loop. It is a challenging route, but you won't run into any mule trains, or many other people.

86

Bright Angel Trail to Three-Mile Resthouse

GRAND CANYON NATIONAL PARK

ARIZONA

Bright Angel Trail is the classic mule-trodden route down into the Grand Canyon from the South Rim. A day hike out and back to the two resthouses at 1.5 miles and 3 miles is a manageable goal for first-time Grand Canyon hikers. Both resthouses offer bathrooms and drinking water. Grand Canyon signs that say "Down is optional, up is mandatory" are a reminder that every step downward will need to be reversed. A hike down to the second resthouse will require climbing 2,100 feet of elevation back up again.

87

Bright Angel Point Trail

GRAND CANYON NATIONAL PARK

ARIZONA

The North Rim of the Grand Canyon sees a fraction of visitors compared to the more popular South Rim, because it is more remote and closed half the year (from November to May). This half-mile hike out to Bright Angel Point offers stunning views of the canyon and the South Rim, which sits about 1,000 feet lower in elevation than the North Rim.

88

Arizona National Scenic Trail

GRAND CANYON NATIONAL PARK

ARIZONA

This trail bisects the state of Arizona, from the Mexican border in the south to the Utah border in the north. The grand finale of the 800-mile trek is the rim-to-rim traverse of the Grand Canyon on the South Kaibab and North Kaibab Trails. Extreme heat and water availability are the most daunting challenges on this desert route.

ABOVE A hike to Bright Angel point provides stunning views over the North Rim and Grand Canyon Lodge.

LEFT Bright Angel to Three-Mile Resthouse involves hiking into the Grand Canyon and up out again.

89

King Canyon Wash Trail

SAGUARO NATIONAL PARK

ARIZONA

The saguaro cactus grows over 75 feet tall and lives for more than a century. This national park is home to around 1.9 million of the striking species, along with twenty-four other varieties of cacti. This easy 2.4-mile loop linking King Canyon Wash and Gould Mine Trail takes you past hundreds of saguaros as well as petroglyphs pecked into the rocks on either side of the wash around 800 years ago by members of the Hohokam tribe.

90

Wasson Peak

SAGUARO NATIONAL PARK

ARIZONA

You'll pass countless saguaros on your way up to the highest point in the Tucson Mountain district of Saguaro National Park. The 7.7-mile round-trip hike gains nearly 2,000 feet of elevation, offering views of the surrounding saguaro forest, the city of Tucson, and several mountain ranges.

91

Long Logs Trail and Agate House Trail Loop

PETRIFIED FOREST NATIONAL PARK

ARIZONA

Petrified Forest National Park is known for its fossilized trees that date back to the time of the dinosaurs. See some of these relics on the Long Logs Trail, which boasts the greatest abundance of petrified wood in the park. Then connect to the Agate House Trail to make a 2.6-mile loop and visit Agate House, a small pueblo constructed using petrified wood, that was last inhabited around 700 years ago. Collecting petrified wood or other objects in the park is strictly prohibited.

92

Chasm Lake

ROCKY MOUNTAIN NATIONAL PARK

COLORADO

The Rocky Mountains run for over 3,000 miles from New Mexico into British Columbia. This national park protects a spectacular pocket of peaks in Colorado's Front Range. A challenging day hike to Chasm Lake takes you to the foot of Longs Peak—at 14,259 feet, it's the highest point in the park.

This trail starts at an elevation of 9,400 feet and climbs into the treeless alpine zone, with outstanding views in every direction. The last mile of the 9.4-mile round-trip hike involves a moderate boulder scramble to reach the alpine lake. The infamously technical east face of Longs Peak—known as the Diamond—looms overhead, beckoning climbers to the summit.

Longs Peak via the Keyhole

ROCKY MOUNTAIN NATIONAL PARK

COLORADO

Longs Peak is one of the most iconic "fourteeners" in Colorado—a nickname for summits over 14,000 feet. The Keyhole route threads through a notch in a rocky ridgeline and traverses along a series of ledges with drop-offs on its way to the summit. The 17-mile out-and-back trail is rated class 3, meaning some scrambling but no technical climbing as it gains more than 4,500 feet of elevation. Getting off-route can be deadly—you should have some rock-climbing experience, a few fourteeners under your belt, and be comfortable with route finding in the alpine environment, or consider hiring a guide.

94

Petroglyph Point Trail

MESA VERDE NATIONAL PARK

COLORADO

For more than 600 years, the Ancestral Puebloan people made their home in dramatic cliff cave dwellings in what is now southwest Colorado before drought and unrest led them to relocate by the end of the thirteenth century. In 1906 Mesa Verde National Park was established to protect more than 5,000 known archaeological sites, including 600 cliff dwellings, several of which can be visited on a ranger-led tour.

The 2.4-mile Petroglyph Point Trail loop passes an overlook of one of these ruins, Spruce Tree House, and then follows a cliff band and climbs some steps to the confluence of Spruce Canyon and Navajo Canyon. Here, you'll find a 20-foot-wide rock festooned with etchings.

LEFT Chasm Lake sits in a glacially carved cirque at 11,823 feet.

BELOW The Petroglyph Point Trail takes you to an overlook of the ancient cave villages.

95

North Vista Trail to Exclamation Point

BLACK CANYON OF THE GUNNISON NATIONAL PARK

COLORADO

Peer into a canyon so deep and dark that parts of it see only thirty minutes of sunlight a day.

DISTANCE
3 miles out and back, elevation gain 364 feet

START
North Rim Ranger Station

DIFFICULTY
Easy

SEASON
May to November; the North Rim is closed in winter

This national park protects a 12-mile stretch of the Gunnison River as it plunges through the deepest, narrowest section of Black Canyon, which it formed through its sheer force. Bring binoculars and you might spot some intrepid rock climbers making their way up the walls in this world-renowned climbing destination.

A hike along the North Vista Trail to the perfectly named Exclamation Point offers some of the best views in the park. The easy path passes several overlooks of the S.O.B. Draw—one of the precipitously steep scramble routes into the inner gorge—and of the Gunnison River, more than 2,000 feet below.

BELOW Looking down on Black Canyon from Exclamation Point.

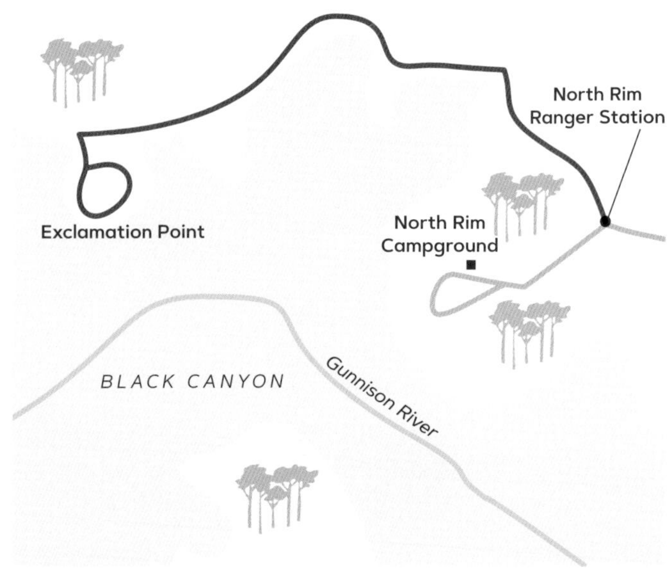

Star Dune

GREAT SAND DUNES NATIONAL PARK AND PRESERVE
COLORADO

In this park, prevailing southwest winds have blown sand gathered from across the San Luis Valley against the foothills of the Sangre de Cristo Mountains. The dunes are always changing, so there are no formal trails. To hike up the tallest sand dune in North America, follow Medano Creek south for about 2 miles until you're lined up with the tallest pyramid-shaped dune, then pick a sand ridge to follow for another 2 miles to the summit.

LEFT Black Canyon is named for its lack of sunlight.

97

Alkali Flat Trail

WHITE SANDS NATIONAL PARK

NEW MEXICO

This 275-square-mile basin of stark white dunes surrounded by mountains is downright otherworldly. The dunes aren't actually made up of sand, which is usually silica, but gypsum crystals. This 5-mile loop takes you through a sea of dunes, into the heart of the dry former lakebed known as Lake Otero. Sunrise, sunset, and moonlight are especially enchanting, but stay vigilant—it's easy to get disoriented in the dunes, especially after dark.

LEFT The Big Room is the largest single cave chamber by volume in North America.

98

Big Room Trail

CARLSBAD CAVERNS NATIONAL PARK

NEW MEXICO

Carlsbad Caverns' Big Room is spangled with limestone formations with evocative names like the Totem Pole, the Chandelier, and the Doll's Theater. They all formed slowly over geologic time as calcium carbonate deposits dripped into the cavern. Join a ranger-led tour of these spectacular limestone caves, but the Big Room is self-guided. The 1.3-mile double loop is well lit and well marked.

99

Natural Entrance Trail

CARLSBAD CAVERNS NATIONAL PARK

NEW MEXICO

The first person to discover Carlsbad Caverns descended into the caves via a homemade wire ladder. These days, you enter via an elevator or by the Natural Entrance—a 1.3-mile vertiginous paved path. Every morning and evening, from mid-April to October, thousands of Brazilian free-tailed bats also use this entrance. At sunset you'll see them leaving for their nightly insect-feeding forays in the surrounding desert. They fly far overhead and are not a threat to people.

100

McKittrick Canyon Trail

GUADALUPE MOUNTAINS NATIONAL PARK

TEXAS

Forget you're in Texas on this scenic out-and-back hike into a deep, leafy canyon cut by the only year-round stream in the park: McKittrick Creek. Pack a backpack for an overnight jaunt to the end of the canyon and back, around 20 miles, or head out for a day hike of any length.

101

Guadalupe Peak Trail

GUADALUPE MOUNTAINS NATIONAL PARK

TEXAS

Reaching the highest point in Texas demands a round trip of 8.5 miles and 3,000 feet of elevation gain. At 8,751 feet, Guadalupe Peak is one of the few places in the state where you can visit a high-alpine ecosystem.

The first 1.5 miles are tough, as you ascend steep switchbacks up from the desert floor, before leveling off a bit at higher elevations. Don't let the first false summit fool you—after surmounting this rocky knob, you have another mile to the true summit, marked by a metal pyramid.

102

Lost Mine Trail

BIG BEND NATIONAL PARK

TEXAS

Big Bend National Park is named for a distinctive 90-degree turn in the mighty Rio Grande as it journeys along the border of Texas and Mexico. This park also contains the entirety of the Chisos Mountains—the only mountain range in the United States to be fully protected within the boundaries of a national park—as well as a vast region of the Chihuahuan Desert.

The 4.2-mile out-and-back Lost Mine Trail is a perfect day hike to experience the diversity of all three ecosystems. A mile down the trail you'll reach a saddle with outstanding views of Casa Grande Peak and Juniper Canyon. Continue another mile up to a ridge that overlooks Pine Canyon and across the Rio Grande into Mexico.

103

Santa Elena Canyon Trail

BIG BEND NATIONAL PARK

TEXAS

You'll get your feet wet on this easy 1.5-mile out-and-back hike along the banks of the Rio Grande. Bring sandals and a walking stick for the crossing of Terlingua Creek, which is usually only a few inches deep. However, following a rainstorm, it may be too high to cross safely. The trail dead-ends where 1,000-foot limestone cliffs meet the river.

LEFT Prepare to get your feet wet on the Santa Elena Canyon Trail.

104

Maah Daah Hey Trail

THEODORE ROOSEVELT NATIONAL PARK

NORTH DAKOTA

Link all three units of this national park on an epic journey through grasslands and badlands.

- **DISTANCE**
  144 miles one way, usually completed in sections or over ten to fourteen days
- **START**
  Various starting points
- **DIFFICULTY**
  Hard due to lack of water
- **SEASON**
  April to October

ABOVE RIGHT At times you'll feel in the middle of nowhere on the long Maah Daah Hey Trail.

RIGHT There are constant elevation changes on the Maah Daah Hey Trail.

Maah Daah Hey means "an area that has been or will be around for a long time" in the Mandan tribe's language, and indeed this indigenous route predates the national park, which was established in 1978, by hundreds, if not thousands, of years.

You'll rack up over 15,000 feet of elevation gain over the entire length of the trail. As it's difficult to find water in this landscape, the Maah Daah Hey Trail Association has installed a series of water cache boxes along the route for people to stash water refills ahead of their trek.

105

Caprock Coulee Loop

THEODORE ROOSEVELT NATIONAL PARK

NORTH DAKOTA

After visiting North Dakota in 1883 on a bison-hunting trip, future president Theodore Roosevelt fell in love with the grasslands and bought two ranches near Medora, both of which are preserved in this national park. Enjoy the wide-open landscape that so inspired Roosevelt on this 4.4-mile loop.

Pick up a brochure for the Caprock Coulee Nature Trail that details the unique geology and ecology of the area. Look for bison and give them plenty of room, as they can charge if they feel threatened.

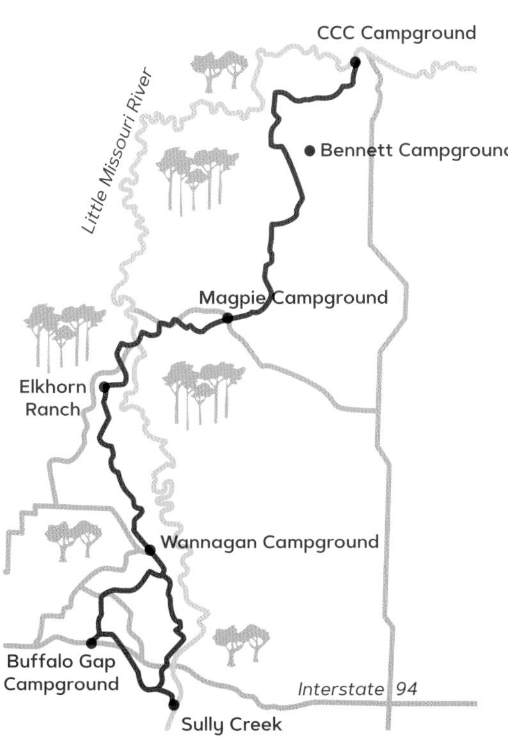
CCC Campground
Little Missouri River
Bennett Campground
Magpie Campground
Elkhorn Ranch
Wannagan Campground
Buffalo Gap Campground
Interstate 94
Sully Creek

106

Notch Trail

BADLANDS NATIONAL PARK

SOUTH DAKOTA

On this 1.3-mile round-trip hike, you have to clamber up a 50-foot wooden stepladder to surmount a sloped hillside. But the payoff is worth the effort—at the top you'll be rewarded with views of the unusual landscape of swaying grasses surrounding islands of artfully eroded badlands.

107

Wild Cave Tour

WIND CAVE NATIONAL PARK

SOUTH DAKOTA

Wind Cave has more than 149 miles of interconnected tunnels that make up the greatest known passage volume per cubic mile of any mapped cave system.

To visit, sign up for a guided tour through the park service. You'll don helmets and kneepads for the four-hour-long Wild Cave Tour, and spend most of the time on your hands and knees, crawling through tight passages. But the rewards are great: Wind Cave is full of beautiful and delicate cave formations.

RIGHT A scramble up a wooden ladder on the Notch Trail takes you to an overlook of the barren badlands.

108

Blind Ash Bay Trail

VOYAGEURS NATIONAL PARK

MINNESOTA

A maze of interconnected waterways makes Voyageurs National Park a world-class canoeing and kayaking destination, but the park also has 50 miles of trails for those who prefer to explore on foot. The Blind Ash Bay Trail starts at a scenic overlook of Kabetogama Lake and skirts the wild shoreline of Blind Ash Bay for a 3-mile round-trip trek.

This national park is a great place to catch the aurora borealis, also known as the northern lights. You're more likely to spot an aurora on dark, new moon nights.

BELOW The colorful northern lights in Voyageurs National Park.

109

Sunset to Hot Springs Mountain Loop

HOT SPRINGS NATIONAL PARK

ARKANSAS

Earn a soak in a modern bathhouse after tackling the trail that circumnavigates Hot Springs Mountain.

- **DISTANCE**
  13.6-mile loop, elevation gain 3,100 feet
- **START**
  Gulpha Gorge Campground or West Mountain
- **DIFFICULTY**
  Moderate
- **SEASON**
  Year-round; fall colors peak in October

BELOW The Sunset Trail is the longest hike in the park.

FAR RIGHT Hot Water Cascade flows down the mountain from one of the springs.

For at least 3,000 years, people have been journeying to the Ouachita Mountains to bathe in the legendary hot springs that emerge from the flank of Hot Springs Mountain.

Before you relax in the soothing waters, conquer the longest trail in the park on the 13-mile Sunset Trail, with a side trip on the Hot Springs Mountain Trail. A short spur also runs over the forested summit of 1,418-foot Music Mountain—the highest point in the park. But the best views are found on Hot Springs Mountain, atop the 216-foot steel observation tower. You'll see the Ouachita Mountains and the historic town in the valley at the base of the mountain.

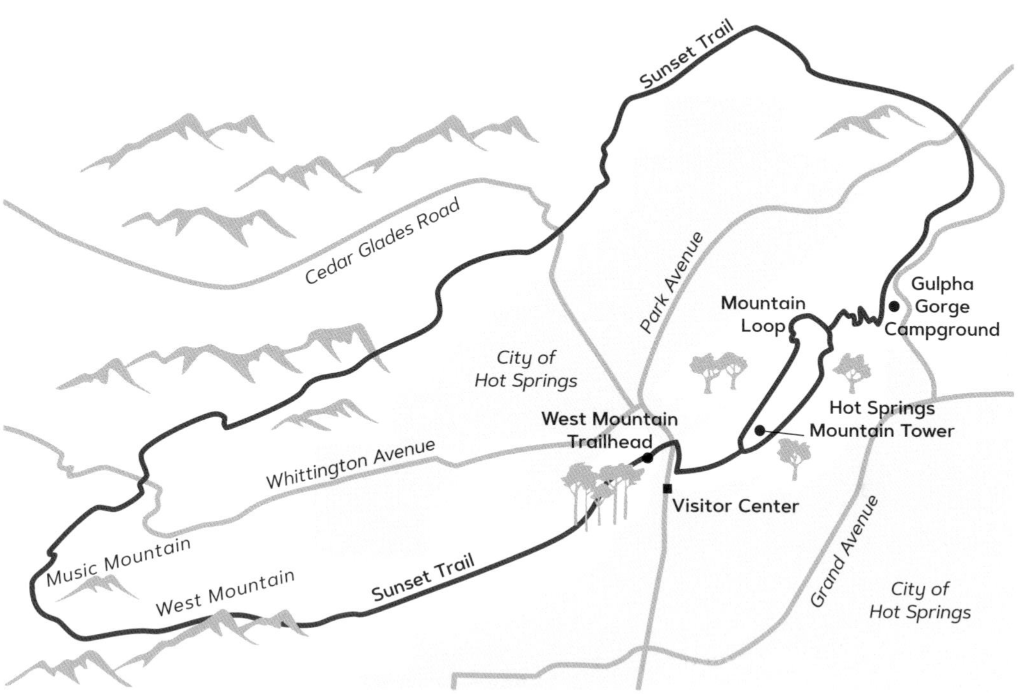

110

Grand Promenade

HOT SPRINGS NATIONAL PARK
ARKANSAS

The Grand Promenade is a redbrick-paved wheelchair-accessible walkway. The 1.2-mile loop runs past eight historic bathhouses on Bathhouse Row, which sit directly on top of natural hot springs—a handful offer soaking and spa services.

You'll pass several fountains where you can taste the mineral-rich water—it has no sulfur smell or taste and is thought by some to have medicinal qualities.

111

Greenstone Ridge Trail

ISLE ROYALE NATIONAL PARK

MICHIGAN

The rocky Isle Royale is the largest island in Lake Superior and supports roughly 1,000 moose and around twenty-five wolves—these numbers fluctuate each season in a classic predator-prey relationship. You may hear wolves howling on the 40-mile Greenstone Ridge Trail, which runs the length of the island on a high ridge. You're unlikely to see one of the elusive canines and no person has ever been attacked in the park. Moose, however, can be aggressive, so give them a wide berth.

112

Scoville Point Loop

ISLE ROYALE NATIONAL PARK

MICHIGAN

Rock Harbor is located on the northeast side of Isle Royale, the opposite end from Windigo Bay, where most visitor services are concentrated. There are no roads on the island, and this quieter side can only be reached by park service ferry or chartered float plane. The 5-mile loop to Scoville Point alternates between dense old-growth forest and exposed rocky shoreline. You'll likely spot moose here.

BELOW Scoville Point is a well-known moose nursery—cow moose hide from wolves with their young calves.

RIGHT More than 350 avian species can be found in Indiana Dunes National Park.

113

Cowles Bog Trail

INDIANA DUNES NATIONAL PARK

INDIANA

Indiana Dunes National Park boasts an incredible diversity of plants and animals. The Cowles Bog Trail is named after an ecologist who spent his career studying plant life here. The 4.7-mile loop trail highlights the park's many ecosystems, including dunes, beaches, ponds, marshes, swamps, and black oak savanna. The plant diversity (more than 1,400 species) is so outstanding that in 1965, the trail was named a National Natural Landmark.

114

Violet City Lantern Tour

MAMMOTH CAVE NATIONAL PARK

KENTUCKY

Experience the underground grandeur of Mammoth Cave on a tour lit only by the light of lanterns carried by the group. In a safe spot, the tour guide will extinguish the lanterns so you can experience the eerie total absence of light, known as cave darkness. On the 3-mile tour, which takes about three hours, you'll walk through huge caverns and wide tunnels.

115

Beneath Your Feet Tour and Sinkhole Trail

MAMMOTH CAVE NATIONAL PARK

KENTUCKY

Discover the caverns and a giant sinkhole on an easy path in the world's longest known cave system.

DISTANCE
2.4 miles out and back, elevation gain 358 feet

START
Mammoth Cave Lodge

DIFFICULTY
Easy; the beginning paved section, called the Heritage Trail, is wheelchair accessible

SEASON
Year-round

ABOVE RIGHT More than 400 miles of passages have been mapped in Mammoth Cave.

RIGHT You have to join a tour to visit the subterranean rooms and passageways in Mammoth Cave.

Mammoth Cave is carved out of limestone, a water-soluble rock, and capped by a thick layer of sandstone, making the cave system remarkably stable. As you walk around on the surface, it's hard to believe that vast caverns and tunnels are hidden underfoot.

Using radio telemetry—which uses radio signals to determine location—the park service has pinpointed where some of the cave's underground features are located on the surface. When you're standing in front of the Lodge, you're standing 140 feet above the Rotunda, one of the largest rooms in the Mammoth Cave system.

A more obvious connection to the underworld can be seen on the Sinkhole Trail. This easy path through the woods leads to the Mammoth Dome Sinkhole, where the earth has collapsed into a limestone cavern, leaving a depression at the surface. Below it lurks a 192-foot shaft that funnels rainwater into the cave system.

Brandywine Gorge Trail

CUYAHOGA VALLEY NATIONAL PARK

OHIO

This national park preserves a scenic, rural stretch of the Cuyahoga River in northeast Ohio. Once one of the most polluted rivers in the United States, the river has been rehabilitated thanks to the Clean Water Act and other environmental efforts. This easy 1.4-mile loop parallels Brandywine Creek through a rocky gorge upstream from the river and leads to Brandywine Falls. In the spring, you may spot salamanders in pools along the creek.

Buckeye Trail

CUYAHOGA VALLEY NATIONAL PARK

OHIO

The 1,444-mile Buckeye Trail loops around the state of Ohio, following blue blazes painted on trees and fence posts. The longest circular trail in any state, it is rarely hiked in its entirety. Dedicated hikers—often proud Ohioans—will instead spend a lifetime hiking individual sections, one weekend at a time.

118

Cadillac Mountain South Ridge Trail Loop

ACADIA NATIONAL PARK

MAINE

Cadillac Mountain is the highest point on the North Atlantic seaboard and therefore the first place to see the sunrise in the United States. You'll have to start hiking dark and early on this loop trail to beat the sun to the summit, or hike the 8-mile round-trip trail any time of day to enjoy expansive views over the Maine coast.

119

Long Point

NEW RIVER GORGE NATIONAL PARK

WEST VIRGINIA

In 2021 the New River Gorge became America's newest national park, but despite its newfound status, the New is one of the oldest rivers on Earth. Flowing from south to north—an unusual direction among North American rivers—the New River was draining the Appalachian Mountains back when dinosaurs roamed the planet.

More than 1,400 established climbing routes snake up the epic canyon's walls. Snap a postcard-worthy shot that includes the gorge's iconic steel arch bridge—a world-famous BASE jumping launchpad—on this 3-mile round-trip hike to Long Point.

ABOVE The Appalachian Trail is famous for the three-sided shelters dotted along its route.

120

Appalachian Trail

SHENANDOAH NATIONAL PARK

VIRGINIA

Perched up high in the Blue Ridge Mountains, Shenandoah National Park is bisected by the relentlessly snaky Skyline Drive. A 115-mile section of the Appalachian Trail (AT) runs the length of the national park.

The AT's huts are spaced about a day's walk apart along the entire length of the 2,190-mile trail. Shenandoah has seven overnight shelters and five that have been designated as day- and emergency-use only.

121

Rose River Trail

SHENANDOAH NATIONAL PARK

VIRGINIA

This spectacular 3.5-mile loop follows the Rose River past dozens of waterfalls. Go in the spring for wildflowers, summer for the incredibly green tree tunnel, fall for the foliage, or winter to enjoy the icy cascades (bring ice-traction devices for your boots). Connect to the Appalachian Trail or Skyland/ Big Meadows Horse Trail for a longer adventure.

122

Old Rag Mountain Loop

SHENANDOAH NATIONAL PARK

VIRGINIA

Old Rag's bald, 3,284-foot boulder summit stands out among the region's mostly forested peaks. It was formed over a billion years ago and once underlied a mountain range longer and higher than the Rockies. All that remains today in this area is Old Rag Mountain.

The 10-mile loop up Old Rag is part hike, part scramble, with painted arrows pointing the way up boulders, down narrow passages, and through crevasses. Wear long pants, long sleeves, and even gloves, as the glittering crystals in the granite are very sharp. Follow signs to descend on the Saddle Trail to the Byrd's Nest Shelter and stroll back to your car on the Weakley Hollow Fire Road.

LEFT The trail up Old Rag follows a series of blue arrows painted on granite boulders.

123

Ramsey Cascades Trail

GREAT SMOKY MOUNTAINS NATIONAL PARK

NORTH CAROLINA AND TENNESSEE

Indigenous people called the southern Appalachians Shaconage, meaning "place of the blue smoke," but the Great Smoky Mountains aren't actually smoky—they're foggy. The fog is produced as trees exhale oxygen and volatile organic compounds during photosynthesis, producing a whitish-blue vapor.

The Smokies may be the busiest national park in the United States, but with more than 850 miles of trails, you're sure to find some peace. This 8-mile out-and-back hike up the creek runs through old-growth forest to 100-foot Ramsey Cascades, the highest waterfall in the park.

124

Boardwalk Loop Trail

CONGAREE NATIONAL PARK

SOUTH CAROLINA

Explore the largest tract of old-growth bottomland hardwood forest in the United States on this elevated boardwalk. Bottomland forests grow in lowland floodplains, where regular flooding helps build up rich alluvial soils that give rise to some of the tallest trees in the eastern part of the country.

Raised 6 feet above the forest floor, this 2.6-mile wheelchair-accessible trail offers a unique perspective on the park's bald cypress and tupelo trees. Congaree is humid in the summer—a perfect breeding ground for mosquitoes. The visitor center has a mosquito meter that ranges from "1: All clear" to "6: War zone!" Visit in the late fall or winter to avoid the bugs.

125

Shark Valley Trail

EVERGLADES NATIONAL PARK

FLORIDA

You'll be grateful for the smooth pavement on this 15.8-mile loop through the wild heart of the Everglades. Many people bike this route, which follows the banks of the Shark River Slough, but you can also walk it. Keep your eyes peeled for alligators and snakes, which sometimes sun themselves on the trail.

RIGHT There are roughly 200,000 American alligators in Everglades National Park.

126

Anhinga Trail

EVERGLADES NATIONAL PARK

FLORIDA

South Florida is saturated by the Everglades' River of Grass that flows slowly from the Kissimmee River near Orlando south to Florida Bay. Along the way, the river system feeds a variety of tropical wetland ecosystems.

This area is home to a vast array of wildlife, and one of the best places to spot it is on the Anhinga Trail, an easy wheelchair-accessible loop that winds through a sawgrass marsh for less than a mile. It is a top bird-watching location, and you might spot alligators here too.

127

Spite Highway and Maritime Heritage Trail

BISCAYNE NATIONAL PARK

FLORIDA

Take a scenic walk on an island trail where 95 percent of the national park is underwater.

DISTANCE
6 miles out and back, minimal elevation gain

START
Elliot Key Ranger Station

DIFFICULTY
Easy

SEASON
December to April

BELOW Kayaking and canoeing are great ways to explore the shallow waters of Biscayne National Park.

Spite Highway is an overgrown former road that runs the length of Elliot Key, an island built up from many layers of coral reefs. The most scenic section of the trail starts at the ranger station and turns around after 3 miles at Petrel Point and Sandwich Cove.

The Maritime Heritage Trail follows a series of six shipwrecks that can be explored by snorkel or scuba. You can sign up for a guided snorkel tour through the park service.

Biscayne National Park can only be reached by boat or seaplane. Mosquitoes are legion here, especially in the spring and summer months. Visit during the dry season between December and April, when the bugs are more manageable.

ABOVE Explore the Maritime Heritage Trail on a scuba-diving excursion.

128

Fort Jefferson Loop

DRY TORTUGAS NATIONAL PARK

FLORIDA

The seven small islands and coral reefs that make up this remote park lie 70 miles west of the Florida Keys. The park is dominated by the remains of Fort Jefferson, a massive brick fortress built in the mid-1800s to help protect shipping lanes in the Gulf of Mexico from pirates. This half-mile loop circumnavigates the fort's walls and moat on Garden Key, providing outstanding beach and reef views. Go in April or May for the annual bird migration—hundreds of different species make their spring journey across the gulf.

129

Petroglyph Trail

VIRGIN ISLANDS NATIONAL PARK

VIRGIN ISLANDS

Hike the 3-mile round trip to a panel of petroglyphs carved into a boulder at the base of the highest waterfall in the Reef Bay valley, on the south shore of Saint John. These mysterious carvings are thought to have been etched by the indigenous Taíno people sometime between the early seventh and late fifteenth centuries.

130

Honeymoon Beach

VIRGIN ISLANDS NATIONAL PARK

VIRGIN ISLANDS

The Virgin Islands are famous for their stunning beaches. This quick hike to Honeymoon Beach doesn't have to end at the edge of the water—you can rent a kayak, paddleboard, or snorkeling equipment on the beach. Return via Salomon Beach to make a 2.3-mile loop back to the visitor center.

131

Boiling Lake

MORNE TROIS PITONS NATIONAL PARK

DOMINICA

Just outside Dominica's capital, Roseau, lies a grayish-blue lake that's always enveloped in vapor. The water in the center is hot enough to boil, producing the copious steam and earning it the name Boiling Lake. Volcanic activity on the island sometimes makes the lake drain rapidly and occasionally roil into a fountain of hot water and steam. The only way to visit is on foot, on an 8.2-mile round-trip hike. Avoid lingering too long—potentially toxic emissions of volcanic gases can be deadly.

132

Douglas Bay Battery Trail

CABRITS NATIONAL PARK

DOMINICA

Cabrits is one of the smallest national parks in the world, covering only 2 square miles. It was once its own island, formed through a series of volcanic eruptions that eventually connected it to the larger island of Dominica, forming a peninsula. Today, Cabrits National Park sits between the two summits of the now-extinct volcano and includes the remains of Fort Shirley, a British garrison built in 1765. On this easy 2-mile stroll, you'll see how the surrounding tropical forest is slowly reclaiming the abandoned fort.

LEFT The flooded fumarole of Boiling Lake is the world's second-largest hot spring.

133

Waitukubuli Trail

CABRITS NATIONAL PARK

DOMINICA

Set out on the longest hiking trail in the Caribbean, which runs the length of Dominica.

DISTANCE
115 miles with shuttle, usually completed in sections or in one go over twelve to fourteen days

START
Multiple access points

DIFFICULTY
Hard due to distance and logistics

SEASON
December to May

ABOVE RIGHT The Cabrits National Park peninsula marks the end of the Waitukubuli Trail.

RIGHT Many start the Waitukubuli Trail at Scotts Head fishing village.

Dominica is the youngest island in the Caribbean—the landform rose out of the sea after a series of volcanic eruptions around 26 million years ago. That volcanism is still active, fueling many geothermal features.

The earliest known settlers arrived here by boat from South America around 3100 BCE. The native Caribs called their island Waitukubuli, meaning "tall is her body"—a reference to the lush tropical forests.

Before roads, the 290-square-mile island was crisscrossed by an extensive network of footpaths. The Waitukubuli Trail makes use of these ancient paths as it meanders across the island. Most people hike the trail in sections, but each year a handful of intrepid trekkers complete the entire route, starting in the south at Scotts Head and finishing at Cabrits National Park in the north. To preserve the ecosystem, camping is not permitted, but you can find nightly lodging in eco lodges, bed-and-breakfasts, and private homes along the route.

134

Rooi Tambu

ARIKOK NATIONAL PARK
ARUBA

The Caribbean island of Aruba is underlain by limestone, volcanic tuff, and pillow lavas that give rise to a desertlike, cactus-studded ecosystem. The Rooi Tambu hike follows a seasonal stream for 3.5 miles through the arid landscape to Dos Playa, two white sand coves frequented by surfers and nesting sea turtles.

135

The Walled City

TULUM NATIONAL PARK

MEXICO

Immerse yourself in history on a picturesque self-guided walking tour of a preserved Mayan city.

DISTANCE
0.8-mile loop, minimal elevation gain

START
Entrance to Walled City

DIFFICULTY
Easy

SEASON
Dry season, November to May

BELOW RIGHT Tulum served as an important trade nexus for the Mayan empire.

Perched on the edge of cliffs overlooking the east coast of Mexico's Yucatán Peninsula, Tulum is protected on the landward side by an expansive limestone wall. These fortifications helped the Mayans fend off the Spanish invasion for around seventy years longer than other Mayan cities, but Tulum was eventually abandoned—likely due to high mortality from introduced Old World diseases.

Today, several notable structures still stand: the Temple of the Frescoes was an observatory for tracking the movements of the sun—it is decorated with murals that date back to the eleventh century; the Temple of the Descending God and the Temple of the Wind God served deities who appear in carvings and sculptures all over the walled city; and El Castillo—the Castle—is a 25-foot tiered building fronted by a flight of steps, which provides fantastic views.

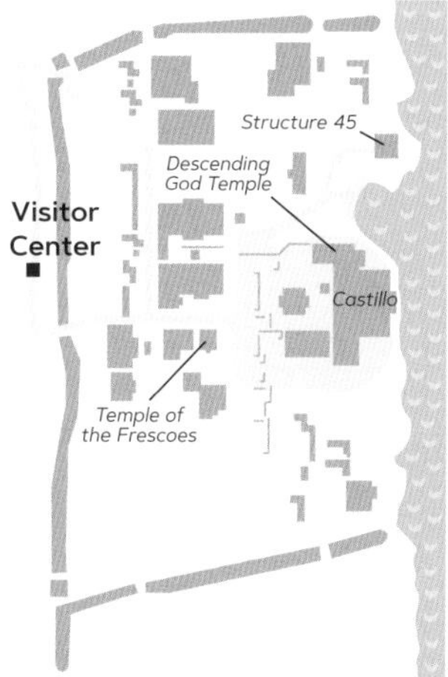

Basaseachic Falls

BASASEACHIC FALLS NATIONAL PARK

MEXICO

Mexico's Copper Canyon produces some of the toughest ultramarathon runners in the world. For generations, the Rarámuri people have traveled the steep canyon systems that drain the Sierra Madre Occidental mountains. Their name means "flying feet" and athletes regularly run for up to 200 miles in a session in ceremonies and competitions.

Test your legs and lungs in the Rarámuri's home training grounds by hiking to the base of 800-foot Basaseachic Falls. The trail to the top is easy, but the views of the falls are limited. Reaching their base is more rigorous, losing and then regaining 850 feet of elevation in a mile, but you'll be able to cool off in the spray before climbing back up to the rim.

LEFT The Temple of the Wind God sanctuary was used for religious purposes.

137

The Causeways

TIKAL NATIONAL PARK

GUATEMALA

During its heyday as one of the most powerful cities in the Mayan empire, Tikal was home to as many as 90,000 people. Located in the Guatemalan rainforest, the city is one of the largest and most thoroughly studied pre-Columbian cities in Central America.

As you walk a 4-mile loop around the city, following the network of causeways, keep in mind that you're walking an astronomical grid—many of Tikal's temples were arranged to align with the sunrise and sunset on the solstices and equinoxes. Climb to the top of the temples to get an aerial view of the complex.

138

Pacaya Volcano

PACAYA VOLCANO NATIONAL PARK

GUATEMALA

Erupting nearly continuously over the past sixty years, Pacaya is one of the most active volcanoes on Earth. Hiking this 3-mile round trip to the top is relatively safe; access to the closely monitored volcano is restricted if an eruption is ramping up. You must go with an experienced guide—they can be hired at the visitor center.

139

Unbelievable Falls

PICO BONITO NATIONAL PARK

HONDURAS

This 3.4-mile round-trip hike starts with a river crossing and then runs through rainforest farmland, where you'll see fields of crops like coffee, bananas, and cacao beans. You might also come across toucans, spider monkeys, tapirs, and deer. You're unlikely to spot a jaguar or a puma, but both large cats live in the park.

ABOVE LEFT AND LEFT Tikal is made up of more than 3,000 excavated buildings.

RIGHT Keep your eyes peeled for spider monkeys on the hike to Unbelievable Falls.

140

Jeannette Kawas Trail

JEANNETTE KAWAS NATIONAL PARK

HONDURAS

Formerly known as Punta Sala National Park, the name was changed in 1995 to honor an environmental activist who was murdered for her efforts to protect the park from development. You will have to catch a boat there, and the trail runs for less than a mile from the dock, across the peninsula, and ends at Puerto Escondido.

141

Crater Hike

MASAYA VOLCANO NATIONAL PARK

NICARAGUA

This notoriously active volcanic complex presides over the landscape just 12 miles south of Nicaragua's capital, Managua. All hikes in the national park are guided, including this 3.6-mile round-trip trek to the crater rim. Sign up for a sunset or nighttime tour to see the red-hot magma glowing down in the Santiago crater from the rim, also known as the "Mouth of Hell."

142

Río Celeste Trail

TENORIO VOLCANO NATIONAL PARK

COSTA RICA

The farther you hike upstream along the banks of the Celeste River, the deeper the hue. The electric blue coloration is due to high concentrations of sulfur and carbonate minerals dissolved in the water, supplied by the nearby Tenorio Volcano. The 3.4-mile round-trip trail leads you through dense rainforest to a stunning turquoise waterfall.

143

La Leona Madrigal Trail

CORCOVADO NATIONAL PARK

COSTA RICA

Corcovado, located on the Osa Peninsula, is Costa Rica's largest national park and a hotbed of ecological diversity, protecting some of the most pristine tropical rainforest in Central America. Look for wildlife on this stunning 3-mile stretch of Corcovado's 23 miles of beaches. Check a tide chart at the ranger station before you leave, as some sections of the coastline are impassable at high tide.

La Trampa

MANUEL ANTONIO NATIONAL PARK

COSTA RICA

Pack a pair of binoculars and a bathing suit for this easy 4.8-mile hike. Capuchin, howler, and squirrel monkeys—as well as sloths, agoutis, and iguanas—are often spotted along this seaside loop. If you do swim, be careful about leaving your bag unattended on the white sand beach—monkeys and raccoons may paw through your belongings looking for food.

LEFT Beautiful beaches attract visitors to Manuel Antonio National Park.

145

Arenal 1968 Volcano Trail

ARENAL VOLCANO NATIONAL PARK

COSTA RICA

Explore the flanks of an active stratovolcano, thought for centuries to be extinct.

DISTANCE
2.9-mile loop, elevation gain 500 feet

START
Arenal 1968 trailhead

DIFFICULTY
Easy

SEASON
November to April

RIGHT Arenal Volcano rises dramatically out of the rainforest in a symmetrical steep-sided cone.

On July 29, 1968, Arenal Volcano came roaring back to life in a series of eruptions that buried three nearby villages and killed eighty-seven people. Since then, the volcano has erupted dozens of times, earning it some notoriety as one of the most active volcanoes on Earth. Today, Arenal Volcano National Park draws volcano enthusiasts and bird-watchers—the surrounding rainforest is home to more than 800 bird species, including the elusive quetzal.

One of the best ways to experience the power of the 1968 eruption is to hike the Arenal 1968 Volcano Trail. This easy loop winds through pristine rainforest before emerging out into a lava field created by the eruption.

146

Poás Volcano Trail

POÁS VOLCANO NATIONAL PARK

COSTA RICA

For the clearest views of the milky blue lake in the Poás Volcano caldera, hike the 1.5 miles to the crater viewpoint early in the morning, before thick fog gathers around the volcano. Lucky visitors may see a geyser erupt from the caldera lake, which occurs when lake water comes in contact with underground geothermal activity, causing steam to shoot upward. The Poás Volcano erupted most recently in 2017; check current conditions and closures before you go.

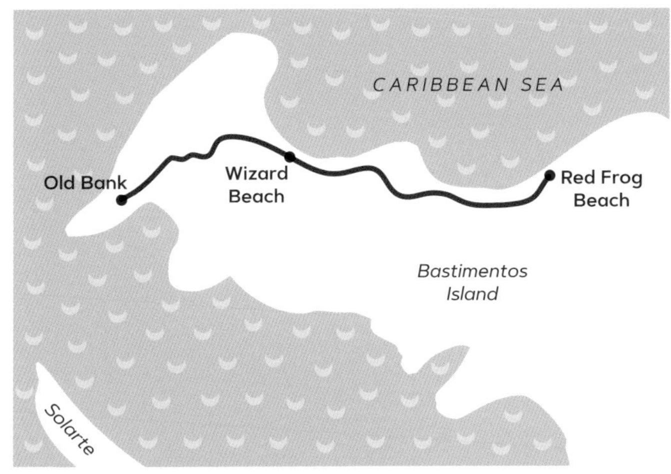
CARIBBEAN SEA
Old Bank
Wizard Beach
Red Frog Beach
Bastimentos Island
Solarte

147

Wizard Beach

BASTIMENTOS ISLAND NATIONAL PARK

PANAMA

Don your hiking boots for this rocky and rooty trail through the jungle to a beautiful beach.

- **DISTANCE**
  4 miles out and back, minimal elevation gain
- **START**
  Old Bank
- **DIFFICULTY**
  Moderate
- **SEASON**
  January to April

LEFT Wizard Beach is known for its striking golden sand.

Most of Bastimentos Island National Park is underwater, where intertidal mangrove forests give way to 10,000-year-old coral reefs. The snorkeling here is top-notch, but you can keep your feet dry on a walking tour to Wizard Beach. Starting in the town of Old Bank, the path crosses the interior of the peninsula, through prime sloth habitat. It then continues down the coast to Second Beach and Red Frog Beach, named for a once-common, now endangered, species of poison dart frog.

Visit nearby Long Beach between April and September to see sea turtles that visit every summer to lay hundreds of eggs in nests they dig in the sand. The hatchlings emerge all at once in a mad dash for the sea, dodging predators. Very few survive to adulthood, but those that do can live for up to eighty years.

148

Volcán Barú

VOLCÁN BARÚ NATIONAL PARK

PANAMA

Located on Panama's narrow isthmus, the 11,398-foot Volcán Barú stratovolcano is the highest mountain in the country. Start your 16-mile round-trip hike before midnight, or camp on the mountain to be on the summit for sunrise, the clearest time of day to enjoy the views.

Quetzal Trail

VOLCÁN BARÚ NATIONAL PARK

PANAMA

Embark on a hike named after a beautiful and elusive Central American bird: the resplendent quetzal.

DISTANCE
11 miles out and back or 5.5 miles one way with shuttle, elevation gain 2,300 feet

START
Cerro Punta or Boquete

DIFFICULTY
Moderate

SEASON
January to April

RIGHT The quetzal is around 1 foot tall and its tail can grow as long as 3 feet.

BELOW The Quetzal Trail follows a ridge on the flank of Volcán Barú.

The quetzal was revered in Mesoamerican mythology by both the Aztecs and Mayans. Today, the bright green bird with a long tail streamer is a once-in-a-lifetime sighting for dedicated birders.

More than 300 pairs of quetzals are known to nest in the Volcán Barú cloud forest, which is rich in the bird's preferred foods. The habitat also supports hundreds of other bird species, including the curiously named buffy tufted cheek, ruddy treerunner, spotted barbtail, and spectacled foliage-gleaner.

This trail can be completed as an all-day, out-and-back hike or you can arrange transportation to make it a one-way shuttle hike.

150

Pirre Mountain Trail

DARIÉN NATIONAL PARK

PANAMA

Take extra precautions—and a guide—on one of the world's most dangerous, lawless wilderness hikes.

DISTANCE
11 miles out and back, elevation gain 2,000 feet

START
Cerro Pirre trailhead

DIFFICULTY
Hard due to logistics

SEASON
January to April

LEFT Lush rainforest abounds on the mountain of Cerro Pirre.

Panama's largest national park protects the virgin rainforest along the border with Colombia. This area is notorious for being the only impassable gap in the 19,000-mile Pan-American Highway that runs from Alaska to Argentina. The missing 66-mile section, known as the Darién Gap, has never been completed due to remote logistics and ecological concerns.

The lack of roads and a reputation for lawlessness and illegal drug smuggling makes this one of the most inaccessible and least-visited national parks in the world. The logistical hurdles are formidable, but the rewards of visiting one of the world's last untrammeled wilderness areas are worth jumping through a few hoops. Panama requires visitors to register in advance with the National Border Police, hire a reputable guide, and stick to the few established trails.

This route climbs Cerro Pirre to the ranger station bunkhouse on the summit, where you'll need your own food, bedding, and water purifier. From here you can enjoy the sunset and sunrise views, and look for jaguars, ocelots, agoutis, sloths, several species of monkeys, and more than 500 bird species.

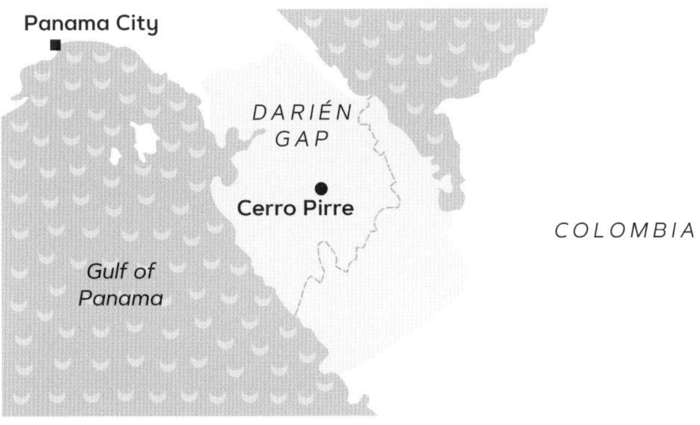

SOUTH AMERICA

Follow in the footsteps of the Incas, from the pristine beaches and jungles of the mighty Amazon River basin, down the high-altitude spine of the Andes, to the literal ends of the Earth in Patagonia.

151

Nine Stones Trail

TAYRONA NATIONAL PARK

COLOMBIA

For a hike that explores the jungle interior of Tayrona National Park, set off on the Nueve Piedras, or Nine Stones Trail, marked by a series of large egg-shaped rocks. On this easy 2-mile loop, keep your eyes and ears open for the sights and sounds of the jungle, home to comically noisy howler monkeys, along with capuchin and cotton-top tamarin monkeys.

152

Cabo San Juan

TAYRONA NATIONAL PARK

COLOMBIA

Tayrona National Park's pristine beaches can only be accessed by boat or on foot. This coastal trek starts at the park's Zaino entrance and runs through lush jungle to Arrecifes. Due to strong surf and rip currents here, walk farther down the coast to La Piscina, which is safe for swimming. Farther yet, 4 miles from the start, is Cabo San Juan, one of Tayrona's largest and most picturesque beaches. If you're feeling brave, walk another 10 minutes down the coast to Tayrona's clothing-optional beach, Playa Nudista.

RIGHT Tayrona's beautiful beaches can only be reached by boat or foot.

FAR RIGHT ABOVE The concrete pyramid on top of Mount Roraima marks the point where three countries meet.

FAR RIGHT Mount Roraima comprises 1,300-foot quartz sandstone cliffs.

153

The Ritacuba

EL COCUY NATIONAL PARK

COLOMBIA

Put your legs and lungs to the test on this high-altitude trek to the edge of the Ritacuba Glacier in the Colombian Andes. The 8.5-mile round-trip hike to see the jumbled blue-ice glacier tops out at 15,000 feet above sea level. Experienced alpinists may be lured even higher, to the looming summit of Ritacuba Blanco, at 17,750 feet above sea level. The northwest ridge route requires glacier travel skills, ice axes, and crampons, and you'll need to hire a local guide.

154

Mount Roraima

CANAIMA NATIONAL PARK

VENEZUELA

Canaima National Park protects a huge swath of Venezuela that is capped with tepuis—tabletop mountains that rise out of the surrounding rainforest. Mount Roraima is the highest sky island in the Pakaraima chain of tepuis. Many of the plants and animals that live here have evolved in isolation and are found nowhere else on Earth.

The Paraitepui Route, the only nontechnical trail to the top of Mount Roraima, starts in the tiny hamlet of Paraitepui, where you'll hire a guide. It usually takes about three days to reach the summit; a few days to explore the plateau and climb to the highest point, 9,220-foot Maverick Rock; and two days to return to Paraitepui. While on top, tag the concrete pyramid that marks where Venezuela, Brazil, and Guyana meet.

Angel Falls

CANAIMA NATIONAL PARK

VENEZUELA

Cast your eyes upon the highest uninterrupted waterfall on Earth—three times as tall as Paris's Eiffel Tower.

DISTANCE
6 miles out and back, elevation gain 500 feet

START
Ratoncito Island Camp

DIFFICULTY
Moderate

SEASON
June to December

BELOW Angel Falls descend from the Auyántepuí plateau ("Devil's Mountain").

Originally named for the American pilot who "discovered" the falls on a flyover in 1933, many have called for Angel Falls to be restored to its indigenous name, Kerepakupai Merú, which means "waterfall of the deepest place."

Laying eyes on this natural wonder isn't easy. First you'll need to fly into the remote Canaima National Park, a place of few roads that is still home to several indigenous tribes. Then from Canaima Lagoon, you'll embark on a five-hour motorized canoe ride up the Churún River.

Once you reach the base camp at Ratoncito Island, it's a 3-mile hike through dense rainforest to a viewing point at the base of the falls. Bring a bathing suit and take a dip in the pool below the thundering falls.

156

Kaieteur Falls

KAIETEUR NATIONAL PARK

GUYANA

Kaieteur Falls is the largest single drop waterfall in the world, as measured by the sheer volume of water that flows over its brink. To visit, you can charter a plane in Georgetown for the ninety-minute flight to the airstrip near the falls and spend the day hiking between the viewing platforms at the base of the cascades. Or sign up for a four- to seven-day trek to reach the falls via a combination of 4x4 vehicles, boats, and hiking up the Potaro River.

LEFT The spectacular Angel Falls drop 3,200 feet.

157

Refugio Route

COTOPAXI NATIONAL PARK

ECUADOR

Conquer the highest continuously active volcano in the world, which rises to an elevation of 19,347 feet.

DISTANCE
6 miles out and back, elevation gain 3,900 feet

START
José Rivas Refuge

DIFFICULTY
Hard due to elevation and glacier travel

SEASON
November to February

LEFT Climbing to the top of Volcán Cotopaxi is no small feat—go with an experienced guide.

Ascending to Volcán Cotopaxi's cratered summit requires ropes, ice axes, crampons, and glacier travel skills to scale the icy fifty-degree slope. An experienced guide can lead you safely around the constantly shifting crevasses—dangerous cracks in the ice. Several Quito-based companies offer training and equipment rentals.

Most summit attempts on Cotopaxi include a night at the José Rivas Refuge at an elevation of 15,744 feet. Set your alarm for just after midnight to climb in the dark, when the snow is firm and safest for travel. Fit climbers can reach the summit by sunrise, taking about six hours. Don't rush the descent—most mountaineering accidents happen on the way down, as fatigue and gravity conspire against tired legs.

158

Limpiopungo Lagoon

COTOPAXI NATIONAL PARK

ECUADOR

If you'd rather admire Cotopaxi's strikingly symmetrical summit across a tranquil lake, head to the Limpiopungo Lagoon at 12,769 feet. A mostly flat 2-mile trail circles the lagoon, providing stunning views of the volcano in clear weather. You may also spot wild horses, hummingbirds, and Andean gulls.

159

Darwin Bay

GALÁPAGOS NATIONAL PARK

ECUADOR

Visit the islands where Charles Darwin famously hatched his theory of evolution through natural selection. The Galápagos Islands are located in the Pacific Ocean some 600 miles off the coast of Ecuador. Santa Cruz serves as a base camp for explorations around the archipelago.

On this short stroll on Darwin Bay, on Genovesa Island, you're likely to see red-footed boobies, frigate birds, swallow-tailed gulls, lava gulls, tropic birds, and storm petrels, earning Genovesa its nickname, "the bird island." You'll also see iguanas, lizards, and sea lions.

160

Sierra Negra Volcano Trail

GALÁPAGOS NATIONAL PARK

ECUADOR

The Galápagos Islands are a group of eighteen volcanic islands that formed atop a mantle plume, similar to the hot spot that spawned the Hawaiian Islands. Over the last century, the nine active volcanoes in the archipelago have erupted dozens of times. The most recent is Sierra Negra on the island of Isabela, which last erupted in 2018. This 9.3-mile out-and-back hike along the caldera rim offers spectacular views and a close look at the recent lava flows that fill the caldera.

161

Santa Cruz Trek

HUASCARÁN NATIONAL PARK

PERU

Follow in the footsteps of the Incas on this four-day trek through the Cordillera Blanca mountains in the central Andes of Peru. Starting in Cashapampa and ending in Vaqueria, the high point of the trail comes on day three at 15,585 feet on Punta Union Pass. From the top you'll enjoy breathtaking views of the world's highest tropical mountain range, including Peru's highest mountain, 22,205-foot Huascarán. You aren't required to hire a guide for this much quieter alternative to the notoriously busy Inca Trail to Machu Picchu.

162

Laguna 69

HUASCARÁN NATIONAL PARK

PERU

If you only have one day to spend in Huascarán National Park, spend it visiting the simply named Laguna 69, or Lake 69. This bright blue alpine lake at the base of snowcapped peaks has a reputation for being the prettiest lake in the park, which is saying something in a place with more than 400 alpine lakes. The 8.6-mile out-and-back trail starts at the Cebollapampa campsite and passes through breathtaking alpine scenery. Most of the trail runs above 15,000 feet of elevation.

LEFT Sea lions are commonly spotted on the Galápagos Islands' Darwin Bay.

163

Lake Otorongo

MANÚ NATIONAL PARK

PERU

Visit a national park that protects a biological hot spot where the Andes Mountains meet the Amazon rainforest.

DISTANCE
2 miles out and back, minimal elevation gain

START
Boca Manú

DIFFICULTY
Easy

SEASON
Dry season, December to April

RIGHT Peru has the second-highest number of jaguars in South America.

BELOW The short stroll beside Lake Otorongo leads to a wildlife observation tower.

Manú is one of the most restricted national parks in the world, with only a fraction of its 6,600 square miles open to visitors. The protections ensure that the local flora and fauna remain undisturbed by people—and that people remain undisturbed by people; several indigenous tribes also live here, completely separate from the modern world.

Keep your eyes peeled for wildlife on this 2-mile stroll along the banks of Lake Otorongo to an observation tower. In addition to more than 350 bird species, you could also spot capuchins, spider monkeys, capybaras (the world's largest rodent), giant river otters, or the rainforest holy grail: a jaguar.

164

Dunes Trek

LENÇÓIS MARANHENSES NATIONAL PARK

BRAZIL

Trek between oases in a unique landscape of dunes and lagoons on the windswept northeast coast of Brazil.

DISTANCE
26 miles with shuttle, minimal elevation gain

START
Atins

DIFFICULTY
Moderate, but walking in sand can be tiring

SEASON
May to August, when the lagoons are full

RIGHT White sand and blue lagoons await in Lençóis Maranhenses National Park.

This national park is adrift in a sea of sand dunes. During the rainy season, from January to May, rainwater pools in the low points between dunes, creating an otherworldly landscape of bright white dunes interlaced with bright blue lagoons.

This three-day trek crosses the dunes from east to west, connecting two famous oases. Tours start in the city of São Luís and travel by car and then boat to Atins on the Preguiças River. From there, you'll hike 9.9 miles through the dunes, occasionally cooling off with a dip in the lagoons.

You'll stop for the night at Oásis Baixa Grande, home to a handful of families, some of whom sell meals and hammock accommodations. The next day, you'll hike west 6.2 miles to Oásis Queimada dos Britos. On the last day, it's another 9.9 miles west to the village of Betânia, where you'll catch a shuttle back to São Luís.

165

Pedra Furada Trail

JERICOACOARA NATIONAL PARK

BRAZIL

Getting to the beautiful Jericoacoara Beach involves hours of driving over sand. Once there, stretch your legs on this 2.5-mile round-trip beach walk to the Pedra Furada arch—a rock eroded into this shape by wave action. Between June 15 and July 30, the sun sets in the middle of the arch, creating a prime photo opportunity.

Dolphin Bay

FERNANDO DE NORONHA NATIONAL MARINE PARK
BRAZIL

Located 218 miles off the coast of Brazil, this national park protects a group of twenty-one volcanic islands and is known for its beautiful beaches, swimming, and snorkeling. This easy 2-mile round-trip hike accesses Curral Beach and Madeiro Beach on the main island, and then climbs to a clifftop overlook where you have an excellent chance of seeing acrobatic spinner dolphins leaping and spinning in the surf.

Lighthouse Trail

FERNANDO DE NORONHA NATIONAL MARINE PARK
BRAZIL

The longest trail in this park leads over rocky bluffs on the main island to an overlook of Lion Beach, a famous nesting ground for sea turtles. The 6-mile out-and-back path then continues out to the Farol da Sapata lighthouse on the western tip of the island, where you can enjoy views of both the mainland and Atlantic sides of the island.

168

Gruta do Lapão

CHAPADA DIAMANTINA NATIONAL PARK

BRAZIL

Chapada Diamantina National Park is famous for waterfalls and caves. Many of these caves are flooded and can only be explored with scuba gear. However, the Gruta do Lapão is dry for part of the year. A 6-mile round-trip hiking trail leads from the town of Lençóis to a massive opening in quartzite sandstone cliffs. The main cave was carved by the Lapão River as it floods underground during the rainy season. Join a tour during the dry season, and admire the beautiful, glittering quartzite cave formations.

169

Black Needles

ITATIAIA NATIONAL PARK

BRAZIL

Tag Brazil's fifth-highest peak in the country's oldest national park.

DISTANCE
3 miles out and back, elevation gain 1,170 feet

START
Rebouças Shelter

DIFFICULTY
Hard due to steep rock faces and route finding

SEASON
Dry season, May to August

LEFT The Black Needles are a collection of dark, vertical rock formations in Itatiaia National Park.

Itatiaia National Park was established in 1937 to protect a region of the Mantiqueira Mountains and the sources of a dozen major rivers. The name Itatiaia means "stone with many sharp points" in the native Tupi language and indeed the mountains here are steep and foreboding, but not impossible to climb.

The highest point is Pico das Agulhas Negras, or the Black Needles, that top out at 9,157 feet above sea level. The route up starts at the Rebouças Shelter. From here, it's almost impossible to believe there's a trail to the summit. Mountaineers will make smooth work of the sloping rocky ramps, but inexperienced climbers may want to hire a guide and rope up for the short scramble sections.

170

Cachoeira da Fumaça

CHAPADA DIAMANTINA NATIONAL PARK

BRAZIL

This national park sits atop a huge plateau, and includes the second-highest waterfall in Brazil. The 1,378-foot Cachoeira da Fumaça, or Smoke Falls, is so named because light winds blow the thin stream of water sideways and upward into a fine mist, creating the illusion of smoke. A 6.7-mile out-and-back hike starts in the village of Capão and climbs 1,600 feet to a viewing point.

171

Iguazú Falls

IGUAZÚ NATIONAL PARK

BRAZIL

Iguazú Falls straddles the border of Brazil and Argentina. The Iguazú River meets the edge of the Paraná Plateau and tumbles over a series of ledges into a gorge called the Devil's Throat. Numerous islands and cliffs divide the water into up to 300 separate falls, depending on the water level. The 2-mile out-and-back trail on the Brazilian side is easy, paved, and wheelchair accessible, with multiple viewing platforms, including an overlook that peers directly into the churning misty maw of the Devil's Throat.

172

Cotovelo Trail

APARADOS DA SERRA NATIONAL PARK

BRAZIL

In southern Brazil, the Perdiz River slices through the landscape, carving out the long and narrow Itaimbezinho Canyon. Waterfalls plunging over the edge fall thousands of feet into the abyss. The 3.7-mile round-trip Cotovelo Trail runs along the edge of the canyon to where Véu de Noiva Waterfall takes its leap, providing stunning views into Itaimbezinho's depths.

BELOW Iguazú Falls is one of the largest and most complex series of waterfalls in the world.

173

Boi River Trail

APARADOS DA SERRA NATIONAL PARK

BRAZIL

Once you've gazed over the edge of Itaimbezinho Canyon, you may want to explore the deep and narrow world 2,160 feet below the rim. The Boi River Trail snakes along the rocky bottom of the canyon for 4.3 miles one way, starting from the Boi River Information and Control Post entrance, near the town of Praia Grande. Flash floods are dangerous in this canyon, so visit in the dry season between July and October, and double-check the weather before you go.

174

El Choro Trek

COTOPATA NATIONAL PARK

BOLIVIA

Embrace the downhill on this Incan road route from the high alpine into the Bolivian jungle.

- **DISTANCE**
  35 miles one way, elevation loss 9,360 feet
- **START**
  La Cumbre Pass
- **DIFFICULTY**
  Moderate
- **SEASON**
  Dry season, May to October

The only climbing you'll do on El Choro is in the first hour, to reach the high point of the route at 15,941 feet—from there, it's all downhill. You'll be following an ancient Incan road from La Cumbre Pass down to the city of Coroico. Downhill can be hard on the knees and joints, especially when carrying a backpack, so stretch this trip over four days and bring trekking poles to help take some of the impact off your legs.

After you descend from the beautiful and barren high-elevation alpine environment, the trail enters the lush green tunnel of the Bolivian rainforest. You'll encounter many villages along the way that offer camping, shelters, and basic supplies.

175

Pomerape Volcano

SAJAMA NATIONAL PARK

BOLIVIA

Tag two countries and two national parks in one summit on Pomerape, where Bolivia's Sajama National Park meets Chile's Lauca National Park. This conical stratovolcano is most easily accessed from the Bolivian side. Although the route isn't technical, you'll need an ice ax and crampons to negotiate the snowy summit.

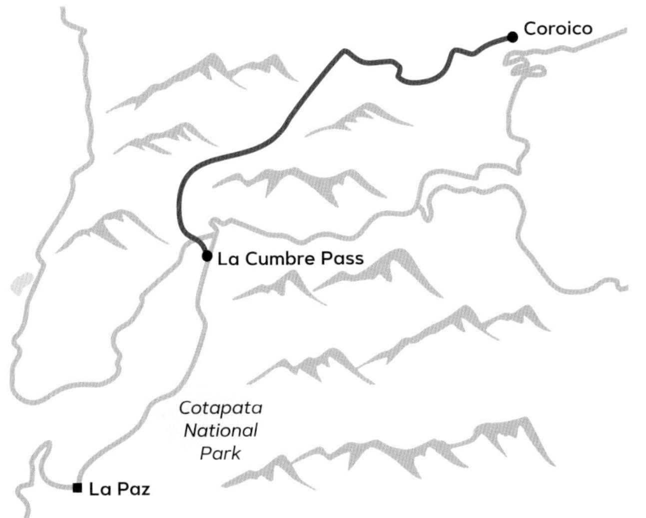

Torotoro Canyon

TOROTORO NATIONAL PARK
BOLIVIA

During the Cretaceous period, around 80 million years ago, what is now an arid region of Bolivia was a vast marshland populated by dinosaurs. They left their footprints in mud, which turned to stone over time. Today, more than 3,500 footprints and trackways from at least eight species have been identified in the park.

This 13-mile out-and-back hike takes you past an impressive collection of tracks—don't step in them, as they are quite delicate. The trail continues to the edge of Torotoro Canyon and into its depths, where you'll be rewarded with a perfect swimming hole at the base of a waterfall.

LEFT Seasonal floods sometimes wash out the bridges along the El Choro route.

177

Rano Raraku via Ara o Te Moai

RAPA NUI NATIONAL PARK

CHILE

Known to its first inhabitants as Te Pito o te Henua, meaning "the end of the world," the island of Rapa Nui (formerly Easter Island) sits 2,200 miles west of Chile, in the South Pacific. People travel to this tiny volcanic dot to see the moai sculptures—massive ceremonial heads carved out of volcanic rock. This easy, 4-mile out-and-back trail runs past several finished and half-carved moai to the Rano Raraku volcanic crater.

178

Monte Terevaka Volcano

RAPA NUI NATIONAL PARK

CHILE

Hike to the highest point on Rapa Nui on this 6-mile round-trip summit trek. Terevaka is the tallest and youngest of Rapa Nui's three extinct volcanoes—each situated at one of the three corners of the triangular island. The views of the entire island are worth the 1,194 feet of elevation you'll gain to the 1,676-foot summit.

LEFT Moai are monolithic human figures carved by the indigenous people of Rapa Nui.

179

Petrohué Waterfalls

VICENTE PÉREZ ROSALES NATIONAL PARK

CHILE

This mile-long out-and-back walk ends at a beautiful waterfall, where the Petrohué River flows through several basalt chutes, just downstream from the picturesque Todos los Santos lake. The waterfall and the lake lie in the shadow of the snowcapped Osorno Volcano, the source of the basaltic lava flow. Osorno erupted eleven times between 1575 and 1869.

180

Desolation Pass

VICENTE PÉREZ ROSALES NATIONAL PARK

CHILE

Take in many of the visual highlights of Chile's oldest national park in one long day hike.

- **DISTANCE**
  14-mile loop, elevation gain 2,900 feet
- **START**
  Petrohué campsite
- **DIFFICULTY**
  Moderate
- **SEASON**
  October to April; yellow retama wildflowers peak in November

LEFT You'll enjoy views of Osorno Volcano and Lake Llanquihue on Desolation Pass.

Desolation Pass runs between the Osorno and Cerro La Picada volcanoes, with panoramic views of the surrounding volcanoes, Patagonian Andes, and Lakes Llanquihue and Todos los Santos. The deep, black volcanic sand underfoot can make the hike seem longer than it is. It's worth the extra energy, however, to make this hike into a loop by following the black sand beaches on the lakeshore of Todos los Santos on the way back.

Looking south from Desolation Pass lies one of the largest protected regions on Earth. Vicente Pérez Rosales National Park is one link in a chain of national parks—along with Puyehue, also in Chile, and Nahuel Huapi and Lanín in neighboring Argentina—that together protect more than 5,700 contiguous square miles of the Andes mountain range.

181

W, O, and Q Circuits

TORRES DEL PAINE NATIONAL PARK

CHILE

In Torres del Paine, you can embark on three overlapping loops called the W, O, and Q circuits. The W is the shortest, hitting several scenic highlights in a 50-mile loop that's completed in three to five days. The O starts with the W route and adds 18 miles around the backside of the Cordillera del Paine—this route takes six to nine days. The Q adds another day of hiking south along Lake Pehoe with stunning views of the Paine Massif. Book all your campsites in advance.

182

Refugio Frey

NAHUEL HUAPI NATIONAL PARK

ARGENTINA

This hike starts at the largest ski area in South America and ends at a small cabin high in the Andes. In the winter, from July to October, the Cerro Catedral Alta Patagonia ski resort chairlifts access more than 3,000 acres of skiable terrain. In the summer, a few lifts stay open to usher hikers high into the mountains. A chairlift will cut a few miles off this 11.6-mile out-and-back trail to the Refugio Frey, but the entire trail is stunning.

183

Cerro Guanaco Summit Trail

TIERRA DEL FUEGO NATIONAL PARK

ARGENTINA

Located on an island at the southern tip of Patagonia, Tierra del Fuego National Park is literally at the ends of the Earth. The southern terminus of the Pan-American Highway is located here, as is the El Parque station for the End of the World Train. Gain over 3,000 feet of elevation from sea level to the summit at 3,192 feet and enjoy views of the island on this 8.4-mile out-and-back trail.

BELOW Book ahead to stay at the Refugio Frey hut.

184

Costera Trail

TIERRA DEL FUEGO NATIONAL PARK

ARGENTINA

Follow the Tierra del Fuego coastline on this easy, rolling 9.2-mile round-trip hike from Ensenada Bay to Lapataia Bay. The signposted trail winds through subantarctic forests and across pebble beaches, with views of Redonda Island and the Beagle Channel, named for the HMS *Beagle*, which carried Charles Darwin around the tip of South America to the Galápagos Islands in 1835.

185

Perito Moreno Glacier Trail

LOS GLACIARES NATIONAL PARK

ARGENTINA

Visit one of the biggest ice caps on the planet, protected by Argentina's largest national park.

DISTANCE
2.9 miles round trip, elevation gain 600 feet

START
El Calafate

DIFFICULTY
Easy

SEASON
Year-round; ice dam ruptures tend to occur between December and March

Nearly a third of the 2,800-square-mile Los Glaciares National Park is covered by a massive ice sheet that feeds forty-seven large glaciers; thirteen of these rivers of ice flow west into the Pacific Ocean—the rest end in stunningly blue alpine lakes. Some of these lakes drain east into rivers that flow to the Atlantic Ocean.

Due to the park's high-latitude location in southern Patagonia and influence of the nearby Pacific Ocean, the glaciers here exist at lower elevations, starting at around 5,000 feet and flowing down to around 600 feet, making several of them accessible to casual hikers. The Perito Moreno Glacier is reached via an easy 2.9-mile round-trip trail. You'll need sturdy boots and crampons to negotiate the often jagged, slippery terrain.

The 3-mile-wide terminus of the glacier towers 240 feet above Lake Argentino, and ice chunks regularly fall off the steep face into the water, creating icebergs. The glacier partially dams a section of the lake called the Rico Arm. Every few years, the water breaks through the ice dam, releasing a spectacular flood—a rare phenomenon to witness.

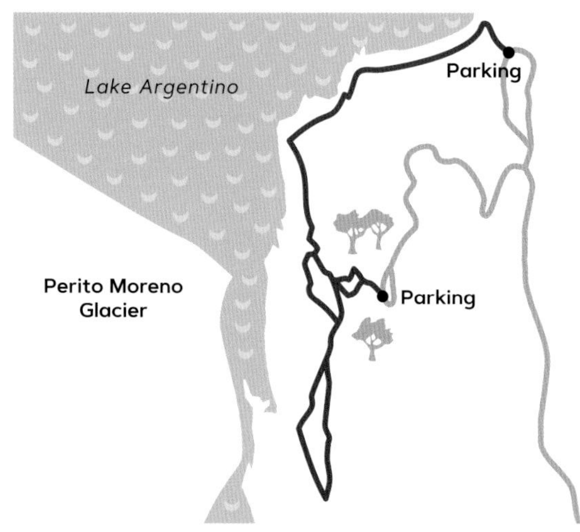

186

Fitz Roy Trail

LOS GLACIARES NATIONAL PARK

ARGENTINA

Most people are familiar with the iconic skyline of the Fitz Roy from Patagonia clothing company labels. Lay eyes on the jagged granite spires in person on this 14-mile round-trip hike to Laguna de los Tres, the lake at the base of the peaks. The last mile to the lake is notoriously steep—bring trekking poles and ice-traction devices in case of snow or ice. Patagonia's founder, Yvon Chouinard, was among the first to summit the highest central peak in 1968; in 2014 Alex Honnold of *Free Solo* fame completed the first Fitz Traverse, climbing all the skyline peaks in one push, with climbing partner Tommy Caldwell.

BELOW Tour companies offer expeditions of varying lengths onto the Perito Moreno Glacier.

EUROPE

Crisscross the Old World on ancient footpaths, from the craggy heights of the Alps to the vast cave systems of Eastern Europe, where hut-to-hut hiking routes have welcomed travelers for generations.

187

Nautastígur Trail

SNÆFELLSJÖKULL NATIONAL PARK

ICELAND

Iceland has three national parks, but only Snæfellsjökull extends to the coastline. Explore several of the country's famous black sand beaches on this 2-mile loop to Black Lava Pearl Beach. Here, you'll find shiny rounded pebbles of dark volcanic rock, while Djúpalónssandur Beach has a collection of *aflraunasteinar*—lifting stones that have been used for hundreds of years to test fishermen's strength. The three rounded stones, named Fullsterkur, Hálfsterkur, and Hálfdrættingur, range from 50 to 340 pounds. Remember to lift with your knees, not with your back!

RIGHT Unique rock formations can be found along Iceland's coast, where hot lava was rapidly cooled by the ocean.

188

Kirkjufellsfoss

SNÆFELLSJÖKULL NATIONAL PARK

ICELAND

A short half-mile stroll will bring you to one of Iceland's most photographed spots: Kirkjufellsfoss Waterfall against a backdrop of Kirkjufell Mountain. Located on the northern shore of Snæfellsjnes Peninsula, near the fishing village of Grundarfjörður, Kirkjufell's imposing profile is the perfect setting for the double-tiered drop of the waterfall. Capture the dancing northern lights behind Kirkjufell and you'll have the makings of an iconically Icelandic image.

189

Vatnshellir Cave

SNÆFELLSJÖKULL NATIONAL PARK

ICELAND

A lava tube under the Snæfellsjökull volcano served as a gateway to the underworld in Jules Verne's 1864 book *Journey to the Center of the Earth.* You won't find any dinosaurs in Vatnshellir Cave, but descending into the 8,000-year-old lava tube does feel like a journey to another world. You'll need to join a guided cave tour, beginning with a steep descent down a spiral staircase to reach the surprisingly colorful chambers, 115 feet beneath the surface.

190

Öxarárfoss Waterfall

THINGVELLIR NATIONAL PARK

ICELAND

Visit an exposed section of the Mid-Atlantic Ridge—and the birthplace of the Atlantic Ocean.

DISTANCE
2.6-mile loop, elevation gain 745 feet

START
Visitor center

DIFFICULTY
Easy

SEASON
Year-round

RIGHT The Öxará River spills over the edge of the Almannagjá ravine, creating a 44-foot-high waterfall.

BELOW Walk between two tectonic plates to this spectacular waterfall.

Over the past 200 million years, plate tectonic movement and volcanic activity along the Mid-Atlantic Ridge has opened the Atlantic Ocean and created a mountain chain on the seafloor that runs from the Arctic Ocean to the southern tip of Africa. Iceland sits directly on top of this ridge, marking one of the few places where vigorous volcanism has raised the spreading ridge above sea level.

In Thingvellir National Park, just outside the capital of Reykjavík, you can walk through an exposed section of the Mid-Atlantic Ridge. The easy 2.6-mile out-and-back trail to Öxarárfoss Waterfall runs between two towering walls of basalt that represent the edges of the North American tectonic plate to the west and the Eurasian plate to the east.

This national park not only protects a geologically significant place, it's also historically important. Between 930 and 1798, Iceland's annual parliament was held in the groove between the tectonic plates.

191

Svartifoss Waterfall

VATNAJÖKULL NATIONAL PARK

ICELAND

Discover the land where fire meets ice—when subglacial volcanoes erupt and melt the overlying glaciers.

- **DISTANCE**
  3-mile loop, elevation gain 550 feet
- **START**
  Skaftafell Visitor Center
- **DIFFICULTY**
  Easy
- **SEASON**
  Year-round

LEFT Svartifoss, meaning "black falls," tumbles 80 feet over a cliff.

Iceland is known as the land of fire and ice. Under the country's extensive ice caps lie thirty active volcanoes. When these subglacial volcanoes erupt, they can rapidly melt the overlying glaciers, unleashing torrential floods called *jökulhlaups*.

Driving to Vatnajökull National Park on the Ring Road from Reykjavík, you'll cross a vast floodplain that was created in 1996 when the Grímsvötn volcano erupted and melted part of the Skeiðarárjökull glacier, destroying a section of this road. The resulting outwash plain, called Skeiðarársandur, is one of the most striking examples of a catastrophic landscape on Earth.

The river that forms the Svartifoss Waterfall flows out of the Skeiðarárjökull glacier, over a cliff of hexagonal basalt columns that form when lava cools slowly and cracks into columns. An easy 3-mile loop hike will take you to a bridge that serves as a viewing platform for the falls.

Falljökull Glacier

VATNAJÖKULL NATIONAL PARK

ICELAND

This 4-mile round-trip trail leads to the blackened toe of Falljökull. The ice is dark because of the glacier's climate-driven retreat through dark volcanic sediments—a reminder that under Iceland's white ice lurk dozens of active volcanoes. The official trail ends at the edge of the ice; to travel on the glacier you'll need crampons or to book a glacier tour.

193

Jökulsárlón Glacier Lagoon

VATNAJÖKULL NATIONAL PARK

ICELAND

This massive national park covers 14 percent of Iceland, including the Vatnajökull Ice Cap—the largest mass of ice in Europe outside of the Arctic. Hike this moderate 4.5-mile out-and-back trail to see the edge of the Breiðamerkurjökull Glacier, where huge chunks of ice regularly break off into a bright blue lagoon, forming icebergs. The trail runs along the shore of the Jökulsárlón Glacier Lagoon, where countless icebergs bob on their way out to sea. Follow the Jökulsá River to its mouth, where you can see icebergs churning in the surf.

LEFT Jökulsárlón Glacier Lagoon is Iceland's deepest lake at 814 feet.

194

Laugavegur Trail

VATNAJÖKULL NATIONAL PARK

ICELAND

This epic 34-mile trek runs past volcanoes, glaciers, ice caves, black sand deserts, mossy rolling plains, and even a forest (Iceland is notoriously treeless), from the hot springs at Landmannalaugar to the glacial valley of Thórsmörk. Most people hike north to south and take four days to complete the trek. You'll need to make reservations ahead of your trip to stay in the series of overnight huts along the way, or pack a tent. Even in the height of summer, expect to spend many miles crossing vast snow and ice fields. Take ice-traction devices and trekking poles.

BELOW You can only hike the Laugavegur Trail in the short summer, between June and September.

195

Cliffs of Moher Coastal Walk

BURREN NATIONAL PARK

IRELAND

Traipse along the towering Cliffs of Insanity on the western coast of Ireland.

- **DISTANCE**
  11.4 miles one way with shuttle, elevation gain 1,650 feet
- **START**
  Doolin; shuttle via bus or taxi
- **DIFFICULTY**
  Moderate
- **SEASON**
  Year-round

The Burren and Cliffs of Moher UNESCO Global Geopark were the perfect setting for the Cliffs of Insanity in the Hollywood classic movie *The Princess Bride*, and more recently appeared in the movie *Harry Potter and the Half-Blood Prince*.

The cliffs are composed of layers of shale and sandstone that were deposited over 300 million years ago at the mouth of a river. Wave action at the base erodes the steep layers, creating numerous sea stacks and sea caves. Thousands of seabirds from twenty species, including Atlantic puffins, raise their young here—nesting season is from March to May.

The Cliffs of Moher Coastal Walk runs for 11.4 miles one way, across the top of the cliffs, from the town of Doolin south to Hag's Head. To avoid the ever-eroding edge, an alternative, parallel route has been built a safe distance inland. Don't walk this trail on windy days.

ABOVE The Cliffs of Moher tower 700 feet above the water.

LEFT Sea pink flowers on the Cliffs of Moher Coastal Walk.

Diamond Hill Loop

CONNEMARA NATIONAL PARK

IRELAND

Mountains in the British Isles are classified by height and prominence into a number of subclasses, including Munros (height over 3,000 feet), Vandeleur-Lynam (over 1,969 feet), and Arderins (over 1,640 feet). At 1,450 feet, Diamond Hill does not meet the height qualifications for any of these categories, but its impressive prominence over the surrounding landscape qualifies it as a Marilyn, which is a peak of any height with a prominence over 492 feet. The 4.5-mile figure-eight loop to the summit is one of the most popular hikes in the park, thanks to its awe-inspiring views over the Connemara coastline.

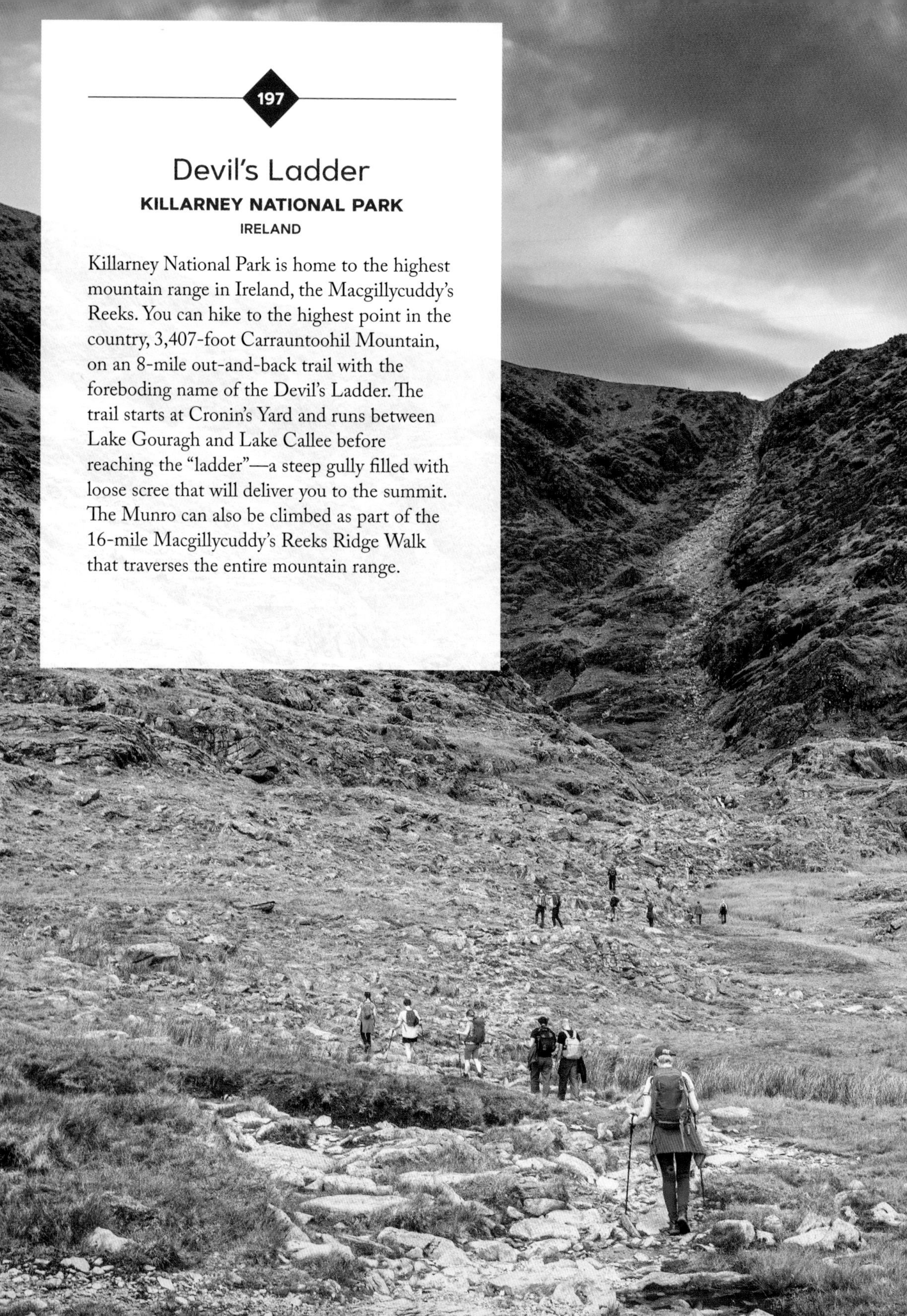

197

Devil's Ladder

KILLARNEY NATIONAL PARK

IRELAND

Killarney National Park is home to the highest mountain range in Ireland, the Macgillycuddy's Reeks. You can hike to the highest point in the country, 3,407-foot Carrauntoohil Mountain, on an 8-mile out-and-back trail with the foreboding name of the Devil's Ladder. The trail starts at Cronin's Yard and runs between Lake Gouragh and Lake Callee before reaching the "ladder"—a steep gully filled with loose scree that will deliver you to the summit. The Munro can also be climbed as part of the 16-mile Macgillycuddy's Reeks Ridge Walk that traverses the entire mountain range.

198

Torc Waterfall Walk

KILLARNEY NATIONAL PARK

IRELAND

Before it was a national park, this region was a private estate that boasted the largest swath of native forest in Ireland. Today, the park is home to the last remaining herd of red deer in the country and is famous for its oak and yew woodlands. Hike through some of these old-growth woods on the 4-mile loop trail to Torc Waterfall. The path runs along the shore of Muckross Lake, one of the three Lakes of Killarney, which cover almost a quarter of the park.

199

Lough Ouler Loop

WICKLOW MOUNTAINS NATIONAL PARK

IRELAND

Hike around a distinctly heart-shaped lake on this 4.6-mile loop. Start at the parking area for Glenmacnass Waterfall, then hop across the Glenmacnass River on often slippery stepping-stones (in the spring and after storms the water might be too high to cross safely). Then head up to the top of the ridge, where you'll see the lake. Hike around it in a clockwise direction, with a short detour to tag the top of 2,680-foot Tonelegee Mountain, whose name translates to "arse to the wind."

BELOW Lough Ouler, or the "Lake of Love," is located just south of Dublin.

200

Lairig Ghru

CAIRNGORMS NATIONAL PARK

SCOTLAND

Follow an ancient drove road through a high mountain pass in the wild heart of the Cairngorms.

DISTANCE
20 miles one way with shuttle, elevation gain 2,600 feet

START
Multiple starting points at both ends

DIFFICULTY
Hard due to long distance and rugged terrain

SEASON
May to October; storms can turn the Lairig Ghru into a brutal wind tunnel

ABOVE RIGHT The Lairig Ghru follows a high pass through the heart of the Cairngorm Mountains.

RIGHT The tame Cairngorm reindeer is the UK's only free-ranging herd of reindeer.

Since medieval times, herders called drovers have moved livestock across Scotland on a network of drove roads. Many of these routes have since been paved for cars, but a few remain in their primitive state. The Lairig Ghru is an ancient droving road that takes advantage of a high mountain pass in the central Cairngorms to link the villages of Strathspey and Deeside. This is not an easy stroll—the route passes through some rugged and remote terrain.

There are several start and end options. From the north, the Lairig Ghru can be approached from Glen More (*glen* means "valley"), through the Chalamain Gap boulder field, or from Aviemore through Rothiemurchus Forest. From the south, routes run from Braemar through Glen Lui or Glen Dee, or from Blair Atholl through Glen Tilt. For a challenging out-and-back day hike from either end, aim to reach the Pools of Dee—shimmering lakes near the high point of the pass.

Ben Macdui

CAIRNGORMS NATIONAL PARK
SCOTLAND

Tagging the second-highest peak in the UK will earn you some bragging rights, but the real prize of this hike is the epic viewpoint down into the Lairig Ghru, a 1,600-foot-deep valley cut between two peaks. Starting from the Cairngorm ski resort, an 11-mile loop runs past Lochan Buidhe—the highest body of water in the British Isles—and across the Cairngorm plateau to the 4,295-foot summit of Ben Macdui.

Glen Clova Mayar and Driesh

CAIRNGORMS NATIONAL PARK
SCOTLAND

Summit two of Scotland's 282 Munros—mountains over 3,000 feet of elevation—on this 9-mile loop. The rocky but seldom steep trail is best tackled in a clockwise direction and can be hiked year-round, with hiking poles and ice-traction devices on your boots in the winter. This loop is known for being one of the most scenic and accessible winter Munro hikes in Scotland.

203

Bracklinn Falls Circuit

LOCH LOMOND & THE TROSSACHS NATIONAL PARK
SCOTLAND

This national park, centered on the largest loch in Scotland, also features a vast region of wooded hills and valleys, known as braes and glens, called the Trossachs. This easy 3.3-mile loop winds through braes and glens, passing fields of Scottish cows, and then over a lovely copper-and-wood footbridge. From the bridge you can feel the spray from Bracklinn Falls, which appears in the classic British movie *Monty Python and the Holy Grail.*

204

Ptarmigan Ridge Path

LOCH LOMOND & THE TROSSACHS NATIONAL PARK
SCOTLAND

Enjoy a bird's-eye view of Loch Lomond by climbing the Ptarmigan Ridge Path to the top of Ben Lomond. Rising to an elevation of 3,196 feet on the eastern shore of the loch, Ben Lomond is the southernmost Munro in Scotland. From the summit, on a clear day, you may be able to see Ben Nevis—the highest point in Scotland—to the north. There are several ways to reach the top of Ben Lomond, but this 7.4-mile loop is arguably the most scenic.

205

The West Highland Way

LOCH LOMOND & THE TROSSACHS NATIONAL PARK

SCOTLAND

Traverse the Lowlands and Highlands of Scotland's first officially designated long-distance hiking trail.

DISTANCE
96 miles one way, usually completed in six to ten days

START
Milngavie

DIFFICULTY
Hard due to long distance and unpredictable weather

SEASON
May to October

ABOVE LEFT The West Highland Way takes in both the Highlands and Lowlands of Scotland.

LEFT A cottage in the scenic Scottish Highlands.

People have been walking and herding livestock across Scotland for millennia. In the 1970s, geographer Fiona Rose hiked more than 1,000 miles searching for a way to link the tangled network of ancient footpaths into a continuous long-distance hiking route. In 1980 the West Highland Way was officially completed, and in 2010 it became part of the International Appalachian Trail, a European extension of the famous American footpath.

Running for 96 miles from Milngavie, north of Glasgow, to Fort William in the Scottish Highlands, the West Highland Way is traditionally walked from south to north, journeying through the Scottish countryside, from the Lowlands to the Highlands.

Each year, around 30,000 people complete the entire route, with most trekkers finishing in about a week to ten days. While a few hardy souls camp along the way, most take advantage of hotels, hostels, and bed-and-breakfasts. An elite few don't need to sleep—the West Highland Way Race is an ultramarathon held on the route, with the fastest runners completing the entire trail in under twenty-four hours.

206

Scafell Pike

LAKE DISTRICT NATIONAL PARK

ENGLAND

Tag the highest point in England on this 9-mile out-and-back trail from Seathwaite to the top of 3,209-foot Scafell Pike. A shorter 5.8-mile round-trip route leads up from Wasdale, but the Corridor Route is often less crowded and arguably more scenic, although it does require some minor scrambling. On top, the striking summit is covered with shattered rocks, produced by relentless freeze-and-thaw frost cycles.

BELOW Scafell Pike in the Lake District viewed from the top of Great Gable.

207

Catbells, Maiden Moor, and High Spy

LAKE DISTRICT NATIONAL PARK

ENGLAND

This all-day ridge walk has a reputation for being the most scenic hike in the Lake District. The 8-mile loop first climbs to the top of Catbells and then follows a horseshoe ridge over two more summits, with stunning views of the surrounding mountains, valleys, and lakes in all directions. The loop can be hiked year-round, but be prepared for snow, ice, and mud in the winter.

ABOVE Catbells, Maiden Moor, and High Spy are located near Keswick, in Cumbria.

208

Coast to Coast Trail

LAKE DISTRICT NATIONAL PARK

ENGLAND

Intrepid hikers can walk all the way across England on this 192-mile footpath. Hikers traditionally dip their feet in the Irish Sea at the start of the hike and in the North Sea at the end. In between, the route crosses three national parks—the Lake District, the Yorkshire Dales, and the North York Moors—each with their own distinctive character, passing through charming towns and villages.

209

Roseberry Topping

NORTH YORK MOORS NATIONAL PARK

ENGLAND

This distinctive summit has long been a beacon—its unique profile can be seen for many miles and has been used by sailors and farmers as a storm sentry, inspiring the old English folk rhyme: "When Roseberry Topping wears a cap, let Cleveland then beware of a clap!" A 3-mile loop trail runs over the 1,050-foot summit, offering splendid views over heather moorlands, where extremely hardy low-growing evergreen shrubs carpet the rolling landscape.

210

Mallyan Spout

NORTH YORK MOORS NATIONAL PARK

ENGLAND

This 70-foot waterfall is the tallest drop in the North Yorkshire Moors. In Victorian times, Mallyan Spout helped put the nearby village of Goathland on the tourism map, and the village has retained its charm. This 2.7-mile loop starts in Goathland—where British television show *Heartbeat* is filmed—and then descends down into a valley to a scenic stretch of the West Beck River, before looping back to the village. Parts of the path are often muddy, and getting close to the waterfall requires some scrambling on slippery boulders, so wear sturdy footwear.

BELOW Roseberry Topping's summit protrudes above the surrounding landscape.

211

Mam Tor

PEAK DISTRICT NATIONAL PARK

ENGLAND

England's first national park preserves an area that has been inhabited since at least the Mesolithic era—artifacts and archaeological sites from the Neolithic, Bronze, and Iron Ages have been identified throughout the park. The 2.4-mile loop up Mam Tor runs past several caves where minerals were once mined and the remains of several Bronze Age and Iron Age forts can be seen near the summit.

Mam Tor's most notable feature is several thousand years in the making: a massive, slow-moving landslide has gradually reshaped the southeast face, ravaging the Mam Tor Road that once ran along its base. Originally built in 1800, the road was abandoned in 1979.

212

South Downs Way

SOUTH DOWNS NATIONAL PARK

ENGLAND

The South Downs Way officially opened as a UK National Trail in 1972, but archaeological evidence indicates that people have been walking this 100-mile route between what is now Winchester and Eastbourne in southern England for at least 8,000 years. The undulating landscape here is underlain by white chalk that peeks through the green grass and at the Long Man of Wilmington—a figure carved into the hillside. Most people hike the route in around eight days, while elite competitors in the Centurion South Downs Way 100 ultramarathon can run the whole trail in less than fifteen hours.

213

Wistman's Wood

DARTMOOR NATIONAL PARK

ENGLAND

A 5-mile loop trail circles through and around Wistman's Wood, a 9-acre copse of gnarled, mossy oaks that is one of the oldest surviving woodlands in the country. The oldest trees here are 500 years old, but studies suggest this hillside has remained forested for thousands of years. The highly contorted trees grow out of a chaotic jumble of rocks called a clatter—their trunks and branches twist to fit between blocks of lichen-coated granite. The trees were likely spared cutting due to the impassable terrain and superstitions inspired by their uniquely tortured growth patterns.

ABOVE Ponies have lived on Dartmoor since prehistoric times.

LEFT See if you can spot the 235-foot Long Man of Wilmington on the South Downs Way.

214

Saddle Tor to Hound Tor

DARTMOOR NATIONAL PARK

ENGLAND

The open rolling moorlands of Dartmoor are topped by tors—craggy granite outcrops that cap many of the hilltops—hinting at the largest expanse of granite in Britain that lies just under the surface. This 5.5-mile loop visits two tors, Saddle and Hound, plus other clusters of rocks, including Smallacombe Rocks and Haytor Rocks. In this ancient, storied landscape, nearly every rock has a name. Keep watch for wild Dartmoor ponies, a small but hardy breed. But don't feed them or any other wildlife—animals that associate people with food can become aggressive.

215

Pembrokeshire Coast Path

PEMBROKESHIRE COAST NATIONAL PARK

WALES

Take a really long walk on the beach on this 186-mile coastal path. Actually, you'll mostly be above the beach, traversing cliff tops that tower as much as 574 feet above the water. The southern end of the path begins in Amroth, Pembrokeshire, and runs north to St. Dogmaels, where it connects to the Ceredigion Coast Path, a 65-mile stretch. Both the Pembrokeshire and Ceredigion trails are part of the Wales Coast Path, an 870-mile designated hiking trail along the coast of Wales from Chepstow to Queensferry—the first footpath in the world to run the entire length of a country's coastline.

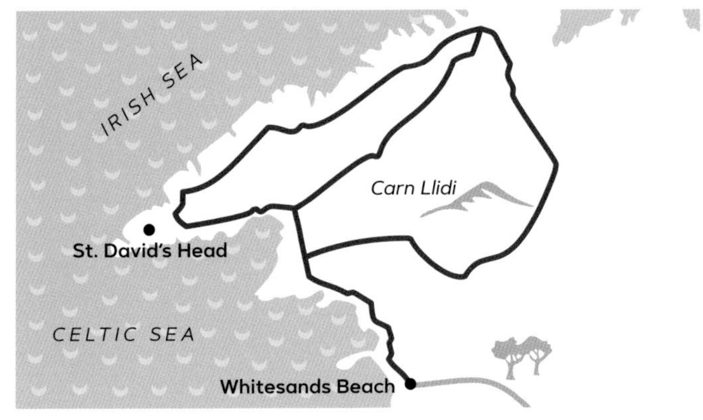

216

St. David's Peninsula Circular Walk

PEMBROKESHIRE COAST NATIONAL PARK

WALES

Discover the colorful wildflowers and seabirds on the windswept coast of west Wales.

DISTANCE
Multiple loop options ranging from 4 miles to 10 miles

START
Whitesands Beach

DIFFICULTY
Easy

SEASON
Year-round; wildflowers peak May to September

LEFT Fantastic views abound from St. David's Head on the Pembrokeshire coast.

BELOW LEFT Whitesands Beach is the starting point for St. David's Peninsula Circular Walk.

As the resting place of Saint David, the patron saint of Wales, this small cathedral city has drawn religious pilgrims for centuries. Since the crowning of Pembrokeshire Coast National Park in 1952, the area has attracted travelers devoted to the soaring headlands and beautiful beaches of the peninsula.

Dominated by the craggy summit of Carn Llidi, the dramatic headland of St. David's Head marks the dividing line between the Irish Sea to the north and the Celtic Sea to the south. Starting from Whitesands Beach, a number of walking paths crisscross the peninsula, offering scenic hiking loops of varying lengths.

Throughout the spring, summer, and fall months, a cacophony of wildflowers light up the bluffs overlooking the water, and dozens of species of seabirds make their homes here. Peregrine falcons, the fastest birds in the world, nest on the cliffs of St. David's Head. You might also spot seals and dolphins playing in the waves.

217

Snowdon via Watkin Path

SNOWDONIA NATIONAL PARK

WALES

Hike the highest mountain in Wales, where Sir Edmund Hillary trained for Everest.

DISTANCE
3.9 miles one way to the summit, elevation gain 3,363 feet

START
Bethania on the A498

DIFFICULTY
Hard due to elevation gain

SEASON
Year-round with ice-traction equipment; usually snow-free from May to October

RIGHT Once you're on the summit of Snowdon, you can return via the same path or choose another route down.

Snowdon is the busiest mountain in Britain; each year, more than half a million people stand on the 3,560-foot summit. There are many ways to the top, the easiest by train via the narrow-gauge rack-and-pinion Snowdon Mountain Railway—it whisks passengers from Llanberis to the summit from May to October.

Several routes up Snowdon involve technical climbing up sheer rock faces. The north face of the mountain, Clogwyn Du'r Arddu, meaning "dark, black cliff" in Welsh, and affectionately nicknamed "Cloggy" by climbers, is considered one of the best traditional mountaineering crags in the UK. Some of these routes are so challenging that world-class mountaineers have trained here to prepare for Himalayan climbing expeditions.

You have a choice of six nontechnical trails to gain the summit. The Watkin Path may be the hardest due to the elevation gained, but it's also the quietest, since most people opt for easier routes.

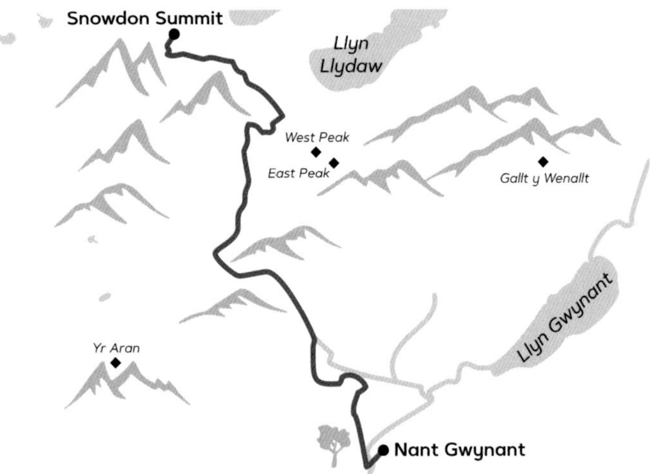

WATKIN
RHYD DDU

218

Llyn Idwal Trail

SNOWDONIA NATIONAL PARK

WALES

This 3-mile loop rings a lovely lake in the heart of the Glyderau mountains. The first part of the trail is paved with native stones, creating a picturesque pathway from the road to Ogwen Cottage, an educational center and bunkhouse, traditionally used as a base camp by mountaineers. On the north end of the lake you'll find a pebble beach, where you might elect to take a chilly dip.

219

The Welsh 3000s

SNOWDONIA NATIONAL PARK

WALES

If you can't decide which of Snowdonia's many mountains to climb, consider tagging them all in this challenge. The Welsh 3000s links the fifteen tallest peaks in the Carneddau, Glyderau, and Snowdon mountain ranges in a 30-mile hike. The fittest hikers can accomplish this feat in under twenty-four hours, but mere mortals may want to budget two to three days for the adventure.

Aberglaslyn Gorge

SNOWDONIA NATIONAL PARK

WALES

Also known as the Fisherman's Path, this 5.7-mile out-and-back hike follows the raging Glaslyn River upstream as it plunges through the narrow Aberglaslyn Gorge. Wear sturdy shoes, because the trail runs across some slippery stone ledges jutting just above the river. About a mile down the trail, you can pay your respects to all good dogs at Gelert's Grave, a monument to the loyal hound in the folk tale about the thirteenth-century Prince Llywelyn.

221

Nigardsbreen Glacier

JOSTEDALSBREEN NATIONAL PARK

NORWAY

Jostedalsbreen National Park protects the largest glacier in mainland Europe: Jostedal Glacier. Hike to a viewpoint of Nigardsbreen, one of fifty branches of Jostedal Glacier, on this 4.5-mile out-and-back trail. Heed the signs to stay well away from the glacier—several people have been killed here by falling ice. This arm of the glacier has advanced and retreated many times over the past few centuries. In the last century, the glacier has been retreating due to the warming effects of climate change.

222

Mount Skåla

JOSTEDALSBREEN NATIONAL PARK

NORWAY

You'll put some serious effort into hiking to the top of 6,063-foot Mount Skåla, an imposing peak in western Norway, but the rewards are worth every step. From the top you'll have an astonishing vantage of the mountains, glaciers, and fjords that carve Norway's intricate coastline. The views are enough to make you forget all about the 6,000 feet of elevation you gained in the 5-mile hike from sea level to the summit. You can spend the night on top in the Skålatårnet round tower or Skålabu hut.

ABOVE Take in the spectacular views of Gjende Lake when hiking Besseggen Ridge.

LEFT Book a guided tour of Nigardsbreen Glacier to see the blue ice up close.

Besseggen Ridge

JOTUNHEIMEN NATIONAL PARK

NORWAY

There are several ways to gain Norway's famed Besseggen Ridge, but the easiest starts with a boat ride from the town of Gjendesheim across Gjende Lake to the Memurubu hut. From there, you can hike the ridge between the two lakes on the way back to town, a 9-mile trek. Throughout your hike, the larger, emerald-green Gjende Lake will be on your right and the higher, bluer Bessvatnet Lake will be on your left, with the rocky finger of Besseggen Ridge in the middle. You'll enjoy legendary views of the Veslfjellet mountain when you look back along the ridge from the high point of the route. Avoid this hike in high winds.

224

Husedalen Waterfalls

HARDANGERVIDDA NATIONAL PARK

NORWAY

Norway's largest national park spans the width of Hardangervidda, the most expansive mountain plateau in Europe. Starting in the village of Kinsarvik, this 8-mile out-and-back trail runs through the picturesque Husedalen Valley, offering views of four striking waterfalls. The falls are created by rivers spilling over the edge of the Hardangervidda plateau, on their way to the spectacular fjords that cut the intricate western coast.

225

Hardangervidda and Mannevasstoppen

HARDANGERVIDDA NATIONAL PARK

NORWAY

People have been living on the Hardangervidda plateau since at least the Stone Age, following the reindeer herds, which still thrive in the lichen-carpeted area. Get a taste of Norwegian nomadic life on this 17-mile out-and-back hike, best tackled as an overnight backpacking trip. The well-marked trail gains 3,900 feet of elevation as it climbs up to Mannevasstoppen, where you'll be rewarded with views across the staggeringly vast and treeless plateau.

226

Aurora Sky Station Loop

ABISKO NATIONAL PARK

SWEDEN

Located in northern Sweden, 120 miles above the Arctic Circle, Abisko National Park is famous for the midnight sun—the sun doesn't set from late May to mid-July—and the aurora borealis, or northern lights, an atmospheric phenomenon that generates dancing lights across the night sky. You can enjoy these on this 3-mile loop to the Aurora Sky Station, a lookout tower with a viewing terrace. The northern lights can occur year-round, but are only visible to the eye against a dark night sky, so you'll need to brave the Nordic winter to experience this awe-inspiring show.

227

The King's Trail

ABISKO NATIONAL PARK

SWEDEN

Experience hut-to-hut hiking and skiing above the Arctic Circle on the king of trails.

- **DISTANCE**
  270 miles one way, usually completed in four weeks
- **START**
  Abisko Turiststation railway station and hostel
- **DIFFICULTY**
  Hard due to distance
- **SEASON**
  Mid-June to late September, on skis mid-February to late April

RIGHT The King's Trail in Sweden is said to be one of the most famous long-distance ski trails in the world.

The Kungsleden Trail, or King's Trail, begins in northern Sweden, then moves south through Abisko National Park. You'll stop every night at a series of backcountry huts spaced a day's walk apart. The route traverses the Scandinavian Mountain Range, which runs north to south for 1,100 miles across the Scandinavian Peninsula. After passing through Sarek National Park, the trail reaches its grand finale in the Vindelfjällen Nature Reserve, one of the largest protected areas in Europe, before ending in the small ski resort town of Hemavan.

The entire 270-mile route is divided into four sections, each requiring about a week of hiking. The well-marked trail can even be completed in winter, usually on skis. In summer, you'll still have to negotiate some snow and ice, as more than half the route lies above the Arctic Circle.

228

Sarek Circular Trail

SAREK NATIONAL PARK

SWEDEN

This 70-mile loop follows the stunningly beautiful Rapa Valley, where thirty glaciers feed into the braided Rapaätno River. Sarek is one of the wildest, most remote national parks in Europe, where you'll be more likely to spot wild animals like elk, lynx, wolverines, moose, and brown bears than other people.

229

Little Bear's Ring

OULANKA NATIONAL PARK

FINLAND

Voted Finland's favorite day hike, this 7.7-mile loop covers a scenic section of the 50-mile Karhunkierros, or Bear's Ring trail. This section can be hiked year-round, but you'll need snowshoes or skis in the winter. Fall is arguably the best season, when the trees turn a vibrant gold called "ruska" and a bejeweled buffet of cranberries, blueberries, lingonberries, and cloudberries can be found nestled among the prodigious lichen, moss, and mushrooms that carpet the boreal forest floor.

230

Rautalampi Hiking Trail

URHO KEKKONEN NATIONAL PARK

FINLAND

Trails in Urho Kekkonen National Park are divided into two categories: the day hikes are collectively called the "Out onto the Fell" trails, while the more challenging multiday treks translate as the "Out into the Wilderness" trails. The Rautalampi trail is a 13-mile loop, best tackled clockwise, that can be hiked as a long day hike or overnight backpack. Both day hikers and backpackers can take advantage of three backcountry campsites along the route, each of which offers a toilet. Reindeer are the most numerous animals in the park and seasonal herd roundups still take place.

BELOW The old watermill at Myllykoski is used as a hut on the Little Bear's Ring hike.

ABOVE You'll cross a suspension bridge over the river Luttojoki on the Iisakkipää Fell day hike.

231

Iisakkipää Fell

URHO KEKKONEN NATIONAL PARK

FINLAND

Each of the "Out onto the Fell" day hikes in Urho Kekkonen National Park has a theme. The 4.5-mile Iisakkipää Fell trail invites you to explore the four seasons on this loop, which can be hiked or snowshoed year-round. Beginning in the village of Saariselkä, the trail crosses the river Luttojoki on a hanging bridge, then climbs to the top of 1,490-foot Iisakkipää Fell, and descends along the Pääsiäiskuru Gorge before looping back to the start.

232

Kirkeby Forest

WADDEN SEA NATIONAL PARK

DENMARK

Stretching from the Ho Bugt bay to the German border, Wadden Sea National Park is the largest park in mainland Denmark. Twelve million birds pass through these vast intertidal mudflats twice a year on their way to and from their summer feeding and breeding grounds in the Arctic. See how many you can spot on this easy 3.3-mile loop on the island of Rømø. In the spring and fall, huge numbers of European starlings gather here, often flocking together in undulating murmurations so thick they block out the sun—a phenomenon called *sort sol*, or the black sun.

233

North Sea Trail

THY NATIONAL PARK

DENMARK

This 58-mile trail runs from Agger to Bulbjerg, with views across the Skagerrak Strait and the North Sea. Most people hike in a south-to-north direction, staying in small seaside towns, with Hanstholm Lighthouse guiding the way. The path mostly follows a grassy rutted road across the dunes; the grass attracts red deer and roe deer.

RIGHT The North Sea Trail hugs the northwest coast of Denmark.

234

Waalsberg-Meinvennen

MEINWEG NATIONAL PARK

THE NETHERLANDS

The Netherlands literally means "lower countries" and the country does have a geographically flat reputation. But this national park in the south has a uniquely terraced landscape—the product of copious sedimentary deposits by the Rhine and Meuse rivers over millennia. This 10.7-mile loop tours the rolling countryside, highlighting the park's varied terrain through forests, fens, and heaths. The park is accessible year-round, but spring is best for wildflowers.

235

Pieterpad

DRENTSCHE AA NATIONAL PARK

THE NETHERLANDS

Cross the Netherlands on this 310-mile route from the North Sea to the country's southernmost tip, marked by its only mountain, 360-foot Sint-Pietersberg. Starting at the coastal village of Pieterburen, the marked trail winds through wide-open fields booming with tulips before passing through the river valley of Drentsche Aa National Park and the quiet woods of the central Netherlands, and then finishing in the southern hill country. Divided into twenty-six stages, each with public transport and overnight accommodations, the Pieterpad is most often hiked in sections.

RIGHT Dutch hikers often make it a lifetime goal to finish the Pieterpad route one section at a time.

236

Hoge Veluwe Rondje Bezoekerscentrum Trail

HOGE VELUWE NATIONAL PARK

THE NETHERLANDS

Visit some of the landscapes that inspired painters like Vincent van Gogh, Claude Monet, and Pablo Picasso; examples of their work are exhibited at the Hoge Veluwe National Park's Kröller-Müller Museum. Originally a privately owned hunting preserve, this park in the central Netherlands boasts a surprisingly varied terrain, including heathlands, sand dunes, and woodlands. The Hoge Veluwe Rondje Bezoekerscentrum Trail is an easy 4-mile loop that highlights the park's beautiful forests. Wildlife viewing platforms create elevated opportunities to spot red deer, roe deer, wild boars, and mouflons, a type of wild sheep.

BELOW A rutting red stag in Hoge Veluwe National Park.

237

Covadonga Lakes Trail

PICOS DE EUROPA NATIONAL PARK

SPAIN

Take in two glacial lakes in the Picos de Europa mountains where the Tour of Spain bicycle race passes through.

DISTANCE
3-mile loop, elevation gain 700 feet

START
Lake Ercina

DIFFICULTY
Easy

SEASON
Year-round

Spain's first national park was established in 1918 to protect the Lakes of Covadonga, named Lake Enol and Lake Ercina. Getting to the lakes is an adventure in itself—the relentlessly steep road that climbs from the parish of Covadonga up to the lakes is infamous for being one of the most punishing stages of the annual Tour of Spain bicycle race (the Vuelta a España). During the busy summer months, the park provides a shuttle bus up to the lakes.

The Covadonga Lakes Trail is a 3-mile loop that starts at Lake Ercina and runs up to a pass, where you have the option to take a short detour into the Bosque Palomberu forest. The trail then heads down to run along the shore of Lake Enol before looping back to the start at Lake Ercina.

238

Cares River Trail

PICOS DE EUROPA NATIONAL PARK

SPAIN

Follow in the sure-footed steps of the rebeco, a small, hardy mountain goat native to the Cantabrian Mountains of northern Spain, on this epic 26-mile round-trip trek through the heart of Picos de Europa National Park. The Cares River Trail extends through three provinces following the river's course through its narrow gorge, surrounded by steep mountains. The 8-mile section between Poncebos, Asturias, and Caín, León, is especially scenic.

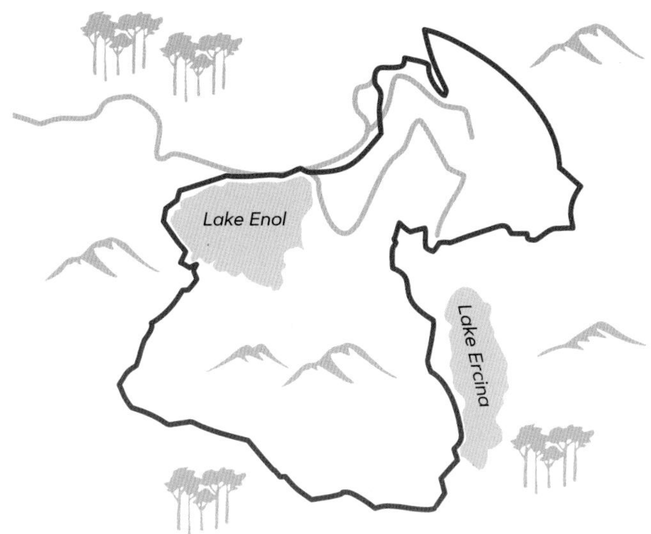

BELOW The spectacular setting of Lake Enol on the Covadonga Lakes Trail.

Ons Island Lighthouse and Castle Route

ATLANTIC ISLANDS OF GALICIA NATIONAL PARK

SPAIN

If you're going to take a ferry out to Ons Island, the main island of an archipelago off the northwest coast of Spain, you might as well make a day of it and hike all the island's trails. Combining the North, South, Lighthouse, and Castle trails adds up to a 9-mile day, and the highlights include the Ons Island Lighthouse. There, on the highest point of the island, you'll have views of O Centolo to the north and Fedorentos on the south.

The Hunter's Trail

ORDESA Y MONTE PERDIDO NATIONAL PARK

SPAIN

The first section of this 12.5-mile loop will get your heart pumping in more ways than one. The trail gains over 3,000 feet of elevation in the first mile and a half, with a few switchbacks cutting across perilously steep cliffs. Acrophobics might want to stick to an out-and-back route on the second half of the loop, which is much tamer. For sure-footed hikers, however, the views overlooking Ordesa Valley—known as Europe's Grand Canyon—will be worth the effort. The rest of the trail follows a long, gradual descent along the Ara River, passing several beautiful waterfalls.

ABOVE Hike to Ons Island Lighthouse for the best panoramic views.

241

Faja de las Flores

ORDESA Y MONTE PERDIDO NATIONAL PARK

SPAIN

Located in the Pyrénées Mountains in northeast Spain, this national park boasts the highest limestone walls in Europe, soaring 3,000 feet above Ordesa Valley. This extreme 21-mile loop follows a ledge eroded across these cliffs, above thousands of feet of air. In some places, you are forced to tiptoe along narrow ledges and cross a short via ferrata section—a route equipped with fixed ladders, cables, or bridges to assist hikers—called the Cotatuero Pegs, where iron spikes have been hammered into the wall. Some hikers elect to bring a climbing harness for this section so they can clip into the metal safety cable that is bolted to the rock.

242

Castle of Monfragüe

MONFRAGÜE NATIONAL PARK

SPAIN

Keep your eyes on the sky on this 7-mile loop to visit the Castle of Monfragüe. The park, located at the convergence of the Tajo and Tiétar rivers in the Cáceres region of western Spain, is known for being one of the best bird-watching spots in Europe—it is home to fifteen species of raptors, including European black vultures, griffon vultures, imperial eagles, and golden eagles.

The castle was originally built in the ninth century, but was rebuilt in the twelfth and fifteenth centuries. Nearby cave paintings date to the Bronze Age; the caves are protected and are open for viewing only at certain times, or you can visit Monfragüe's Rock Art Interpretation Center to learn more about the region's abundance of ancient underground art.

ABOVE RIGHT Castle Monfragüe sits in a lovely location overlooking the river Tagus.

RIGHT You'll cross several rope bridges on the Cahorros de Monachil trail.

243

Mulhacén

SIERRA NEVADA NATIONAL PARK

SPAIN

Tag the highest point on the Iberian Peninsula on this strenuous 15-mile out-and-back route up Mulhacén. On a clear day, you'll be able to see all the way to Morocco from the 11,414-foot summit. Mulhacén can be approached from several directions, but the shortest and least technical route is from the south, from the village of Capileira.

Cahorros de Monachil

SIERRA NEVADA NATIONAL PARK

SPAIN

Save this beautiful 4.5-mile loop for spring, when the wildflowers and apricot, cherry, and almond trees are in bloom. The hike starts in Monachil, home of the Sierra Nevada ski resort, and follows the Monachil River as it tumbles over waterfalls and through a narrow, rocky gorge, crossing several rope bridges along the way.

245

Geira Roman Road

PENEDA-GERÊS NATIONAL PARK

PORTUGAL

Portugal's only national park is located on the northern border, in the Gerês mountains. A 200-mile Roman road, built to connect the Roman civitates of Asturica Augusta (now Astorga, Spain) and Bracara Augusta (now Braga, Portugal) in the first century CE still runs through the park. This 2.6-mile out-and-back trail follows a flagstone-paved section of the ancient road, crossing the Homem River on bridges several times and passing Portela de Homem Waterfall.

246

Pedra Bela Trail

PENEDA-GERÊS NATIONAL PARK

PORTUGAL

This trail starts with an astonishing viewpoint over the Gerês mountains and Cávado River, and then follows an 8-mile loop clockwise through the surrounding forest. The route, marked by a series of rock piles called *mariolas* (elsewhere known as cairns or ducks), also accesses Arado Waterfall.

LEFT Take a dip in the swimming hole at the base of Arado Waterfall on the Pedra Bela Trail.

247

Cascades du Pont d'Espagne Trail

PYRÉNÉES NATIONAL PARK

FRANCE

You'll get to see six major waterfalls and countless cascades on this 5-mile out-and-back trail that follows the Gave de Marcadau River through lush wildflower meadows. The trail begins at the Pont d'Espagne, a striking stone bridge that spans the Gave de Marcadau at its whitewater confluence with the Gave de Gaube. The waterfalls are most spectacular in the spring and early summer months, when snowmelt is pouring out of the high country.

ABOVE The Pont d'Espagne stone bridge marks the start of the Cascades du Pont d'Espagne Trail.

RIGHT The Pyrénéan Way covers 550 miles from the Atlantic Ocean to the Mediterranean Sea.

248

Pyrénéan Way Trail

PYRÉNÉES NATIONAL PARK

FRANCE

Hike from the Atlantic Ocean to the Mediterranean Sea on an intense 550-mile backpacking trek. Most people tackle the Pyrénéan Way, or GR10, from west to east, starting at the Bay of Biscay and ending two months later at Banyuls-sur-Mer. The entire route, which traverses the Pyrénées, paralleling the border between France and Spain on the French side, is marked with red and white blazes.

The trail runs deep into the mountains, but reemerges regularly in towns and villages. Brown bears still live in the Pyrénées, but the big white Pyrénéan mountain dogs raised to protect sheep are more of a threat to hikers—give sheep a wide berth and never get between a dog and its flock.

PORT DE
Saleix
1794M
GR10 Refuge de Bassiès 1h30
GRP Cabane de Carol 40mn
1h GRP Mont Ceint

249

Calanques de Sugiton and Morgiou

CALANQUES NATIONAL PARK

FRANCE

The Mediterranean coast of France is riddled with deep, steep-sided inlets carved into vertical limestone cliffs called *calanques*. This 6.7-mile loop visits two of the nine calanques in Calanques National Park. Going clockwise, you'll first come to Calanque de Sugiton, a narrow crevice where you can jump off the rocky shoreline into the inviting crystalline water. Then head south and west to round the peninsula into Calanque Morgiou. A partially submerged sea cave here contains cave paintings created 27,000 years ago when the sea level was much lower and people could walk into the cave. Now only experienced divers can access it.

250

Calanques de Port-Miou, Port-Pin, and d'En-Vau

CALANQUES NATIONAL PARK

FRANCE

Check off three more calanques on this 5-mile loop in the French Riviera. These steep-sided crevices were cut into the white limestone coastline by rivers and wave action. Beginning near Cassis, the trail follows the edge of Calanque de Port-Miou before crossing a small peninsula to Calanque de Port-Pin. Then you'll reach an overlook that juts out in between Calanque de Port-Pin and the neighboring Calanque d'En-Vau before circling around to the head of Calanque d'En-Vau, where you'll want to take a dip in the clear blue water. Due to sweltering hiking conditions, access to many of the calanques is restricted during the hottest part of the summer.

251

Lac du Saut to Lac de la Sassière

VANOISE NATIONAL PARK

FRANCE

Vanoise National Park was established in 1963 to protect the alpine ibex, a mountain goat with spectacular 3-foot-long, backward-curving horns. After balancing on the edge of extinction, today around 2,000 ibex live in the park, along with 5,000 chamois, a smaller type of goat-antelope. Keep your eyes peeled for both species on this easy 4.3-mile loop between the smaller Lac du Saut and the larger Lac de la Sassière. The trail stays above 8,000 feet the entire time and gains only 675 feet of elevation.

252

Grand Tour

VANOISE NATIONAL PARK

FRANCE

France's first national park is surrounded by ski resorts and bordered on the Italian side by Gran Paradiso National Park, making this one of the largest protected regions in the European Alps. Starting in the village of Pralognan-la-Vanoise on this 100-mile loop through the heart of the park, you'll be able to keep your pack light by utilizing the mountain refuges and village accommodations along the way. Highlights of the legendary route include views of the highest peak in the Vanoise, the 12,648-foot Grande Casse, the Vanoise glaciers, and a summit of 9,173-foot Col dè Chaviere.

LEFT Take a refreshing dip in Calanque de Sugiton's crystal-clear waters on this hike.

ABOVE Hiking in the Vanoise Massif mountain range on the Grand Tour.

253

Black and White Glaciers

ÉCRINS NATIONAL PARK

FRANCE

Pay your respects to the ghosts of glaciers past in the French Alps, which is teeming with these rivers of ice.

DISTANCE
12.7 miles out and back to both glaciers, elevation gain 3,800 feet

START
Upper Saint Pierre Valley Nature Reserve

DIFFICULTY
Hard due to distance and elevation gain

SEASON
June to October

Écrins National Park boasts dozens of glaciers tucked into the heart of the French Alps, but most have retreated substantially due to warming and diminished snowfall. This 6.7-mile out-and-back trail follows a rocky moraine of glacial debris that marks the original extent of the Glacier Noir, or the Black Glacier, which earns its name from the dark smattering of rock scree on its surface.

In the next valley lies the Glacier Blanc, or White Glacier, which can be reached via a 6-mile round-trip offshoot of the Glacier Noir trail, following a glacially carved hanging valley. Strong hikers can visit both glaciers in a long day or plan to spend a night at the backcountry Écrins Refuge.

254

Lauvitel Lake

ÉCRINS NATIONAL PARK

FRANCE

Pack a picnic and a bathing suit for this 3.5-mile loop to Lauvitel Lake, the largest lake in Écrins National Park. The steep but well-maintained trail follows a creek, gaining 1,820 feet to the lake, which sits at an elevation of 5,020 feet. Due to avalanche danger, this trail is best hiked in the summer months from May to October.

ABOVE The colossal Glacier Blanc in Écrins National Park.

255

Lacs des Millefonts Trail

MERCANTOUR NATIONAL PARK

FRANCE

With more than 340 miles of hiking trails, you could spend an entire summer hiking in this park and not see everything. A network of trails connects the park's seven picturesque valleys and twenty-eight time-capsule villages tucked within the Alps. The challenging Lacs des Millefonts Trail is a 4.7-mile loop that passes five lakes on its way to the 8,773-foot summit of Mount Pépoiri.

256

Westweg

BLACK FOREST NATIONAL PARK

GERMANY

Spend a few weeks in the woods that inspired the brothers Grimm's fairy tales like *Hansel and Gretel* and *Sleeping Beauty*. The Westweg runs from north to south for 178 miles through the Black Forest. Marked by red and white signs, the route frequently passes through towns and villages. A baggage service can shuttle your backpack ahead to the next town so you'll only need to carry a day pack with essentials.

257

The Lothar Path

BLACK FOREST NATIONAL PARK

GERMANY

You won't need to leave a trail of bread crumbs on this unique path that delves into the deep, dark woods that frightened Hansel and Gretel. This loop, less than a mile long, tunnels through a section of the Black Forest that was decimated by Cyclone Lothar in 1999. The gale-force winds snapped and uprooted many trees, the remains of which were left in place so scientists can study how a forest recovers from destructive storm events.

258

Elbe River Canyon

SAXON SWITZERLAND NATIONAL PARK

GERMANY

Rising in the Czech Republic and flowing into Germany, the Elbe River cuts a steep and narrow defile through the Elbe Sandstone Mountains, helping to expose this region's intricate landscape. Smooth bike paths run on either side of the river, with inspiring views of the cliffs, fissures, and spires that line the deepest sandstone canyon in Europe (984 feet). You can walk a section of the path and take public transportation back to your starting point.

LEFT The Black Forest National Park was founded in 2014 and has many hiking routes.

259

Bastei Bridge

SAXON SWITZERLAND NATIONAL PARK

GERMANY

Discover the place where human ingenuity meets fabulous rock formations on a bridge to nowhere.

- **DISTANCE**
  3.5-mile loop, elevation gain 850 feet
- **START**
  Take a ferry to Rathen
- **DIFFICULTY**
  Easy but some stairs
- **SEASON**
  Year-round; fall colors peak in October

LEFT Nineteenth-century Bastei Bridge seems to lead to nowhere.

The imposing sandstone spires in this national park look like the ramparts of a castle fortress and were indeed once part of the defensive ring around Neurathen Castle. Today, the castle remains are preserved in an open-air museum and a striking stone bridge, built in 1851, runs across the top of the towers, cleverly making use of the natural stone spires as supports.

This easy 3.5-mile loop starts in the car-free village of Rathen, reached by boat across the Elbe River. Best hiked counterclockwise to save the bridge for last, the loop also runs through a narrow sandstone slot canyon called the Swedish Holes, which features a pretty waterfall. This popular loop can get very busy, so go early in the morning or in winter.

260

Schrammsteine

SAXON SWITZERLAND NATIONAL PARK

GERMANY

Rock climbers from all over Europe are drawn to the 17,000 climbing routes established in Saxon Switzerland. However, you don't need to be a rock climber to summit at least one spire. If you can climb a ladder, you can conquer the Schrammsteine monolith. A 4.5-mile loop winds through a labyrinth of rocks, leading to a metal staircase, ladders, and elevated walkways that safely escort you to a viewing platform, where you'll be rewarded with sweeping views of the forested, rock-dotted landscape.

261

Watzmann Peak

BERCHTESGADEN NATIONAL PARK

GERMANY

Set a date with Destiny Mountain on this hike across three summits that involves some climbing skill.

DISTANCE
4 miles one way to Hocheck, 14 miles total, elevation gain 7,400 feet

START
Car park in Ramsau

DIFFICULTY
Hard due to vertical terrain and route finding

SEASON
July to October; do not attempt if there's snow on the route

Part hike, part rock climb, this adventurous route traverses across the triple summit of one of Germany's highest mountains using a series of iron spikes and cables bolted to the rock. You'll need to be comfortable with scrambling and route finding in the vertical world to attempt this route. Alternatively, aim to only reach the Hocheck, the first of the three peaks.

Starting in the village of Ramsau, follow the hiking trail to the Watzmannaus hut at 6,332 feet, where you may opt to spend the night. From there it's another two hours of steep but nontechnical hiking to Hocheck. To go beyond this point, you'll need to don a helmet, rock-climbing shoes, and a harness. The route runs across the jagged skyline to the Mittelspitze, the highest point at 8,901 feet, and then to the third high point, Südspitze, followed by a steep, 2,000-foot descent to loop back down to the valley. The entire route can take ten to eighteen hours to complete.

Sections of this ferrata route were removed to dissuade inexperienced climbers, who often needed to be rescued mid-route. Experienced alpinists should have no trouble free soloing the missing sections, but be vigilant and remember that Watzmann has earned its nickname Schicksalsberg, or the Destiny Mountain, many times over.

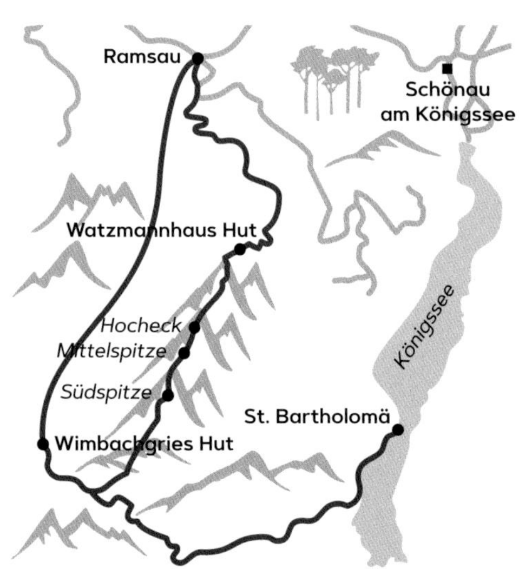

RIGHT You'll need some climbing skills—and daring—to conquer Watzmann Peak.

262

Malerwinkel

BERCHTESGADEN NATIONAL PARK

GERMANY

This easy 2-mile loop has a big payoff: epic views of the large Königssee. This lake sits in a tectonic rift that opened during the Jurassic period, which was later deepened by glaciers, creating Germany's third-deepest lake. From the Malerwinkel overlook you'll also be able to spy the red onion-style domes of Saint Bartholomä, a Roman Catholic pilgrimage church on the western shore of the lake.

263

Königssee to Kärlingerhaus am Funtensee

BERCHTESGADEN NATIONAL PARK

GERMANY

Beginning with a boat ride across the Königssee to Saint Bartholomew's church, this 12-mile out-and-back hike follows the ancient pilgrimage trail along the lakeshore for 2 miles before climbing to breathtaking views of Königssee and the smaller Obersee. If you think you're out of breath now, just wait for the Saugasse—a section of thirty-six hairpin switchbacks that gains 1,300 feet of elevation on its way up to Steinerne Meer, a high limestone plateau. If you're out for a day hike, return the way you came, or stay at the Kärlingerhaus mountain hut.

BELOW Hike the Malerwinkel and you'll be rewarded with breathtaking views of Lake Königssee.

ABOVE Val Trupchun is located in the Western Rhaetian Alps in eastern Switzerland.

Val Trupchun

SWISS NATIONAL PARK

SWITZERLAND

Switzerland has eighteen natural parks but only one national park. Swiss National Park is the only wilderness area in the country where hunting, livestock grazing, forestry, and mining are all prohibited and where natural processes like floods, fires, avalanches, and predation are left unchecked.

This trail runs up Val Trupchun Valley, along the Ova de Trupchun River, into the heart of this pristine wilderness. Footpaths run on both sides of the river, with multiple bridge crossings, so you can customize an out-and-back hike of any length. You're almost guaranteed to see marmots—a type of ground squirrel—on your hike, but keep your eyes open for ibex, deer, and chamois. You may hear the eerie bugles of the males during the mating season at the end of September.

265

Vittorio Sella Refuge

GRAN PARADISO NATIONAL PARK

ITALY

Hike in the footsteps of King Vittorio Emanuele II on this overnight trek to the Vittorio Sella Refuge in Aosta Valley. The trail follows a stream from the Valnontey River into the high country of Gran Paradiso National Park. After 3 miles you'll reach the refuge, a lodge built by the king in 1860 for ibex hunting. Today, the refuge has a restaurant and beds for 150 people. You can use it as a base camp to explore the surrounding mountains and valleys, or return the way you came.

266

Valnontey River Trail

GRAN PARADISO NATIONAL PARK

ITALY

From this family-friendly trail that follows the Valnontey River, you'll be able to admire the 13,323-foot Gran Paradiso mountain for which the park is named, as well as numerous glaciers on surrounding peaks. The mostly flat, wide trail runs along the river for 4 miles before it gains altitude into the mountains. It can be hiked year-round, but is especially scenic when the larch trees turn bright yellow in the fall.

RIGHT The Valnontey River Trail runs through a beautiful valley enclosed by towering mountains.

267

Mount Lagazuoi

DOLOMITI BELLUNESI NATIONAL PARK

ITALY

The natural ramparts of the Dolomites have played a role in many battles since Roman times. During World War I, Italian and Austro-Hungarian troops faced off on either side of Mount Lagazuoi, with both factions building extensive networks of tunnels. A 3.6-mile loop trail summits the 9,115-foot Lagazuoi, making use of the tunnels on the Italian side, and a steep trail known as the Austrian troop path on the descent. Bring a helmet, headlamp, and extra batteries for the tunnels section, which takes about forty-five minutes to complete.

268

High Paths of the Dolomites

DOLOMITI BELLUNESI NATIONAL PARK

ITALY

Trails in the Dolomites are renowned for spectacular alpine scenery and extreme difficulty. Experienced hikers may wish to tackle the legendary Alta Via, or High Paths. These ten trails, numbered from 1 to 10, connect a series of alpine huts spaced about a day apart. Alta Via 1, a 93-mile stretch from Pragser Wildsee to Belluno, is considered the most scenic and least technical.

269

Alta Via Dei Monzoni

DOLOMITI BELLUNESI NATIONAL PARK

ITALY

The Dolomites are not known for easy hikes, but this one qualifies as a moderate day hike. Starting at the Passo San Pellegrino ski area, cut off a few thousand feet of vertical gain by hitching a ride on a chairlift. The 10-mile loop begins by traversing through lush green cow pastures before ascending to the Passo delle Selle mountain refuge at an elevation of 8,293 feet, where you'll enjoy views of the surrounding peaks.

You'll then follow a narrow trail through the World War I Austrian and Italian trenches, where sniper stations, cannon stations, and artillery tunnels have been preserved as an open-air museum. Hiring somebody with historical knowledge will greatly add to the experience.

ABOVE RIGHT The Dolomites in northeastern Italy are one of the world's most spectacular mountain ranges.

RIGHT The Dolomites are topped by hundreds of peaks up to 10,968 feet.

270

The Blue Trail

CINQUE TERRE NATIONAL PARK

ITALY

Hug the Mediterranean coast of Italy on a cliff-top footpath between colorful seaside towns.

DISTANCE
7.5 miles one way with shuttle, elevation gain 1,700 feet

START
Monterosso or Riomaggiore

DIFFICULTY
Moderate

SEASON
Very busy in summer; September and October are cooler and quieter

Italy's smallest national park is also the most densely populated—around 5,000 people live in five towns within the 15-square-mile park. The rainbow-painted buildings perched on cliff edges overlooking the Mediterranean were declared a UNESCO World Heritage Site in 1997 and a national park in 1999 in recognition of the area's scenic, historic, and cultural value.

The five towns within the Cinque Terre—Monterosso al Mare, Vernazza, Corniglia, Manarola, and Riomaggiore—are connected by the Sentiero Azzurro, or the Blue Trail, a 7.5-mile footpath that runs from Monterosso to Riomaggiore. The trail hugs the edge of precipitous sea cliffs, offering spectacular views of the multicolor coast. Shorter sections can be hiked between the towns—bear in mind that some sections require climbing and descending lots of steps.

Erosion is an ongoing problem here, especially in the summer months, when as many as 5 million people visit. Check trail conditions before setting out on a hike, in case trails are closed due to maintenance, repairs, and closures after rainstorms.

ABOVE RIGHT The Blue Trail's stone pathway section between Corniglia and Vernazza.

RIGHT You'll pass through the colorful town of Manarola on the Blue Trail.

271

Riomaggiore Ring Trail

CINQUE TERRE NATIONAL PARK

ITALY

This 2.2-mile loop begins and ends in Riomaggiore, and provides sweeping views of the coastline and crystalline waters of the Ligurian Sea in the northern Mediterranean. Best hiked clockwise, the loop visits the Sanctuary of Montenero, an eighteenth-century church with ornately painted ceilings that offers pilgrims stone benches at a lofty overlook of the coastline more than 1,000 feet below.

272

Jorio Refuge

ABRUZZO, LAZIO, AND MOLISE NATIONAL PARK

ITALY

See wolves and bears in their natural habitat as you explore one of their last refuges in Europe.

- **DISTANCE**
  5-mile round trip, elevation gain 750 feet
- **START**
  Pescasseroli
- **DIFFICULTY**
  Moderate
- **SEASON**
  May to October

LEFT Italian wolves are protected in Italy's Abruzzo, Lazio, and Molise National Park.

BELOW The town of Pescasseroli is the starting point of a hike to the Jorio Refuge.

According to legend, Rome was founded in 753 BCE by Romulus and Remus, who were raised by a she-wolf, and killing a wolf was long considered taboo. However, by the 1970s, extermination campaigns almost wiped out the Italian wolf, a subspecies unique to the Italian peninsula.

Thanks to protections, around 700 Italian wolves live in Italy today, with several packs thriving in Abruzzo, Lazio, and Molise National Park. Around fifty Marsican brown bears also call the park home—the last remaining population of the critically endangered species. These massive bears live almost entirely on berries and rarely show aggression toward humans.

One of the best places to see wolves and bears is at the Jorio Refuge, a beautiful valley reached by a 5-mile round-trip hike from Pescasseroli. For most of the year, you're required to go with a guide.

ABOVE You'll enjoy vast panoramic views from the top of Montalto Mountain.

Montalto Mountain

ASPROMONTE NATIONAL PARK

ITALY

Located on the toe of Italy's high-heeled boot, these imposing mountains overlook the Strait of Messina—the narrow strip of water between Sicily and the Italian mainland that connects the Tyrrhenian Sea to the Ionian Sea. For a bird's-eye view of this magnificent landscape, long the hiding place of hermetic monks and the Italian mafia, hike to the top of Montalto Mountain, a 9-mile round-trip trek. At 6,414 feet above sea level, you'll have an epic view of the central Mediterranean and the Aspromonte mountains. Bring a small camping stove to enjoy a cup of Earl Grey tea on the summit; the beloved flavor comes from the rare bergamot fruit that grows here.

274

Pietra Cappa to Saint Peter's Rocks

ASPROMONTE NATIONAL PARK

ITALY

Aspromonte means "rough mountains," and for centuries, hermits and outlaws sought refuge in this rugged region near Calabria. This 3.5-mile loop hike in the Valley of the Great Stones circles the 460-foot glacier-carved monolith Pietra Cappa. Numerous other rock formations jut out of the earth here, each with their own names and stories. By the time you reach the Rocche of Saint Peter, where Byzantine monks scooped a hermitage out of rocks and earth, you'll see why this region remains a place of mystique and legend.

LEFT The rock formation Rocca tu Dracu, or Rock of the Dragon, in Aspromonte National Park.

275

Cala Napoletana

ARCIPELAGO DI LA MADDALENA NATIONAL PARK

ITALY

This marine geopark protects a cluster of islands in the Mediterranean Sea off the coast of Sardinia, known as the Maddalena Archipelago. The easiest way to reach the park is by boat or by taking a car ferry from Palau on Sardinia to La Maddalena and then driving over a bridge to Caprera.

This 5-mile loop circles the northern tip of the island, which was named for the prolific herds of wild goats that still inhabit the place (*capra* means "goat" in Italian). Follow the red-and-white wooden trail markers so you don't get sidetracked onto the countless goat trails that crisscross the island.

You'll reach private sandy beaches tucked between rocky alcoves, with inviting calm and crystal-clear water. The islands of the Maddalena Archipelago are made of granite and the trail is quite rocky, so wear sturdy hiking shoes.

276

Plechý

ŠUMAVA NATIONAL PARK

CZECH REPUBLIC

Šumava National Park, also known as Bohemian Forest National Park, boasts the largest forested region in central Europe. Unfortunately, much of the forest was logged and replanted with non-native spruce trees, large swaths of which have been affected by bark beetle infestations. However, a few primeval patches of native forest remain. Get a bird's-eye view of the forest from the top of Plechý, the highest point in the park. A 10-mile out-and-back trail gains 2,000 feet of elevation to the 4,524-foot summit, which sits on the border between the Czech Republic, Austria, and Germany.

277

Cave of Fairies

BOHEMIAN SWITZERLAND NATIONAL PARK

CZECH REPUBLIC

The mystique of the Elbe Sandstone Mountains also extends underground—the region is riddled with caves. From the village of Krasna Lipa, a 2.5-mile round-trip trek will take you to the Cave of Fairies in Kyjov Valley. As with most caves, the temperature underground is much cooler than at the surface and the walls and ceilings are decorated with glittering icicles and icy stalactites and stalagmites all year. Guided cave tours are available year-round, but in the winter you may need snowshoes to reach the cave.

278

The Prebisch Gate

BOHEMIAN SWITZERLAND NATIONAL PARK

CZECH REPUBLIC

The Elbe Sandstone Mountains extend across the border from Germany into the Czech Republic's Bohemian Switzerland National Park. An 11.7-mile loop hits many of the park's highlights, including Pravčická Brána, or the Prebisch Gate. For a shorter day, you can hike out and back to the Gate, a 6-mile round trip. Either way, it's worth the effort—with a span of 86 feet, the Gate is the largest natural stone arch in Europe and the second-largest arch of its kind in the world.

ABOVE The Prebisch Gate was featured in *The Chronicles of Narnia* movies.

LEFT Candles placed among icy stalagmites create a magical atmosphere in the Cave of Fairies.

279

Celts, Sumpters, and Romans Path

HIGH TAUERN NATIONAL PARK

AUSTRIA

Follow an ancient trade route over the Austrian Alps where the highest mountain in the country is located.

DISTANCE
2 miles out and back, elevation gain 400 feet

START
Car park at Hochtor Pass

DIFFICULTY
Easy

SEASON
Road usually open from May to October

LEFT Tread where others have for thousands of years, over the ancient Celts, Sumpters, and Romans Path.

The largest of Austria's national parks stretches for 62 miles across the Austrian Alps—also known as the Central Eastern Alps. People have been crossing the Austrian Alps on foot for millennia, but the route became much easier in 1935 with the opening of the Grossglockner High Alpine Road. This paved toll road connects Bruck in Salzburg with Heiligenblut in Carinthia over the Hochtor Pass, at 8,215 feet.

Archaeological and historical studies show that people have been crossing the Alps at Hochtor Pass for at least 3,500 years. During the construction of the road, a bronze Roman statuette of the demigod Hercules, as well as Celtic and Roman coins, were unearthed. These and other relics are on display at the Hochtor Pass Sanctuary at the top of the pass. An easy 2-mile round-trip trail called the Celts, Sumpters, and Romans Path leads from a car park to the original ancient footpath.

280

Grossglockner Peak

HIGH TAUERN NATIONAL PARK

AUSTRIA

Tag the highest point in Austria on this strenuous 10-mile round-trip hike to the top of 12,461-foot Grossglockner Peak. Known as the "Normal Route," this trail starts on the west side of the mountain in Kals and runs up to the Erzherzog Johann hut—the highest mountain hut in Austria, at 11,332 feet. Most people spend the night here and get an early start for the summit the next morning. You'll need crampons, an ice ax, and glacier travel experience or consider hiring a guide.

281

Krimml Waterfalls and Old Tauern Trail

HIGH TAUERN NATIONAL PARK

AUSTRIA

As it pours out of Krimml Ache Valley, the Krimml River plunges over three tiers of cliffs for a combined height of 1,247 feet, making this the highest waterfall in Austria. Visit the falls and circle back on a historic footpath on this 5-mile loop hike. More than 400,000 people visit these falls each year and the trail can get very busy. You'll see far fewer people by making a loop on the Old Tauern Trail, which dates back to the sixteenth century.

BELOW Reach Austria's highest point by climbing to the top of Grossglockner Peak.

282

Wurbauerkogel Loops

KALKALPEN NATIONAL PARK

AUSTRIA

Topping the Northern Limestone Alps of Austria, this national park is crowned by a glass lookout tower called the Wurbauerkogel. From the top, on a clear day, you'll count twenty-one peaks over 6,000 feet in the surrounding Sengsengebirge and Reichraminger Hintergebirge mountain ranges. Numerous hiking trails of varying lengths and difficulties spiderweb out from the Wurbauerkogel, which is reached from the town of Windischgarsten via a chairlift. You can also descend the mountain via a summer toboggan track.

283

Merkersdorf and Umlaufberg

THAYATAL NATIONAL PARK

AUSTRIA

Austria's smallest national park sits on the northern border across from its sister park, Czech Podyjí National Park, in the Czech Republic. Together, the parks protect a meandering section of the Thaya River. This 6.3-mile forested loop follows an oxbow turn in the river, where it loops back on itself, nearly creating an island. The park is known for being a refuge for the rare steppe polecat—a ferretlike animal that preys on ground squirrels.

LEFT The Wurbauerkogel lookout tower offers views over several Austrian mountain ranges.

284

Mostnica Gorge

TRIGLAVSKI NATIONAL PARK

SLOVENIA

Pack a quality camera and tripod to capture long-exposure images of the rushing water on this hike.

DISTANCE
8-mile loop, elevation gain 1,300 feet

START
Stara Fužina

DIFFICULTY
Moderate

SEASON
May to October

RIGHT Look for the Little Elephant rock formation on the Mostnica Gorge hike.

At the end of the last Ice Age, meltwater from retreating glaciers roared through this narrow, sinuous canyon. Today, the Mostnica creek flows year-round through Mostnica Gorge, creating one of the most photo-worthy waterways in eastern Europe.

Starting in the village of Stara Fužina, the trail winds through the meandering gorge, offering splendid views of the emerald water as it rushes over intricately carved rock formations. The most photographed spot, called the Little Elephant, is a trunklike arch. Follow the creek for 4 miles to the Mostnica Waterfall, and then return on the other side of the creek, making use of several bridges that span the gorge.

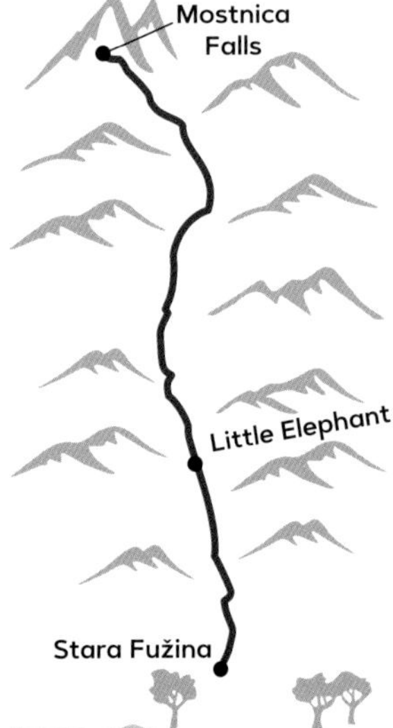

285

Vintgar Gorge Loop

TRIGLAVSKI NATIONAL PARK

SLOVENIA

Hike the easy 3.5-mile loop around the Vintgar Gorge and you'll understand why this is Triglavski's most-visited attraction. The crystal-clear water running through the gorge is so blue it has to be seen to be believed. Go early in the morning to avoid crowds.

286

Mount Triglav

TRIGLAVSKI NATIONAL PARK

SLOVENIA

At 9,395 feet, Mount Triglav is the highest point in Triglavski National Park and the highest peak in the Julian Alps. This strenuous 15.5-mile round-trip hike gains 7,100 feet of elevation, including a via ferrata section of metal cables. Most people summit Triglav as an overnight trek, starting in the town of Trenta and spending a night at the Kredarica hut in the picturesque Krma Valley. Hire a guide if you're not familiar with via ferrata routes.

287

Valley of the Seven Lakes

TRIGLAVSKI NATIONAL PARK

SLOVENIA

The name Valley of the Seven Lakes is a bit of a misnomer, as there are actually ten lakes in this valley between Bohinj and Trenta. This 16-mile out-and-back trek passes through idyllic scenery in the Julian Alps—a little-known subrange of the European Alps. A multitude of backcountry huts offer basic accommodations and meals. You can also visit the valley on a longer hut-to-hut trek on the Slovenian Mountain Trail, which runs for 370 miles.

288

Veliki Risnjak

RISNJAK NATIONAL PARK

CROATIA

Summit the highest point in the park on this 4-mile out-and-back trail up 5,013-foot Veliki Risnjak. The route only gains 1,400 feet, making it a moderate summit climb, but some hikers choose to stay at the Šloserov hut. Open from June to October, it has a reputation for being the most beautiful mountain hut in Croatia.

LEFT Tag the highest peak in the Julian Alps by climbing Mount Triglav.

289

Roški Waterfall

KRKA NATIONAL PARK

CROATIA

Krka National Park is centered on a turbulent, cascading stretch of the Krka River, famous for its series of dramatic waterfalls. This 1.6-mile loop circles Ogrlice Lake to an overlook of Roški Waterfall. Blue-green water flows over the terraced falls into a beautiful blue swimming hole. Bring a bathing suit and swim behind the falling water for a unique view of the falls.

BELOW The vibrant cascading Roški Waterfall in Croatia's Krka National Park.

290

Plitvice Lakes Loop

PLITVICE LAKES NATIONAL PARK

CROATIA

Admire a spectacular set of lakes and intricate waterfalls in this picturesque national park.

DISTANCE
9-mile loop, elevation gain 1,450 feet

START
Plitvička Jezera

DIFFICULTY
Moderate

SEASON
Year-round; very crowded in summer

ABOVE RIGHT With more than ninety waterfalls, Plitvice is the world's largest waterfall network.

RIGHT Veliki Slap is the highest waterfall in Croatia.

Several rivers meet to form the Plitvice Lakes, in a valley in the Dinaric Alps, about 45 miles upstream of the Adriatic Sea. Each of the sixteen lakes has its own distinctive color, and is separated by naturally forming dams of travertine—a mineral that precipitates out of the water and gives it a preternaturally blue hue. These dams are often damaged and rearranged by floods, creating uniquely dynamic waterfalls that change over time.

There are many trails and overlooks along the 5-mile valley that contains the lakes. This 9-mile loop circles the northern half of the lakes basin, starting at Kaluđerovac Lake in the north and weaving around eight of the lakes before circling back, passing dozens of waterfalls along the way. The route, which sometimes follows boardwalks and bridges across the water, is long but the hiking is easy, with some restaurants and restrooms along the way.

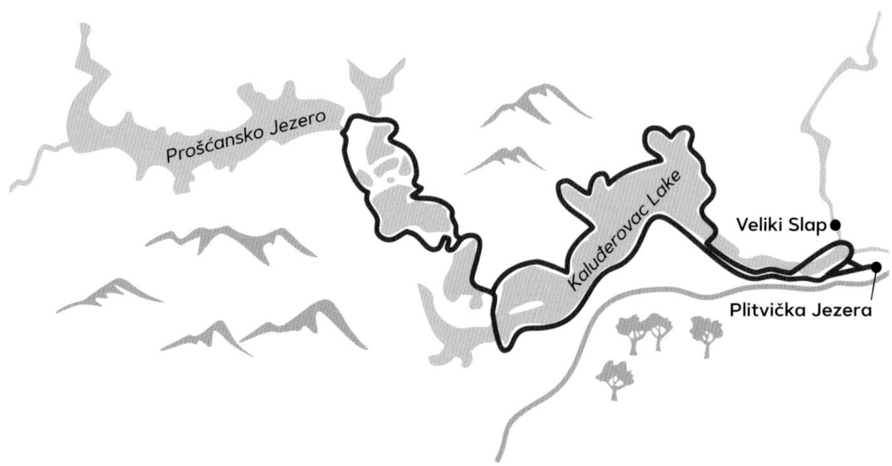

Trail A

PLITVICE LAKES NATIONAL PARK

CROATIA

This 2.2-mile loop encircles the four lower Plitvice Lakes: Milanovac, Gavanovac, Kaluđerovac, and Novakovića Brod, each with their own local legend. Gavanovac is supposedly the hiding place of the Gavanovo treasure, although the water is so clear that it looks like there's nowhere for it to hide. Along the route you'll pass several breathtaking waterfalls, including the 255-foot Veliki Slap, or Great Waterfall.

292

Štrbački Buk

UNA NATIONAL PARK

BOSNIA AND HERZEGOVINA

Bosnia and Herzegovina's largest national park was established to protect the Upper Una, Krka, and Unac Rivers, which meet in the heart of the park. The Una hosts the International Una Regatta, a kayaking competition utilizing the river's whitewater rapids and waterfalls. If you'd prefer to experience the often raging river from the safety of the bank, set out on this 7-mile out-and-back trail that runs from Cukovi to Štrbački Buk, the largest waterfall in the park.

293

Via Dinarica

SUTJESKA NATIONAL PARK

BOSNIA AND HERZEGOVINA

Established in 1962, Bosnia and Herzegovina's oldest national park is one gem in a 1,260-mile string of crown jewels along eastern Europe's most epic long-distance trail. The Via Dinarica passes through Slovenia, Croatia, Serbia, Bosnia and Herzegovina, Montenegro, Kosovo, Albania, and Macedonia, following the spine of the Dinaric Alps across the Balkan Peninsula. The scenic 40-mile section from Sutjeska National Park to Durmitor National Park in Montenegro was the first section to be built.

ABOVE Water activities are popular on the Štrbački Buk rapids.

RIGHT Durmitor Ice Cave is a 130-foot-long cave that is icy year-round.

294

Durmitor Ice Cave

DURMITOR NATIONAL PARK

MONTENEGRO

From December to March, the Durmitor mountains are home to Montenegro's biggest ski resort. If you visit in summer, you can still enjoy a small blast of winter by ducking into the Durmitor Ice Cave, or Ledena Pécina. A vigorous 7.7-mile double loop starts at the twin lakes Mlínski Potok and circles around two 7,000-foot peaks on its way to the cave. Bring ice-traction devices, as the sloping floor is paved with ice year-round. Do not disturb the fragile stalactites and stalagmites made from dripping ice water.

295

Bobotov Kuk

DURMITOR NATIONAL PARK

MONTENEGRO

Tag the highest peak in the Durmitor mountains on this 6-mile round-trip jaunt up Bobotov Kuk. This mountain was long thought to be the highest point in Montenegro, but surveys found three higher summits along the border with Albania. The signed trail to the top gains nearly 3,000 feet from Sedlo Pass. From the 8,278-foot summit, the landscape falls away in sheer cliffs and tumbling talus slopes that lead into the alpine lake basins that grace the high country of this national park.

296

Valbona Pass

VALBONA VALLEY NATIONAL PARK

ALBANIA

Cross a once-forbidden pass that now lies in the heart of the Balkans Peace Park.

DISTANCE
6 miles with shuttle, elevation gain 3,200 feet

START
Valbona or Theth

DIFFICULTY
Moderate

SEASON
July to September

Valbona Valley National Park is part of a transboundary national park that connects a vast swath of Albania, Kosovo, and Montenegro called the Balkans Peace Park. This region hasn't always been so inclusive; the Albanian Alps are also known as the Accursed Mountains, and for decades was a forbidden zone, where people suffered crippling oppression and poverty under communist rule. Today the area welcomes travelers, and tourism is revitalizing long-forgotten villages.

One of the scenic highlights of the park, Valbona Pass is famous for the overlook at the top of the expansive and rugged terrain. You can hike up and over the pass from either direction; both Valbona and Theth offer vans for hire, overnight accommodations, and restaurants. The well-marked route runs for 3 miles up to the pass, where you'll be treated to epic views of the Accursed Mountains, and then another 3 miles downhill to the next village.

ABOVE Valbona Pass is a high mountain pass in northern Albania.

LEFT The Albanian Alps, aka the Accursed Mountains, are now open to the public.

Cape of Stillo

BUTRINT NATIONAL PARK

ALBANIA

Visit some of the best-preserved ruins in Europe at Butrint National Park. You can roam the 2,500-year-old Temple of Asclepius and an Ottoman castle. A network of hiking trails also lead beyond the town's crumbling walls into the surrounding wetlands, forests, rocky shorelines, and sandy beaches. A 3.2-mile round-trip hike up a mountain to the Cape of Stillo provides sweeping panoramic views.

298

Rebäse Landscape Trail

KARULA NATIONAL PARK

ESTONIA

This 4.5-mile trail begins at the Tornimäe observation tower near Rebäse and hits two other high points: the local Mount Ararat and Linnamägi Hill, all with excellent views of the surrounding bucolic rolling landscape. The region is steeped in history; traces of an Iron Age settlement can be found on Linnamägi Hill and you'll pass a farmstead that dates back to the sixteenth century. Keep your eyes peeled for wild boar, beavers, and elk. Visit in the spring, when the snowdrop anemones bloom white flowers with golden hearts.

299

Turaida Castle Museum Reserve Loop

GAUJA NATIONAL PARK

LATVIA

Latvia's largest national park is set around Gauja River Valley, where people have been congregating and building for centuries. More than 500 historic buildings and monuments are protected within the park's Museum Reserve. This 3-mile loop through hills and forests circles Turaida Castle. Climb the castle's main tower for outstanding views of the river. Numerous sculptures, relics, ruins, and caves dot the route.

ABOVE Turaida Castle dates back to the thirteenth century.

300

Great Ķemeri Bog Boardwalk

ĶEMERI NATIONAL PARK

LATVIA

After glaciers retreated at the end of the last Ice Age, parts of what is now Latvia began forming bogs—a type of wetland where accumulated plant matter forms into peat. This ancient landscape has been evolving for millennia, creating one of the most biologically unique ecosystems in eastern Europe.

Follow this 3-mile double-loop trail through the Great Ķemeri Bog on a series of raised planks and look for sundew, a carnivorous plant that traps insects on its glistening sticky leaves. This bog is also famous for bird-watching—several species like the wood sandpiper and European golden plover raise their chicks here.

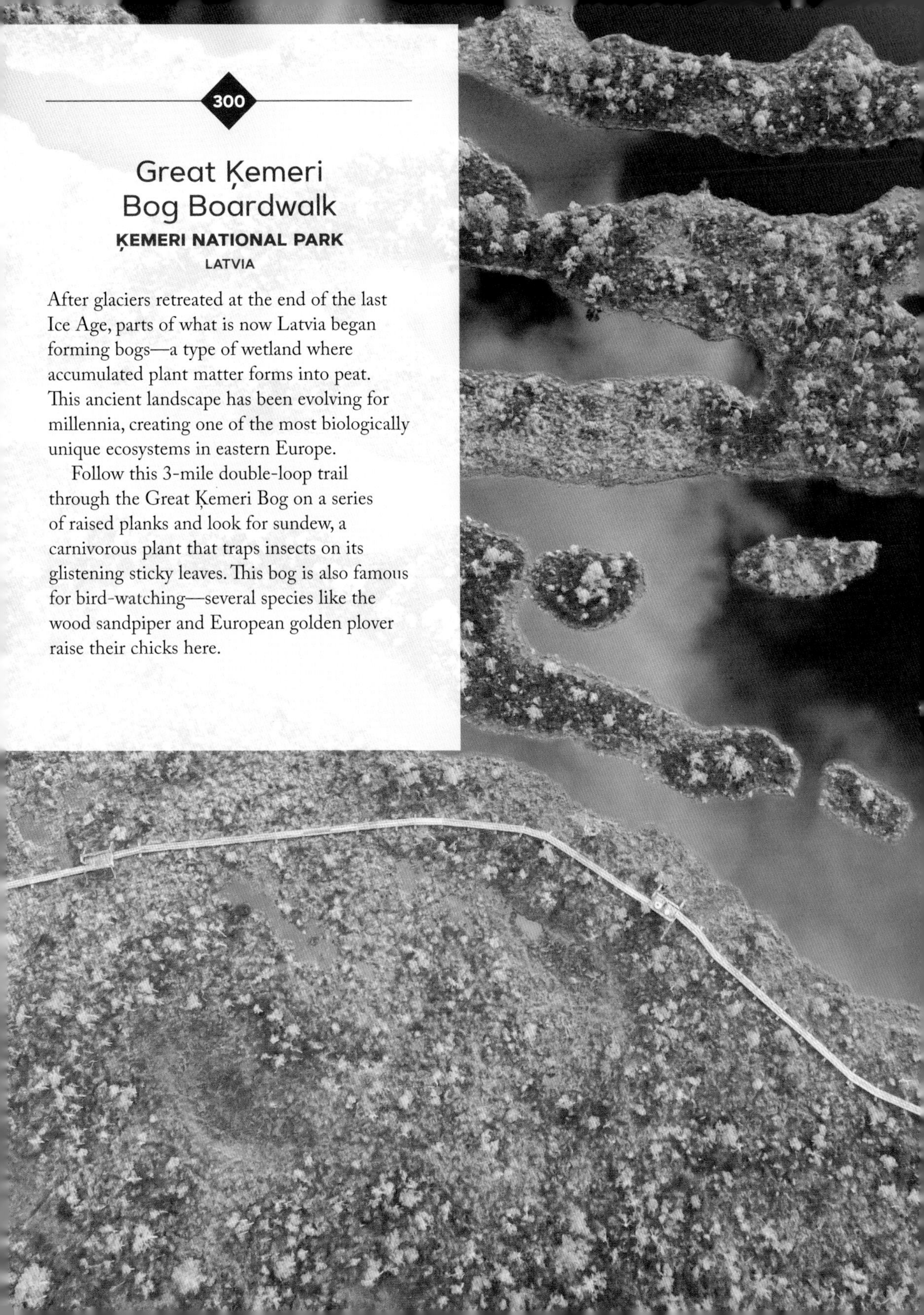

301

Wydma Łacka

SŁOWIŃSKI NATIONAL PARK

POLAND

Perched on the coast of the Baltic Sea, this park is famous for its rapidly shifting sand dunes. This 8-mile loop explores a narrow strip of land between Łebsko Lake and the Baltic Sea. The trail loops between the oceanside coastline and the lakeside shoreline, passing several stands of pine trees where the sand dunes have been blown deep into the forest, creating an eerie scene reminiscent of snowy woods. Keep watch for white-tailed sea eagles, which hunt fish in both the lake and the sea. If you see one hovering, wait for the plunge as the massive bird folds its wings into a torpedo for splashdown, then takes to the sky again with a thrashing fish gripped in its talons.

302

Obszar Ochrony Ścisłej

BIAŁOWIEŻA FOREST NATIONAL PARK

POLAND

Białowieża Forest is the largest surviving remnant of the primeval forests that once covered the central interior lowlands of Europe. The national park protects a pristine 41-square-mile pocket, while the Białowieża Forest UNESCO World Heritage area covers nearly 550 square miles of the forest. Hiding among the 800-year-old oak trees is the largest remaining population of European bison, managed by the European Bison Breeding Center. Large areas of the park are closed to the public to protect the forest and enable scientists to study an untouched temperate forest ecosystem. A number of trails, including this 4-mile lollipop-shaped loop, are open, but you must be accompanied by a guide.

ABOVE The Three Crowns loom above Pieniny National Park.

LEFT Experience the Łeba desert dunes on the picturesque Wydma Łacka hike.

Three Crowns

PIENINY NATIONAL PARK

POLAND

This national park on the Polish border with Slovakia is best known for whitewater rafting trips through the Dunajec River Gorge, but the park has an extensive network of hiking trails as well. This strenuous 5.7-mile out-and-back trail climbs to the top of the Three Crowns—a group of limestone peaks that tower over the river. An observation deck sits at the top of the highest peak, 3,222-foot Okrąglica, offering spectacular views.

304

Priečne Sedlo Loop

TATRA NATIONAL PARK

POLAND

If you have time for only one hike in Tatra National Park and you're up for a challenge, this 10.5-mile loop has it all: spectacular mountain scenery, high alpine lakes, multiple waterfalls, and a dose of adrenaline. You'll feel the jolt where the trail climbs up a steep rocky gully—a set of chains and a few metal ladder rungs are bolted to the rock here to help you. This loop is only accessible in the dry summer months between June and September.

305

Kościeliska Valley

TATRA NATIONAL PARK

POLAND

Time your visit for the spring crocus bloom and you may find yourself in the most beautiful purple valley. The Dolina Kościeliska, or Kościeliska Valley, in southern Poland opens in a deep and rocky gorge at the foot of the Tatra Mountains. An 8.5-mile loop circles the valley, passing several cave entrances. The Jaskinia Mroźna, or Frost Cave, is accessible without a guide. Bring a headlamp and extra batteries.

BELOW Pretty Kościeliska Valley is located near the resort town of Zakopane, in southern Poland.

306

Morskie Oko

TATRA NATIONAL PARK

POLAND

Circle Tatra's most famous lake on this classic 1.6-mile loop. Morskie Oko might be the most-visited spot in the national park—for good reason. The turquoise-blue waters of the lake reflect the surrounding peaks of the Tatra Mountains, including Mount Rysy, the highest point in Poland at 8,199 feet. Hike an extra mile up to Czarny Staw—another lake with even more epic views.

307

Dry White Gorge

SLOVAK PARADISE NATIONAL PARK

SLOVAKIA

Named for the Slovak Paradise Mountain Range, this region of Slovakia is blessed with numerous rivers and streams that have riddled the park's karst limestone plateau with deep valleys, gorges, canyons, and caves—not to mention countless waterfalls.

Hike this 5.5-mile loop through the Roklina Suchá Belá, or Dry White Gorge. You'll follow the creek upstream past waterfalls and make use of metal ladders and chains in steep, scrambling sections. You'll cross the creek many times—sometimes the creek is the trail—and the rocks can be slippery, so wear hiking boots with tread. The second half of the trail circles back to the start on an easy path through a lush green forest.

Štrbské Lake to Popradské Lake

HIGH TATRAS NATIONAL PARK

SLOVAKIA

The best way to start getting to know High Tatras National Park is with a walk around Štrbské Pleso (*pleso* means "lake"), the most accessible alpine lake in the park. An easy 2-mile loop encircles the lake, with views of the forested slopes and rocky peaks of the High Tatras. You can stop here in a lakeside coffee shop for refreshments. Next, take the scenic red trail for 2 miles to Popradské Pleso, a neighboring alpine lake that's more remote, but the Majláthova Mountain Hut offers a full bar and restaurant.

LEFT Majláthova Mountain Hut beside the serene Popradské Lake.

ABOVE The Tatranská Magistrála is a long-distance trail through Slovakia's High Tatras Mountains.

Tatranská Magistrála

HIGH TATRAS NATIONAL PARK

SLOVAKIA

Traverse the High Tatras Mountains on this 26-mile hut-to-hut route. Most hikers take four days to complete the trek from the village of Podbanské to Vel'ké Biely Pleso; both ends of the route can be accessed by bus or train, and there are numerous side excursions off the main trail. The mountain huts along the way supply shelter and food; all you need to bring is a sleeping bag and day-hiking supplies. Weather can change quickly in the mountains, so pack plenty of layers and rain gear.

Green Lake

HIGH TATRAS NATIONAL PARK

SLOVAKIA

The hike to Green Lake starts with a cable-car ride from the town of Tatranska Lomnica to Skalnaté Pleso. From there you'll hike 10 miles to Green Lake and back to town, skipping the cable-car ride on the way back. The trail offers splendid views of the jagged mountains and iridescent green valleys of the High Tatras and a bit of excitement too—you'll need to negotiate a steep descent by holding on to a set of chains that are bolted to the rock.

311

Zádielska Valley

SLOVAK KARST NATIONAL PARK

SLOVAKIA

Delve into Slovakia's deepest gorge on a fairly easy hike in the striking Slovak Karst landscape.

DISTANCE
5-mile loop, elevation gain 2,000 feet

START
Zadiel

DIFFICULTY
Moderate

SEASON
May to October

LEFT Expect stunning scenery on this half-day walk through Zadielská Valley.

Karst landscapes form when water-soluble rocks like limestone and dolomite are dissolved by running water, creating gorges, canyons, and cave systems. The Slovak Karst mountains in southeast Slovakia are cut by numerous steep canyons and riddled with hundreds of caves and karst pits—deep vertical sinkholes that plunge hundreds of feet underground.

One of the most spectacular hikes in the park delves into Zádielska Valley and over its adjoining plateau in a 5-mile loop. Also known as Zádielska Gorge, it is the deepest in the land (980 feet), and only 30 feet wide at its narrowest point. The trail follows an old road, so while the gorge itself is an extreme place, the hiking path is moderate. The trail circles back to the start across a high plateau with stunning views of the surrounding mountains.

312

Ďumbier and Chopok Peaks Loop

LOW TATRAS NATIONAL PARK

SLOVAKIA

Slovakia's largest national park protects the Low Tatras Mountains, which are lower in elevation and more heavily forested than the High Tatras. This 9.5-mile loop summits two peaks—6,703-foot Ďumbier and 6,640-foot Chopok—that are connected by a spectacular ridge walk.

313

Lake Tisza

HORTOBÁGY NATIONAL PARK

HUNGARY

This park in eastern Hungary preserves a swath of the Hungarian Great Plains. People have been raising livestock on these grasslands for millennia and the region is known for its unique shepherding culture, featured at the Shepherd Museum here. Lake Tisza was created in the 1970s by damming the Tisza River, creating a wetlands habitat that serves as a sanctuary for migrating birds. Lake Tisza Water Nature Reserve follows a series of wheelchair-accessible boardwalks along the lakeshore for a mile. Bring binoculars to spot the hundreds of bird species that either live in or migrate through the park.

314

Baradla Cave

AGGTELEK NATIONAL PARK

HUNGARY

Like much of eastern Europe, Hungary is underlain by limestone, which erodes into dramatic canyons and caves typical of karst landscapes. Aggtelek National Park is riddled with at least 280 caves, including the largest stalactite cave in Europe—Baradla Cave.

Take a guided tour of Baradla's massive tunnels and giant caverns, decorated with spectacular formations with names like the Mother-in-Law's Tongue, Santa Claus, and the Tiger. This tour covers about 1.5 miles underground, climbing up and down numerous steps.

315

Bükk Plateau

BÜKK NATIONAL PARK

HUNGARY

The Bükk Plateau is a wide-open area with epic views, intriguing rock formations, and carpets of wildflowers in the spring. Numerous marked trails crisscross the plateau, so you can customize a hike of almost any length. The 7-mile out-and-back route from Lake Gyári to the 3,146-foot summit of *Istállós-kő* affords panoramic views of the heavily forested park, which is also home to the country's longest cave and highest waterfall.

316

Hany Istók Nature Trail

FERTŐ-HANSÁG NATIONAL PARK

HUNGARY

Located on the border of Austria and Hungary, Lake Fertő is the largest saltwater lake in central Europe. The unique habitat attracts millions of birds from hundreds of species, including the rare red-breasted goose, hen harrier, and white-tailed eagle. You'll start this 3.5-mile nature trail at the Esterházy bird watchpoint, where you'll find a quality exhibit. The trail then runs through prime bird-watching territory and along the lakeshore.

LEFT The entrance to Europe's largest stalactite cave system, Baradla Cave.

BELOW Baradla Cave dripstone columns form when stalactites and stalagmites meet.

317

Ochiul Beiului

CHEILE NEREI-BEUȘNIȚA NATIONAL PARK

ROMANIA

Tucked away in a remote part of Romania, this national park protects a region of the Aninei Mountains known for deep gorges and bright blue rivers. This 2-mile round-trip hike from Podu Beiului to the spring-fed lake Ochiul Beiului highlights the unusual tropical blue of the water here, a product of minerals dissolved in the water. Local legends say, on the night of Sânziene, Romania's midsummer solstice celebration, fairies gather at Ochiul Beiului to dance and bathe in its waters.

318

Raiskoto Praskalo Waterfall

CENTRAL BALKAN NATIONAL PARK

BULGARIA

Falling 400 feet over a cliff, Raiskoto Praskalo Waterfall is the highest in the Balkans. Its name means "spray from heaven" and its idyllic setting above wildflower fields and below the highest peaks in the park is indeed heavenly. The 13-mile round-trip hike to the falls is strenuous, at one point climbing a steep hill named Dzhendema, meaning "hell." Make this an overnight trip and stay at the Rai Hut, or Heaven Chalet, near the base of the falls. You can climb the highest peak in the Balkans, 7,795-foot Botev Peak, from here too.

BELOW Ochiul Beiului never freezes—its temperature remains constant throughout the year.

319

Seven Rila Lakes

RILA NATIONAL PARK

BULGARIA

Bulgaria's most famous natural attraction is this series of seven glacially carved lakes connected by small streams and waterfalls in the Rila Mountains. A 6.2-mile loop hike starts with a ride up a ski lift and then circles around to the lakes, each with its own unique character. Okoto, named "the Eye" after its oval shape, is the deepest lake in Bulgaria; the distinctly shaped Babreka, or "the Kidney," has the steepest shoreline. Spend a night in the chalet on the northeastern shore of Ribnoto Ezero, or "the Fish Lake," so you can admire the sunset and sunrise over the surrounding peaks.

320

Musala Peak

RILA NATIONAL PARK

BULGARIA

At 9,596 feet, Musala Peak is the highest point in the Rila Mountains, but thanks to a ski lift from Borovets, the 4-mile round-trip hike to the top can be done as a casual day hike—or plan to stay at the nearby Musala Chalet for a night. From the summit, all the major mountain ranges of Bulgaria are visible, including the surrounding Rila peaks, Vitosha to the northwest, Sredna Gora to the northeast, the Balkans to the north, the Rhodopes to the southeast, the Pirin to the south, and the Osogovo and Ruy ranges to the west.

BELOW Each of the Seven Rila Lakes has a name determined by its shape or characteristic.

321

Samariá Gorge Trail

SAMARIÁ GORGE NATIONAL PARK

GREECE

Hike through Europe's longest gorge in southwestern Crete. This 10-mile one-way hike follows the length of the gorge as it descends 4,000 feet of elevation from the mountains to a beach on the Libyan Sea at the coastal village of Agia Roumeli. The most famous section of the walk goes through the Portes, or Gates, a narrow stretch where the imposing walls narrow to a width of 13 feet.

322

Vikos Gorge Trail

VIKOS–AOÖS NATIONAL PARK

GREECE

Guinness World Records lists the Vikos Gorge in the Pindus Mountains of northern Greece as the world's deepest gorge relative to its width. The spectacular 7-mile gorge plunges to depths 3,300 feet below its rim, and widens to 3,600 feet. A point-to-point trail runs along the Voidomatis River at the bottom of the gorge for 7.3 miles, starting in Monodendri and hiking north to Vikos. The seasonal Voidomatis River runs year-round only in the lower reaches of the gorge.

LEFT The narrowest part of Samariá Gorge, the Portes, is only 13 feet wide.

323

Oxya Viewpoint

VIKOS–AOÖS NATIONAL PARK

GREECE

This easy half-mile out-and-back walk follows a ledge to a spectacular overlook of the Vikos Gorge, where the sheer white limestone walls of the gorge plunge into a narrow green canyon more than 2,000 feet below. The viewpoint is positioned directly west of the junction where the Megas Lakos side canyon meets the Vikos Gorge, providing a unique perspective of the tremendous scale of the gorge.

324

Orlias Waterfalls

MOUNT OLYMPUS NATIONAL PARK

GREECE

Bathe in the waters of the gods in a seemingly endless series of waterfalls and pools along the Orlias River as it rushes through Orlias Canyon on the northeastern slopes of Mount Olympus. The white noise in this canyon is deafening, as the emerald-green water tumbles through the boulder-choked channel. A 14.5-mile out-and-back trail runs through the canyon, starting in Litochoro.

ABOVE The views of Vikos Gorge from Oxya Viewpoint are simply breathtaking.

325

Mount Olympus

MOUNT OLYMPUS NATIONAL PARK

GREECE

You'll probably ask Zeus for strength a few times on the strenuous 11-mile round-trip hike to the top of Mount Olympus. The trail from Prionia gains over 6,300 feet on its way to the 9,573-foot summit. The massif actually has fifty-two peaks—Mytikas is the highest. Most of the hike is nontechnical, except for the final scramble from the lower Skala summit up to Mytikas, which is rated class 3—you'll want to use both hands and feet here. You can stay a night at one of the six refuges on the mountain.

BELOW The looming Mount Olympus was home to the mythical Greek gods.

326

Pindus Horseshoe

PINDUS NATIONAL PARK

GREECE

Situated in northern Greece in the Pindus Mountains, this is one of the least-visited national parks in Europe because it is located far off the beaten tourist path. But these mountains have a lot to offer intrepid travelers looking for a quieter national park experience. This four- to six-day, 36-mile trek starts in Monodendri and ends in Vradheto. The scenic route follows centuries-old footpaths past the Vikos Gorge, high alpine lakes, limestone peaks, and over a series of striking semicircular stone bridges that link ancient stone Zagori villages, many of which can still be reached only on foot.

BELOW Aristi is one of the Zagori villages in Pindus National Park.

327

Zemi Valley Loop

GÖREME NATIONAL PARK

TURKEY

Explore the intriguing maze of hoodoos and human-made caves in this volcanic region of central Turkey.

DISTANCE
2-mile loop, elevation gain 250 feet

START
Trailhead half a mile east of Göreme

DIFFICULTY
Easy

SEASON
Year-round

RIGHT The open-air archaeological museum in Zemi Valley is full of unusual rock formations.

BELOW Zemi Valley's hoodoos are rock columns that have eroded into spires.

Millions of years ago, a series of volcanic eruptions covered what is now central Turkey in ash topped by basaltic lava flows. Over time, the ash solidified into basalt-capped volcanic tuff that eroded into hoodoos, rock chimneys, towers, and tent rocks.

Thousands of years ago, people discovered that the volcanic tuff was easily carved into caves and shelters, and over time, they hollowed out a vast network of interconnected rooms that include painted chapels and entire subterranean villages that extend eight stories underground. People still live in these rooms, and a few hotels in the area offer subterranean rooms for visitors seeking an authentic Göreme experience.

Visit the picturesque phenomena on this easy 2-mile loop through Zemi Valley. The trail begins with a walk through an open-air archaeological museum and winds through a collection of unique rock formations and fascinating cultural sites.

Rose and Red Valleys

GÖREME NATIONAL PARK
TURKEY

Set off on a longer excursion through the natural and cultural wonders of Göreme National Park on this 5-mile loop through the Rose and Red Valleys. Starting just north of Göreme, the trail passes several historic churches and traditional tea gardens, as well as cave villages, some of which are open for exploration. There are many overlapping trails in this area, so pick up a map of the park to help you navigate. The valley gets very hot in the summer, so visit in the spring and be treated to the wildflowers that bloom throughout the valleys.

329

Lycian Way

BEYDAĞLARI COASTAL NATIONAL PARK

TURKEY

Turkey's first long-distance hiking trail follows an ancient network of Roman roads for 316 miles along the Mediterranean coast. Starting south of Antalya, the trail runs through the archaeologically rich Beydağları Coastal National Park before curving west, following the coastline to Hisarönü. Along the way, the route is marked by red and white stripes painted on rocks and trees every 50 feet. The trail can be done in sections and you can camp or stay in hotels and hostels.

330

Mount Nemrut

NEMRUT DAĞI NATIONAL PARK

TURKEY

Pay your respects to various Greek, Roman, and Iranian gods on this pilgrimage to the top of Mount Nemrut. This 7,001-foot summit is scattered with the toppled remains of massive statues of lions, eagles, and various gods, including Zeus, Hercules, and Apollo. The decapitated heads of these statues have been excavated and placed in upright positions, creating an eerie gallery of faces. A road runs to a parking lot near the summit and then a 2-mile round-trip trail leads to the western temple. Spend a few hours exploring the area.

RIGHT Colossal head statues abound on Mount Nemrut.

331

Köprülü Canyon

KÖPRÜLÜ CANYON NATIONAL PARK

TURKEY

People have been living and walking through Köprülü Canyon for millennia, and this area is rich in history and archaeological relics. An ancient Roman-era footpath paved with cobblestones runs through the canyon, connecting neighboring villages. Along the way, the path crosses several striking arched stone bridges; the Eurymedon Bridge dates to the second century CE. Choose an out-and-back hike of any length along the 8.7-mile canyon to experience a slice of life in ancient Turkey.

AFRICA AND THE MIDDLE EAST

From the mountains of Morocco to the deserts of Arabia to the big game parks of South Africa, get your hiking boots on the ground on the world's wildest continent.

332

Mount Teide

TEIDE NATIONAL PARK

CANARY ISLANDS, SPAIN

Stand on the highest point in the Canary Islands atop an active volcano.

- **DISTANCE**
  10 miles out and back, elevation gain 4,470 feet
- **START**
  Car park two miles past cable car station
- **DIFFICULTY**
  Moderate
- **SEASON**
  Year-round; be prepared for snow in winter

RIGHT Mount Teide is the highest point in Spain, yet it's far from the mainland, on the island of Tenerife.

Located on the island of Tenerife in the Canary Islands, measured from sea level, Mount Teide is a respectable 12,188 feet tall. However, a huge portion of the volcano lurks below the waves—from the seafloor, it is 24,600 feet tall. Still-active Teide is one of sixteen "Decade Volcanoes" on an international watch list for its potentially destructive capacity.

Summiting Teide via the Montaña Blanca trail isn't too strenuous. It is steep at times but well-maintained and clearly marked. The views of the Canary Islands, Atlantic Ocean, and coast of Africa from the summit crater are legendary. You can take a cable car partway down, but you'll then have to hike 3 miles back to your car.

333

Chinyero Volcano Loop

TEIDE NATIONAL PARK

CANARY ISLANDS, SPAIN

This easy 4-mile loop inscribes a circle through the jagged lava fields ejected during the 1909 Chinyero eruption—you'll see how the landscape has since recovered. Keep your ears tuned for rhythmic tapping and your eyes peeled for a flash of red—great spotted woodpeckers are often sighted among the pine trees.

334

Mirador de los Brecitos a Barranco

CALDERA DE TABURIENTE NATIONAL PARK

CANARY ISLANDS, SPAIN

During the Spanish conquest of the Canary Islands in the fifteenth century, the last stand of the indigenous Benahoaritas people took place inside of what is now Caldera de Taburiente National Park, on the island of La Palma. This gargantuan caldera was formed over 2 million years ago by slow erosion of an existing crater, leaving a gaping hole. The caldera is now covered in lush vegetation, in stark contrast to other, more recently formed islands in the Canary chain. This 8-mile one-way trek crosses the 6-mile caldera following the Taburiente River, with views of Idafé rock, a natural stone pillar worshipped by the Benahoaritas.

335

El Golfo

TIMANFAYA NATIONAL PARK

CANARY ISLANDS, SPAIN

Located on the island of Lanzarote, Timanfaya National Park was originally called Tyterogaka, meaning "one that is all ocher." On this 5.6-mile clockwise loop, you'll constantly be stepping on and over black volcanic rocks, but dashes of yellow and red are scattered throughout the landscape. The trail runs to the black sand El Paco Beach.

BELOW You'll be walking on volcanic soil on the El Golfo loop in an eerie landscape.

336

The Forgotten Forest Loop

IFRANE NATIONAL PARK

MOROCCO

Stroll through a forest of 800-year-old Atlas cedar trees on this 4.4-mile loop through an old-growth forest. The hike follows a network of old logging roads, then enters a dark cluster of ancient trees that were somehow overlooked. For decades these cedars were harvested for commercial use, but a protection and replanting campaign is restoring Morocco's Atlas cedar forests to their former glory.

337

Monkey Trail

IFRANE NATIONAL PARK

MOROCCO

Located in Morocco's Middle Atlas mountain range, this national park is the primary refuge for the Barbary macaque—an endangered species of monkey. Keep your eyes peeled for the light-tan to orange primate on this 4.6-mile loop. Servals and caracals, two small species of wildcats, also live here but are rarely seen by people.

RIGHT Discover ancient Atlas cedar trees on the Forgotten Forest Loop.

338

Tislit and Isli Lakes

HAUT ATLAS ORIENTAL NATIONAL PARK

MOROCCO

Pay your respects to the two lakes where a traditional marriage festival has been held for more than 500 years.

- **DISTANCE**
  10 miles round trip, elevation gain 1,300 feet
- **START**
  Imilchil
- **DIFFICULTY**
  Moderate
- **SEASON**
  June to October

The names Tislit and Isli mean "bride and bridegroom" in Berber, an ancient North African language that is still spoken in villages in the Atlas Mountains. Inspired by a Moroccan version of *Romeo and Juliet*, the twin lakes are said to have been filled with the tears of two star-crossed lovers from warring tribes.

For the past 500 years, the Imilchil Marriage Festival has been held in the village of Imilchil, near Lake Tislit, usually around August/September. This three-day festival has traditionally served as a matchmaking event for young people from the surrounding villages.

The 10-mile round-trip hike from Lake Tislit to Lake Isli crosses an arid high plateau and climbs a ridge between the two lakes, offering splendid views of the Atlas Mountains. You can bring a tent and spend a night at Isli, or arrange for a taxi shuttle to make this a one-way hike.

339

Mount Lakraa

TALASSEMTANE NATIONAL PARK

MOROCCO

Talassemtane National Park protects a surprisingly green region of Morocco, which is a mostly arid country. Get a bird's-eye view of the scenery from the top of 7,083-foot Mount Lakraa. A 5.7-mile out-and-back trail gains 1,650 feet, making this a moderate summit climb.

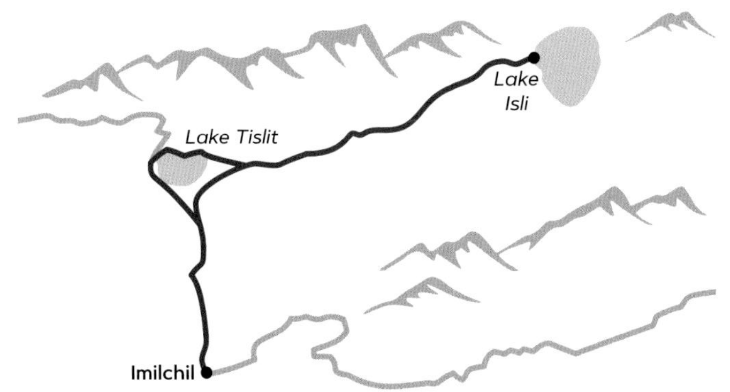

BELOW Lake Tislit near Imilchil is the location of a centuries-old marriage festival.

340

Kasbah du Toubkal

TOUBKAL NATIONAL PARK

MOROCCO

The village of Imlil, located 37 miles from Marrakech, is the gateway to Toubkal National Park. The striking historic hotel Kasbah du Toubkal is perched above the town on the flanks of Jebel Toubkal, and is only reachable via a mile-long trail. If you plan to stay at the Kasbah, arrange for mules to carry your luggage and leave your hands free for taking photos of the village and surrounding mountains. Several trails branch off from the Kasbah, including a route to the top of Jebel Toubkal.

341

Toubkal Circuit

TOUBKAL NATIONAL PARK

MOROCCO

Bag the highest peak in the Atlas Mountains on this 45-mile loop. Starting in Imlil and completed in four to six days, the route follows a trail system established by Berber tribespeople that links ancient villages and crucial oases with high mountain passes and panoramic ridges. The climax is the 13,671-foot peak of Jebel Toubkal. You don't need a guide and can find food and accommodations along the route.

ABOVE You'll feel on top of the world on the Toubkal Circuit in the Atlas Mountains.

342

Akchour Cascades and Bridge of God

TALASSEMTANE NATIONAL PARK

MOROCCO

This two-pronged, 8.5-mile out-and-back hike follows a scenic stretch of river to an overlook of the Akchour Waterfall. You'll then double back, cross the river, and hike up to a natural stone span called the Bridge of God—an arch that links the two sides of the impressive gorge.

343

Gandiol Lighthouse

LANGUE DE BARBARIE NATIONAL PARK

SENEGAL

This coastal national park was created in 1976 to protect a hawksbill sea turtle nesting beach and migratory bird sanctuary. During the fall, winter, and spring, large flocks of pelicans, flamingos, and spoonbills descend on the park to rest and forage before continuing their long migrations. Bring binoculars for the 3.7-mile one-way hike to the now-defunct but still elegant Gandiol Lighthouse. Take the circular staircase to the top for sweeping views of the Langue de Barbarie coastline.

344

Lake Ichkeul

ICHKEUL NATIONAL PARK

TUNISIA

Located in northern Tunisia, this lake is another important stopover for migrating birds before and after they cross the Mediterranean Sea. During the peak of the biannual migration, as many as 300,000 ducks descend on the lake and surrounding wetlands. A 33-mile trail encircles the lake, offering the ultimate bird-watching experience.

LEFT Little egret on Lake Ichkeul—a stopover for migrating birds.

345

Oued Djerat Gorge

TASSILI N'AJJER NATIONAL PARK

ALGERIA

Examine 12,000-year-old petroglyphs created when this plateau was a lush savanna.

- **DISTANCE**
36 miles out and back, elevation gain 1,500 feet
- **START**
Northern end of Oued Djerat Gorge
- **DIFFICULTY**
Moderate
- **SEASON**
April to October

ABOVE RIGHT The walls of Oued Djerat Gorge are decorated with numerous carvings and paintings.

RIGHT One of more than 300 rock arches in Oued Djerat Gorge.

Algeria is the largest country in northern Africa and most of it is covered by the Sahara desert. However, it's not all sand. Tassili n'Ajjer National Park is located on a high plateau dominated by sandstone rock formations and rock arches.

The black and red rocks make for a beautiful landscape, but the real treasures are the thousands of engravings and paintings that decorate the rock walls.

The Oued Djerat Gorge runs through the northern part of the park, cut by a now-dry river system. Rock engravings can be seen along an 18-mile stretch of the gorge, starting from the dry river's mouth and running south. You can hike all or part of the gorge. Due to the remote nature of the park and fragility of the carvings, guides are required for all backcountry travel.

346

Yemma Gouraya

GOURAYA NATIONAL PARK

ALGERIA

Overlook the Mediterranean coast of Algeria on this 4-mile round-trip jaunt to the top of Yemma Gouraya. From the summit you'll enjoy views of the village of Béjaïa and the Mediterranean Sea, where you might catch a glimpse of a sperm whale, dolphin, or harbor porpoise. You might also spot Barbary macaques on this walk.

347

Sahara Desert Hike

WHITE DESERT NATIONAL PARK

EGYPT

Located in the heart of the Farafra depression—a 380-square-mile sunken region within the Sahara desert—this surreal landscape is famous for its white sands and white rock formations. Live out your desert bedouin dreams on this twelve-day loop through the world's largest desert. This guided trek is best tackled between October and April to avoid the summer heat, but Sahara winters can bring frigid temperatures and even snow.

348

Chicken and Mushroom Trail

WHITE DESERT NATIONAL PARK

EGYPT

A half-mile stroll takes you to the base of two of the White Desert's most unusual rock formations: side-by-side wind-sculpted towers of chalk that resemble a chicken sheltering under a mushroom. These are textbook examples of ventifacts—rock formations carved by wind-driven sand particles over geologic timescales.

BELOW The distinctive chicken and mushroom rock formations in White Desert National Park.

349

Geech Camp to Chenek

SIMIEN MOUNTAINS NATIONAL PARK

ETHIOPIA

Ethiopia's largest national park protects a spectacular swath of the Ethiopian Highlands, including the country's highest peak, 14,928-foot Ras Dejen. The Simien Mountains are famous for their dramatic cliffs and for being one of the few places in Africa that sees regular snowfall. A 9-mile one-way trek between the villages of Geech and Chenek follows a ridge with stunning views to the summits of Imet Gogo and Inataye, before descending through a giant hazel forest and across open grasslands to the historic Chenek Camp.

350

Bekalikali

SALONGA NATIONAL PARK

DEMOCRATIC REPUBLIC OF THE CONGO

How do you find an elephant in the jungle? By seeking out a salt lick. This 14-mile round-trip hike runs from Lokofa Patrol Station on the Luilaka River through the rainforest to the Bekalikali *baï*. A *baï* is a clearing in the forest where animals gather to feed on mineral salts and bathe in clay mud. At Bekalikali, a two-story viewing platform has been built for observing the animals. You might also see antelopes, bonobos, and numerous bird species.

BELOW You might spot the iconic Ethiopian wolf on the trail from Geech Camp to Chenek.

351

Mount Nyiragongo

VIRUNGA NATIONAL PARK

DEMOCRATIC REPUBLIC OF THE CONGO

Created in 1925 to protect the watersheds of the Nile and Congo rivers, this was one of the first national parks on the African continent. The landscape is dominated by two active volcanoes, Mount Nyiragongo and Nyamuragira. Nyiragongo has erupted at least thirty-four times since 1882, most recently in 2002. The 10-mile guided hike to the top of the mountain is strenuous, but the payoff is the view down into the summit crater that contains the world's largest red-hot lava lake.

352

Gorilla Trek

VIRUNGA NATIONAL PARK

DEMOCRATIC REPUBLIC OF THE CONGO

Virunga's most famous residents are the mountain gorillas; approximately a third of the world's 1,000 remaining mountain gorillas live in the park. You can join a ranger-led trek to one of the park's habituated gorilla groups—these animals are wild but are used to seeing people. The treks are up to 6 miles on a round trip, depending on the location of the gorilla troop. The park encompasses parts of Uganda, the Democratic Republic of the Congo, and Rwanda.

353

Weissman's Peak

RWENZORI NATIONAL PARK

UGANDA

Located in southwest Uganda, the Rwenzori Mountains boast some of the highest mountains in Africa. This 27-mile, five-day guided trek culminates on 14,157-foot Weissman's Peak. The trail starts in the grasslands and ascends into the jungle and then a bamboo forest before reaching the alpine tundra of the high country. You usually spend a night at the Bugata Hut at 13,400 feet before heading to the snowcapped summit.

354

Ivy River Trail

BWINDI IMPENETRABLE NATIONAL PARK

UGANDA

Follow the Ivy River for 9 miles on this out-and-back hike that starts at the Nkuringo Park office. The rolling Ivy River Trail is also used by local people traveling between Nkuringo and the markets in Nteko. The diversity of animal and plant life here is legendary. More than 1,000 types of flowering plants, 163 species of trees, and 104 species of ferns are found here, along with 350 species of birds, and more than 300 species of butterflies.

RIGHT The Ivy River Trail takes you through one of Africa's oldest and densest rainforests.

Chimpanzee Trek

KIBALE NATIONAL PARK

UGANDA

See wild chimps and other primates in their natural habitat on this ranger-led trek.

DISTANCE
Varies

START
Ranger station

DIFFICULTY
Easy to moderate

SEASON
Dry season, June to October

ABOVE RIGHT A young chimpanzee in Uganda's Kibale National Park.

FAR RIGHT Chimps have grown accustomed to having people observe them.

BELOW Ugandan red colobus monkeys are hunted by chimps.

Kibale National Park in western Uganda boasts some of the greatest diversity and concentration of monkey species in Africa. Spot chimpanzees and twelve other primate species, including red colobus and L'Hoest's monkeys, on a ranger-led trek.

Chimpanzees are social animals that live in communities of up to a hundred individuals. Park rangers engage with some of the wild groups on a regular basis to get them used to seeing people. This process, called habituation, ensures the chimps are comfortable enough to go about their business while being observed by people from a safe distance.

The chimp troops roam freely in the park, so the length of the hikes varies. Expect to walk through dense rainforest for up to 4 miles on a round trip; treks usually last from two to five hours, with an hour allotted for observing the chimps.

356

Murchison Falls

MURCHISON FALLS NATIONAL PARK
UGANDA

See the frothing waters of the Nile River squeeze through a narrow chute in Uganda's oldest and largest national park. After it emerges from Lake Victoria, at the top of Murchison Falls, the mighty Nile drops into a 23-foot gap in a cliff band before falling into a basin on its way to Lake Albert. A 3-mile round-trip trail delivers you to the top of the falls, where you'll be rewarded with the rumbling power of the falls underfoot, and epic views of the Nile flowing into the expansive Albert Delta—the park's premier bird- and wildlife-watching location.

357

Sipi Falls

MOUNT ELGON NATIONAL PARK

UGANDA

Sip coffee by a series of three waterfalls that cascade downhill from the upper slopes of Mount Elgon.

- **DISTANCE**
  4.5-mile loop, elevation gain 1,800 feet
- **START**
  Budadiri
- **DIFFICULTY**
  Moderate
- **SEASON**
  Year-round

LEFT The lush location of Sipi Falls, named for the sep plant.

Visit all three dramatic drops of Sipi Falls on this 4.5-mile loop on the flanks of Mount Elgon—an extinct volcano that straddles the border between Uganda and Kenya. The trail begins at the 320-foot main drop of the falls and circles through dense vegetation and coffee plantations on its way to the 240-foot middle falls and 280-foot lower falls, each linked by stretches of cascading whitewater. Sipi Falls is also the jumping-off point for expeditions up Mount Elgon via the Sasa Trail.

Sipi Falls is named for the sep plant, which is found only on the banks of the Sipi River. This medicinal plant has been used by indigenous tribes to treat measles and fevers for generations. The area is also known for locally grown Bugisu Arabica coffee. Join a tour where you can harvest and brew your own cup from start to finish.

358

Kitum Cave

MOUNT ELGON NATIONAL PARK

KENYA

Kitum Cave is one of five named caves on the flanks of Mount Elgon, where elephants go to scrape salt from the walls with their tusks. Buffaloes and hyenas are also known to visit the cave's salt licks. The nontechnical cave can be explored with a flashlight, but go with a guide who knows how to avoid wild animals and will provide protective equipment like gloves and a face mask—this cave is infamous for its resident bats that can carry Marburg virus, a deadly relative of Ebola.

359

Central Tower Trail

HELL'S GATE NATIONAL PARK

KENYA

Hell's Gate is named for a narrow break in the cliffs that enclose the Great Rift Valley, a long, escarpment-lined valley that bisects Kenya from north to south. Rife with active volcanoes, this setting was the model for the landscape in the original *Lion King* animated movie. This easy 1.7-mile out-and-back trail runs along the base of Central Tower, a volcanic plug that formed when lava hardened inside the neck of a volcano.

360

Ol Njorowa Gorge

HELL'S GATE NATIONAL PARK

KENYA

Home to giraffes, zebras, warthogs, and antelopes, this national park lacks lions and other large predators, making it one of the few in Kenya that allows backcountry hiking and camping. The 30-mile round-trip trek through Ol Njorowa Gorge makes for an excellent one- or two-night trip. A small stream with occasional hot springs bubbling along its banks runs through the dramatic gorge.

BELOW In some places the narrow Ol Njorowa Gorge riverbed is dry.

ABOVE You'll traverse between traditional Maasai villages on a Maasai Mara Walking Safari.

361

Maasai Mara Walking Safari

MAASAI MARA NATIONAL PARK

KENYA

Kenya's most famous game reserve is home to the big five: lions, leopards, elephants, buffaloes, and rhinos, as well as huge herds of wildebeest and zebra. Because of the potentially dangerous wildlife, hiking is restricted here. The best way to experience this landscape on foot is to sign up for a Maasai Mara Walking Safari. These guided treks are led by the Maasai people—a seminomadic tribe that has lived here for thousands of years. Trips typically last several days, moving between traditional Maasai camps and villages.

Mount Longonot

MOUNT LONGONOT NATIONAL PARK

KENYA

Mount Longonot is a 9,108-foot stratovolcano—a volcano built up of various layers of lava and ash—that last erupted in 1863. Starting from the park entrance, a 1.8-mile trail runs up to the crater rim, then a 4.5-mile loop trail encircles the massive summit caldera. The quiet but not extinct caldera is forested with small trees and dotted with active steam vents, and the abundant plant life supports a variety of grazing wildlife.

ABOVE Mount Longonot is located in Kenya's Great Rift Valley.

Mount Kenya via Sirimon Route

MOUNT KENYA NATIONAL PARK

KENYA

Tag the highest point in Kenya on this multiday trek to the 17,057-foot summit of Mount Kenya, an imposing stratovolcano. The tallest summits can be reached only by challenging rock climbs, so most nontechnical treks settle for the third-highest peak, 16,355-foot Point Lenana. Eight different hiking routes run to the top, but the Sirimon Route is the most scenic and has the most gradual ascent profile—but still gains over 9,100 feet to the top. Most people attempt this 31-mile route over three days, stopping at the Austrian Hut.

364

Nairobi Safari Walk

NAIROBI NATIONAL PARK

KENYA

Unfurling just 4 miles south of Kenya's capital city, Nairobi National Park is fenced on three sides, to keep the wildlife away from the sprawl of Nairobi, with the southern boundary left open to allow animals to migrate freely between the park and the adjacent Kitengela Conservation Area. The Nairobi Safari Walk is a 4-mile nature trail that follows a winding boardwalk through three different habitats. It starts in a wetland before entering a savanna grassland, and then a woodland, with signs detailing the plant and animal life you might see along the way.

365

Lake Tanganyika

MAHALE MOUNTAINS NATIONAL PARK

TANZANIA

Stroll along the shoreline of one of the largest and deepest freshwater lakes in the world, contained within the Albertine branch of the East African Rift. The blue waters of the lake are lined with white sand beaches against a backdrop of the Mahale Mountains. There are no roads in the park and the mountains can only be accessed by boat and explored on foot. Start your walk from the Mbali Mbali Mahale Lodge or charter a boat to access some of the lesser-explored areas of the lakeshore.

BELOW Charter a boat to explore different areas around Lake Tanganyika.

366

Mount Kilimanjaro

KILIMANJARO NATIONAL PARK

TANZANIA

Reach the roof of Africa on a slow hike to allow for acclimatizing to the thinner air at altitude.

- **DISTANCE**
  35-mile loop, elevation gain 16,800 feet
- **START**
  Machame Gate
- **DIFFICULTY**
  Hard due to elevation gain and altitude
- **SEASON**
  Dry seasons: January to March, August to October

RIGHT Walk above the clouds on Kilimanjaro, Africa's highest mountain.

At 19,341 feet above sea level, Mount Kilimanjaro towers over the broad plains of Tanzania. Reaching the summit via one of the seven official trekking routes requires gaining over 15,000 feet of elevation, usually over the course of a week. Due to the extreme elevation change, altitude sickness is common, so you must ascend slowly to allow your body to acclimate to the thinner air.

On the 35-mile Machame Route, guides keep the daily hiking mileage low to ease you into the higher elevations. The trail begins in a cloud forest on the southwest side before entering a moonlike alpine landscape. The semi-technical crux of the route comes on day four, with an easy scramble up the Great Barranco Wall, a class 3 section of steep rock that requires both hands and feet.

Most climbers will reach the broad, snowy summit on the second-to-last day of the trek at sunrise. Kilimanjaro is made up of three volcanic cones; the true summit is on Kibo, on a point called Uhuru Peak, where a wooden sign marks the top. Most climbers then descend via the Mweka Route.

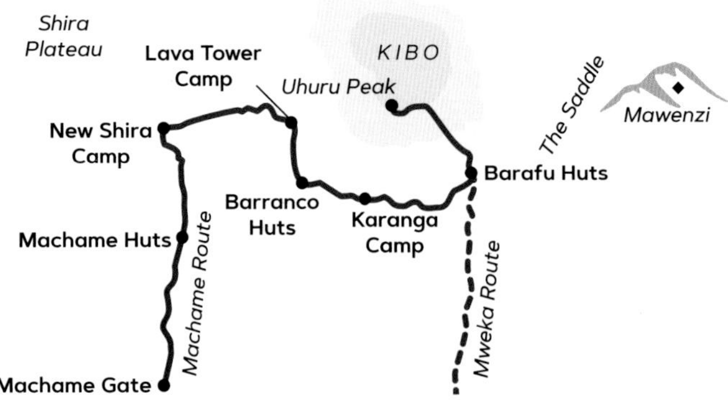

367

Walking Safari

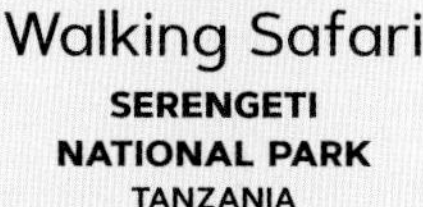

SERENGETI NATIONAL PARK
TANZANIA

The name Serengeti comes from the Maasai word *siringet*, meaning "the place where the land runs on forever." Indeed, this 5,700-square-mile park in northern Tanzania does seem endless. Due to the density of wild animals here, hiking opportunities are limited. Most visitors explore by safari vehicle, but a few companies offer guided walking tours. These typically span two to five days, where you follow an armed guide to animal-viewing areas, and nights are spent in traditional safari camps.

368

Mount Meru Waterfall Loop

ARUSHA NATIONAL PARK
TANZANIA

Prepare for your trek up Mount Meru on this 5.6-mile loop that follows a pretty stream through grasslands and forests to an impressive waterfall. At the park's entrance you'll pay a fee for an armed ranger to accompany you. You have a good chance of spotting giraffes, buffaloes, elephants, warthogs, and monkeys on this walk.

369

Mount Meru

ARUSHA NATIONAL PARK

TANZANIA

Enjoy views of Mount Kilimanjaro from the top of the still-active neighboring Mount Meru.

DISTANCE
17 miles out and back, elevation gain 11,000 feet

START
Momella Gate

DIFFICULTY
Hard due to elevation gain and altitude

SEASON
Dry seasons: January to March, August to October

At 14,968 feet, Mount Meru is the second-highest peak in Tanzania, after Kilimanjaro. The two stratovolcanoes sit about 43 miles apart, and each is visible from the summit of the other on a clear day. The only official route up Meru starts at the Momella Gate. Most people take three days to tackle the 17-mile round trip, spending nights in the Miriakamba Hut at 8,202 feet and Saddle Hut at 11,713 feet.

The trail follows the edge of Meru's horseshoe-shaped summit ridge, the result of a massive collapse of part of the summit crater thousands of years ago. Meru is still active, having last erupted in 1910, and an ash cone is currently growing inside the crater, hinting that another eruption may occur in the future.

370

Sanje Waterfall

UDZUNGWA MOUNTAINS NATIONAL PARK

TANZANIA

This national park is nicknamed "the Galápagos of Africa" for the high numbers of endemic species that are found here and nowhere else on Earth, including the highly endangered Sanje crested mangabey monkey, the Kipunji ape, and the Udzungwa forest partridge. Pack a bathing suit for this 7-mile round-trip hike to Sanje Waterfall, which pours into a deep plunge pool at the base, perfect for swimming.

ABOVE Savor spectacular views from the summit of Mount Meru.

371

Lumemo Trail

UDZUNGWA MOUNTAINS NATIONAL PARK
TANZANIA

No roads run through this national park, so the only way to explore it is on foot. The 40-mile Lumemo Trail is the longest in the park, usually hiked over five days. The trail runs along the Lumemo River, through dense rainforest; it's best to tackle this route in late summer, after the park crew conducts an annual trail clearing in June. You are required to hire an armed ranger, as the Udzungwa Mountains are home to two of Africa's most dangerous animals: forest elephants and Cape buffalo.

372

Beach Walk

KISSAMA NATIONAL PARK

ANGOLA

After decades of civil war, Kissama National Park nearly went extinct, with most of the animals either being killed or fleeing elsewhere. However, the park has been revitalized through Operation Noah's Ark—a large animal transport operation that has brought hundreds of wild animals from countries like South Africa to repopulate the park. You're sure to see birds and marine life on a walk of any length along the park's South Atlantic coastline.

373

Olive Trail

NAMIB-NAUKLUFT NATIONAL PARK

NAMIBIA

This arid and rocky national park protects a slice of the world's oldest desert, the Namib, and the Naukluft mountain range, sandwiched between the Atlantic Ocean and the Great Escarpment—the ring of imposing cliffs that follows the southern coastline of the continent. The 7-mile Olive Trail is a self-guided clockwise loop that starts on top of a small plateau before dropping into a gorge. The crux of the route are several open pools of water that you can either swim across or balance on a series of chains that stretch across the water.

LEFT If you don't want to swim, you'll have to balance on a series of chains to cross this part of the Olive Trail.

ABOVE There are plenty of swimming spots along the Waterkloof Trail.

374

Waterkloof Trail

NAMIB-NAUKLUFT NATIONAL PARK

NAMIBIA

The 10.5-mile Waterkloof Trail follows the Naukluft River through a deep gorge. After rainstorms, the pools in this gorge are filled with bright blue water, perfect for swimming. The trail culminates on top of a high point at 6,266 feet, with outstanding views of the Naukluft mountains.

375

San Walking Safari

CHOBE NATIONAL PARK

BOTSWANA

Nomadic hunter-gatherers have thrived in what is now Chobe National Park for thousands of years, living off the land and coexisting with an incredible diversity of wildlife. Around 50,000 elephants live in the park, along with several prides of lions that specialize in hunting elephants. Join a trek accompanied by a member of the San bushmen tribe—called Walking with the San—to learn about how indigenous people make a living in this harshly beautiful landscape.

376

Zambezi River Walk

VICTORIA FALLS NATIONAL PARK

ZIMBABWE

Stretching over a mile wide, Victoria Falls—also known as Mosi-oa-Tunya, or the Smoke That Thunders—is the largest curtain of falling water in the world. The 1.5-mile out-and-back Zambezi River Walk follows the river upstream from its 350-foot plunge. It starts near the Devil's Cataract and the turnaround point is the Big Tree—an enormous baobab tree. The trail meanders along the lush banks of the river, where you may spot warthogs, hippos, and even elephants in the river. Beware of the water's edge—it looks calm, but the current is strong.

377

The Boiling Pot

VICTORIA FALLS NATIONAL PARK

ZIMBABWE

Once you've seen Victoria Falls from eye level, hike downstream to see the falls from below. This 1.5-mile round-trip trail descends into the gorge below the falls, with awe-inspiring views. The hike ends at an overlook of the Boiling Pot—an exhilarating stretch of rapids. High above, Victoria Falls Bridge stretches across the gorge and you may see and hear shrieking daredevils bungee jumping from the arched metal span.

BELOW Head upstream of the magnificent Victoria Falls for the Zambezi River Walk.

Alexandria Hiking Trail

ADDO ELEPHANT NATIONAL PARK

SOUTH AFRICA

Check off Africa's iconic animals in this national park that includes a marine protected area.

DISTANCE
22-mile loop, elevation gain 2,000 feet

START
Woody Cape headquarters

DIFFICULTY
Moderate

SEASON
September to April

ABOVE RIGHT Give African elephants a wide berth if you stumble upon them on the Alexandria Hiking Trail.

FAR RIGHT A breeding colony of Cape fur seals in the Woody Cape Nature Reserve.

BELOW A bottlenose dolphin—one of the marine big five.

When this park was established in 1931, only eleven elephants lived in the area. Today, more than 600 roam the park, which has been expanded south from the Zuurberg Mountains to include the Woody Cape Nature Reserve and a marine reserve on the coast.

The addition of the marine reserve means that as well as hosting Africa's famous big five, the park is also home to the marine big five: African penguin, Cape fur seal, bottlenose dolphin, great white shark, and southern right whale.

The trail is a two-day hike along the coast, in the Woody Cape section of the park. It begins in the forest and then enters the Alexandria dune field, where hiking on the golden sand can be slow going. The path, marked with tall poles that remain visible above constantly shifting sands, leads to the coast, where crumbling cliffs make for slightly easier walking. You can stay in Langebos Huts—cabins with electricity, a porch, and an outdoor firepit.

379

Zuurberg Trail

ADDO ELEPHANT NATIONAL PARK
SOUTH AFRICA

This 7-mile loop combines the Cycad and Doringnek trails in the Zuurberg Mountains section of Addo Elephant National Park. The route runs through an open valley lush with fynbos—a type of shrubland vegetation. Visit between September and December to experience the spring wildflower bloom. Elephants are not typically seen in this part of the park, but you may spot hartebeest and blue duikers, two disparately sized species of antelope.

Otter Trail

GARDEN ROUTE NATIONAL PARK

SOUTH AFRICA

Hug the South African coastline on the continent's most famous hiking trail.

DISTANCE
28 miles one way with shuttle, elevation gain 8,500 feet

START
Storms River Mouth

DIFFICULTY
Moderate

SEASON
Year-round

ABOVE RIGHT Cape clawless otters are famously elusive creatures.

RIGHT You'll hike from sea level to a height of more than 490 feet on the Otter Trail.

The 28-mile Otter Trail follows the spectacular coastline of South Africa from Storms River Mouth to Nature's Valley, passing white sand beaches, rocky cliffs, and waterfalls.

Most hikers complete the trail over five days, leaving plenty of time each day for enjoying beaches and observing wildlife, such as seals, dolphins, deer, and monkeys. You're unlikely to see the trail's namesake, the Cape clawless otter, which is mostly nocturnal. Nights are spent in simple huts along the route, but you'll have to pack your own food and cookware.

On day four you'll have to cross the Bloukrans River. Plan to cross at low tide (bring a tide chart), when the water should be between knee and waist deep. Bring a trash bag for the crossing to keep your backpack dry, and unbuckle the hip belt of your pack so that if you fall, the weight of your backpack won't pull you underwater.

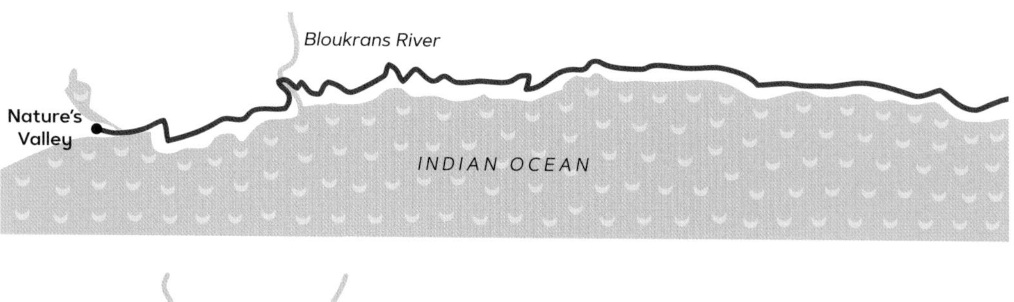

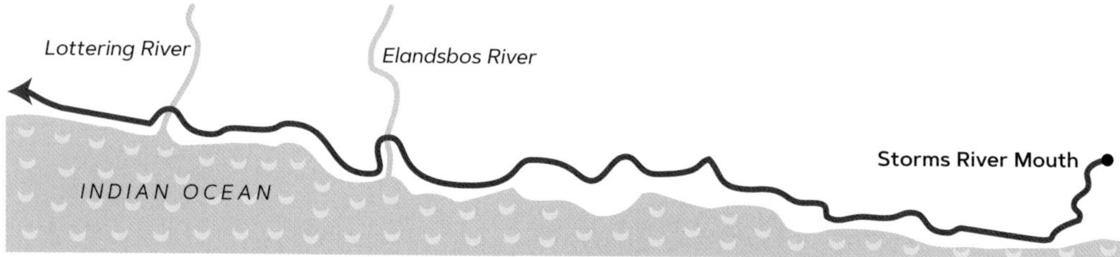

381

Skeleton Gorge Trail

TABLE MOUNTAIN NATIONAL PARK

SOUTH AFRICA

Hike to the summit plateau of Cape Town's iconic Table Mountain on this relentlessly steep but stunning trail. It begins with a pleasant stroll through the Kirstenbosch National Botanical Garden before quickly gaining elevation on a series of rock scrambles and ladder climbs up through Skeleton Gorge. On the summit plateau, enjoy unparalleled views of Cape Town and the coast. You can either return the way you came for a 3.8-mile round-trip hike, or hitch a ride back down on the cable car.

382

Olifants Wilderness Trail

KRUGER NATIONAL PARK

SOUTH AFRICA

Traverse one of the largest game reserves in Africa, following the Olifants River. Kruger National Park boasts more species of large mammals than any other African park, including a population of endangered African wild dogs and more than 20,000 elephants. Exploring Kruger on foot is not for the fainthearted, but each expedition is led by at least two armed guards with expert knowledge of the park and resident animals. Each day, the trek covers about 4 miles of ground, with several stops at elevated wildlife-viewing areas. Nights are spent in A-frame log cabins at the Olifants Camp.

LEFT You'll be rewarded with fantastic views after conquering the Skeleton Gorge Trail up Table Mountain.

383

Sacred Waterfall Circuit

ANDASIBE-MANTADIA NATIONAL PARK

MADAGASCAR

The island of Madagascar was once covered by lush rainforest, but centuries of deforestation have left the once-impenetrable forests fragmented. Andasibe-Mantadia National Park protects three remaining swaths of rainforest in the east. The Sacred Waterfall Circuit is a 1.2-mile loop hike that runs past several waterfalls that were sacred to the indigenous inhabitants of this rainforest. Along the way, you might see or hear one of the eleven species of lemurs that live in the park. The indri is one of the easiest to spot, thanks to its distinctive black and white coloration and hair-raising shriek.

384

Piscine Naturelle

ISALO NATIONAL PARK

MADAGASCAR

Located in the southwest corner of the island, Isalo National Park features Triassic-era sandstone that has been eroded into deep canyons, sandstone domes, and flat-topped mountains. The sandstone layer also makes for beautiful pools of crystal-clear water. This 7-mile round-trip hike to Piscine Naturelle ends at a stunningly blue pool fed by a waterfall. Along the way, watch for lemurs in the trees—these small primates are found only in Madagascar.

385

Pic Boby

ANDRINGITRA NATIONAL PARK

MADAGASCAR

Known to the indigenous Malagasy people as Imarivolanitra, meaning "close to the sky," Pic Boby is the second-highest mountain on the island. It is sometimes called Madagascar's Yosemite for the sheer granite walls that grace the park's impressive skylines. The 22-mile round-trip trek to the 8,720-foot summit of Pic Boby is an epic tour through the park's many eco zones, from the lush forest to the rocky, windswept peaks.

ABOVE Time your Pic Boby trek for sunrise to find yourself in magical surroundings.

RIGHT The hike to Cap Noir will lead you to Réunion Island's mountainous interior.

386

Cap Noir and Roche Verre Bouteille Circuit

RÉUNION NATIONAL PARK

RÉUNION ISLAND, FRANCE

Before the 1600s, Réunion Island in the Indian Ocean, east of Madagascar, was uninhabited and the arrival of people led to widespread extinctions of many unique species. Established in 2007, Réunion National Park protects nearly half of the island, hopefully providing a haven for the remaining endemic species. You may spot the Réunion cuckooshrike bird or the Réunion day gecko on this easy 2-mile loop to Cap Noir—a spectacular viewpoint of the island's densely mountainous interior. You'll need to climb up and down metal ladders in a few steep sections.

387

Peak of the Furnace

RÉUNION NATIONAL PARK

RÉUNION ISLAND, FRANCE

Réunion Island is one of the most volcanic places on Earth. This 7.5-mile out-and-back hike takes you on a tour of the island's volcanic features. The trek starts by descending into the Enclos Fouché caldera, where you'll follow a line of white dots painted across the black lava flow. Take a short detour to climb Formica Leo—a small, reddish scoria cone that offers expansive views—before climbing the eastern wall of the caldera to the Balcon du Dolomieu overlook. Wear sturdy boots and stay well back from the edge of the crater—landslides occur here frequently.

388

Snake Path

MASADA NATIONAL PARK

ISRAEL

In 37–31 BCE, King Herod built a winter palace on top of this flat-topped plateau surrounded by steep, crumbling cliffs. This natural fortress would later withstand several attacks. Today, Masada's fortifications are considered the most complete surviving ancient siege system in the world. The 2-mile round-trip Snake Path starts at the Masada Museum and follows a steep, switchbacking trail to gain nearly 1,000 feet of elevation to the top of the plateau. You'll find an impressive collection of restored and crumbling ruins, and views of Jordan and the Dead Sea. Return the way you came or ride the cable car back down.

389

The Beach Trail

CAESAREA NATIONAL PARK

ISRAEL

The ancient city of Caesarea Maritima was built during the reign of King Herod around 22–10 BCE. The city's impressive ruins, including an amphitheater, a Roman aqueduct, and the Herodian hippodrome, were excavated in the 1950s and incorporated into a national park in 2011. Most of the trails in the park are short, and exploring the entire city takes about half a day. The 1.4-mile beach walk follows the Mediterranean coastline, past many historical structures. You'll find ruins and artifacts off the coast here too, and the park offers scuba-diving tours of the underwater museum.

RIGHT Explore the ancient ruins of Israel's Caesarea Maritima on the Beach Trail.

390

Wadi Wurayah Trail

WADI WURAYAH NATIONAL PARK

UNITED ARAB EMIRATES

This national park is home to the world's largest ophiolite complex, where slabs of ancient oceanic crust have been exposed at the surface, revealing clues about the interior of the Earth. The 14.5-mile out-and-back trail runs through a *wadi*, or river canyon, so you'll have to wade or swim across numerous pools. Year-round water is rare in this arid region, making this a uniquely beautiful oasis on the Arabian Peninsula. It is one of the best places in the world to see dragonflies—twenty-four of the thirty known Arabian species can be found here. The park is also one of the last refuges for several critically endangered species, including the Arabian leopard and Arabian tahr—a type of long-haired wild goat.

ASIA

From the world's highest national park to the planet's most vast cave systems, the largest continent on Earth has stoked the spirit of exploration for thousands of years.

391

Yauza River

LOSINY OSTROV NATIONAL PARK

RUSSIA

The largest urban park in Europe lies within the city limits of Moscow. This national park—a swath of mostly forested land—was originally a game reserve for Russian grand princes and tsars. Despite the close proximity to the city, wildlife thrives here—moose, beavers, wild boars, and red foxes live under the watchful eyes of birds of prey like kestrels, goshawks, and red-footed falcons. See how many of Moscow's wildest residents you can spot on a 3-mile out-and-back hike along the Yauza River, starting from the Yauza Ecological Center.

392

Alpine Meadows and Medvezhiy Waterfall

SOCHI NATIONAL PARK

RUSSIA

Russia's oldest national park protects a region of the Western Caucasus mountains near Sochi—host city for the Winter Olympic Games in 2014. This 3.3-mile out-and-back hike begins with a ride up the K3 chairlift at the Gorky Gorod Ski Resort—which runs in the summer to deliver people high into the mountains—and combines two neighboring trails to a lovely open meadow and a picturesque waterfall.

393

White Rocks Canyon

SOCHI NATIONAL PARK

RUSSIA

This 2.6-mile loop begins at the top of Navalishinsky ("White Rocks") canyon and then descends along the Khosta River through white cliffs and past a waterfall to a small pebble beach before looping back around to the start. The deep canyons and dense forests are prime habitat for the Persian leopard, but you're unlikely to see the shy and perfectly camouflaged big cat. The Russian Center for Reintroduction of the Leopard in the Caucasus was established here in 2007 and the captive breeding program has since released several litters of kittens into the park and neighboring reserve.

394

Mount Zyuratkul

ZYURATKUL NATIONAL PARK

RUSSIA

Stretching for 1,600 miles from the Arctic Sea to Kazakhstan, the Ural Mountains form a rugged natural boundary between Europe and Asia. Several national parks dot the Polar, Northern, Middle, and Southern Urals, protecting many large predatory mammals, including brown bears, foxes, wolves, wolverines, and lynx. In Zyuratkul National Park in the Southern Urals, an 8-mile round-trip hike to the top of 3,796-foot Mount Zyuratkul affords the best views of the park's distinctive namesake lake. Zyuratkul, meaning "heart lake" in the Bashkir language, is considered to be the highest lake in the range.

LEFT You might see deer on a hike along the Yauza River in Losiny Ostrov National Park.

ABOVE At 2,473 feet of elevation, Lake Zyuratkul is the highest lake in the Southern Urals.

395

Mount Markova

ZABAIKALSKY NATIONAL PARK

RUSSIA

Scale a mountain overlooking the world's oldest, deepest, and largest freshwater lake by volume.

DISTANCE
8.7 miles round trip, elevation gain 5,000 feet

START
Trailhead on Svyatoy Nos

DIFFICULTY
Hard due to elevation gain

SEASON
June to October

ABOVE RIGHT Mount Markova is the highest point on the Svyatoy Nos peninsula.

RIGHT You can also visit the frozen Lake Baikal and ice rocks of Horin-Irgi in winter.

Cradled in a massive rift in southern Siberia, Lake Baikal contains nearly a quarter of the planet's fresh surface water—that's more than all the North American Great Lakes combined.

Zabaikalsky National Park protects the central section of the eastern shoreline of the lake, including the western slope of the Barguzin mountains, the Ushkany Islands in the lake, and the Svyatoy Nos "Holy Nose" peninsula that juts out into the lake.

One of the most unique hikes in the park is to the top of 6,160-foot Mount Markova. The steep and strenuous 8.7-mile, round-trip hike to the top gains over 5,000 feet, with astonishing views of the lake.

Keep an eye out for seals—despite being hundreds of miles from the closest ocean, the freshwater Baikal seal has thrived here for more than 2 million years, though how it got to Baikal from the Arctic Ocean is a mystery.

396

Great Baikal Trail

PRIBAIKALSKY NATIONAL PARK

RUSSIA

Since the early 2000s, a Russian nonprofit organization called the Great Baikal Trail has been working to expand recreational opportunities at Lake Baikal by blazing a hiking trail around the lake. So far, only sections of the eventual 1,300-mile lakeshore trail have been completed. One of the most scenic of these is the 14-mile stretch on the southwest shore between the villages of Listvyanka and Bolshie Koty. You can hike it as an out-and-back overnight trek or as a one-way day hike with a ferry shuttle.

397

Semivyorstka Trail

LAND OF THE LEOPARD NATIONAL PARK

RUSSIA

When Land of the Leopard National Park was established on the western banks of the Razdolnaya River in 2012, the Amur leopard was one of the rarest animals in the world, with fewer than thirty left in the wild. By merging three wildlife refuges, the park helped knit together the large spotted cat's protected home range and boost its population—in less than a decade, kittens born within the park nearly tripled the world's wild population.

Siberian tigers and Eurasian lynx are also captured on motion-activated game cameras installed throughout the park. You're unlikely to see any of these elusive cats in person, but your best bet is to hike the Semivyorstka Trail, a 6-mile hiking, biking, and Nordic skiing route that features rolling hills, panoramic overlooks, and viewing platforms. For safety, hike in groups of two or more, avoid the early morning and evening—when big cats are most active—and make noise to scare away the typically shy animals.

398

Singing Dunes

ALTYN-EMEL NATIONAL PARK

KAZAKHSTAN

Sand dunes can be found on every continent on Earth (even Antarctica!), but only a few places have the right combination of conditions to produce "singing" sand dunes. The noises are produced when silica sand grains of a certain diameter and humidity rub together, creating an audible vibration. The effect can be produced by wind or by footsteps on the dunes. See if you can conduct a singing sand orchestra on this 4.5-mile round-trip hike that runs to the top of the singing barchan dunes. If the wind is blowing from the west, you may hear sounds like that of a low pipe organ playing across the sand.

RIGHT Stepping on the Singing Dunes in Altyn-Emel National Park just might create a tune.

399

Mother Sea

KHÖVSGÖL NUUR NATIONAL PARK

MONGOLIA

Explore the shore of Mongolia's largest lake, which holds 70 percent of the country's fresh water.

DISTANCE
Varies

START
Khatgal

DIFFICULTY
Moderate

SEASON
June to September

LEFT The name of Mongolia's Lake Khövsgöl translates to "Mother Sea."

Perched at the transition zone between the boreal forests of the Siberian taiga and the vast grasslands of the central Asian steppe, Lake Khövsgöl is an important source of drinking water in this arid landscape. The lake is a popular summer vacation destination for Mongolians, who flock to the western shore, where most of the accommodations are located. Most trips start from Khatgal, a village at the southern end of the lake. The eastern and northern shores are comparatively less developed and can only be reached by boat or on foot via a rough dirt road.

A hike or horseback ride along the lakeshore will give you an appreciation for the Mongols' nomadic culture and famous hospitality. Consider renting a horse and aiming for the Bolnain hot springs on the eastern shore, 45 miles from Khatgal. After a three-day ride, you'll appreciate the hot springs even more. Along the way you'll pass remote villages and you may even be invited into a yurt for a meal and a game of Mongolian checkers.

400

Eagle Valley

GOBI GURVAN SAIKHAN NATIONAL PARK

MONGOLIA

Named for the Gurvan Saikhan Mountains, meaning "the three beauties of the Gobi," Mongolia's largest national park is centered where the Gobi desert meets the mountains. The deep and narrow Eagle Valley is cut into the Eastern Beauty subrange, where you can spot golden eagles and bearded vultures. Each winter, an ice field several feet thick forms in the valley—it usually melts by late summer.

A hike of any length on the trail that runs across the valley floor is a beautiful introduction to this remote and rugged region of Mongolia. To really cover ground, rent a Mongol horse—these small but hardy equids are the pride of the Mongolian people. As you walk or ride, keep an eye on the surrounding cliffs for Argali sheep and Siberian ibex. Only the supremely lucky will spot the elusive and perfectly camouflaged snow leopard.

BELOW You can hike through the deep and narrow Eagle Valley or rent a Mongol horse.

401

Khongoryn Els Singing Dunes

GOBI GURVAN SAIKHAN NATIONAL PARK

MONGOLIA

The Gobi desert stretches across southern Mongolia, tucked into the massive rain shadow cast by the world's largest mountain range, the Himalayas. In the northern Gobi, the Khongoryn Els Singing Dunes sprawl for more than 60 miles, where countless sand grains have been blown into golden piles along the base of the Altai Mountains. Hiking to the top of the massive dunes takes about an hour, and if the wind is blowing just right, you may be treated to a concert as the sand grains vibrate against one another.

BELOW Hike to the top of Khongoryn Els Singing Dunes and wait for the blowing wind to treat you to some music.

402

Rainbow Rocks

ZHANGYE DANXIA NATIONAL GEOPARK

CHINA

Step into a real-life candyland in China's Rainbow Mountains—a colorfully striped layer cake that dates from the Cretaceous period. Over geologic time, wind and water have sculpted the soft sandstone layers into towers, pillars, and steep ravines, creating a landscape found nowhere else on the planet. Most trails in the park run across boardwalks to preserve the fragile formations, and this 5-mile trek circles between four viewpoints overlooking the Danxia scenic spot. Go at sunset to see the sun's rays play across the red, orange, and yellow striped rocks.

403

The Great Wall

BADALING NATIONAL PARK

CHINA

This section of the Great Wall of China was built more than 500 years ago, during the Ming dynasty, to protect the Juyongguan Pass and the city of Beijing to the south. After extensive restorations, a 2.3-mile section of the Badaling Great Wall opened to tourists in 1957 and remains the most-visited segment. A 3.4-mile loop trail runs along the top of the wall, passing several watchtowers, and then returns along the base, offering differing perspectives above and below the imposing 20-foot-wide, 26-foot-high brick wall. Visit early to catch the sunrise and avoid the crowds.

ABOVE The vibrant Five-Color Pond is one of the smallest bodies of water in the park.

LEFT Follow boardwalks through China's colorful and mystical Rainbow Rocks landscape.

Five-Color Pond

JIUZHAIGOU VALLEY NATIONAL PARK

CHINA

Visit the broad-leaved forests, home to the giant panda, in Jiuzhaigou Valley, on the edge of the Tibetan Plateau. This park is famous for its vividly blue turquoise lakes and streams, colored by a high concentration of calcium carbonate minerals in the water. The 9.6-mile out-and-back trail to Five-Color Pond begins at Long Lake, then runs through dense forest. This may be one of the smallest lakes in the park, but it's also the most colorful, featuring many shades of blue, green, and yellow. Visit in the fall to witness the red and orange hues added to the park's already colorful palette.

405

Pearl Shoal Waterfall

JIUZHAIGOU VALLEY NATIONAL PARK
CHINA

The famously blue waters of Jiuzhaigou Valley are even more beautiful in motion. An easy 1.6-mile out-and-back trail runs along the shore of Mirror Lake to Pearl Shoal Waterfall. Here, the Bailong River cascades over a shelf of tufa rock, dropping 130 feet down into a bright turquoise pool.

RIGHT Some of Zhangjiajie's pillars soar 1,500 feet high.

406

Yuanjiajie Mountain

ZHANGJIAJIE NATIONAL FOREST PARK

CHINA

Hike in the mystical mountains that were the inspiration for the 2009 blockbuster film *Avatar*.

DISTANCE
3.6 miles round trip, elevation gain 2,300 feet

START
Trail begins near the Hundred Dragons elevator

DIFFICULTY
Moderate

SEASON
April to November

BELOW The Hundred Dragons Sky Lift ferries people 1,000 feet up and down Yuanjiajie Mountain.

When Hollywood went looking for an otherworldly landscape to stand in for the floating Hallelujah Mountains in *Avatar*, director James Cameron chose the Heavenly Pillar in China's Zhangjiajie National Forest Park. Here, thousands of vertical pillars of quartzite sandstone emerge out of a near-constant mist that makes the towers appear to be hovering in the clouds.

The best views of the 500-foot Avatar Hallelujah Mountain—as the Southern Sky Column is now known—are from the top of Yuanjiajie Mountain. The 1.8-mile one-way route to the top is steep and rocky, gaining 2,300 feet of elevation up carved stone steps. At the top, you can hike back the way you came for a 3.6-mile round-trip hike, or hitch a ride down on the Hundred Dragons Sky Lift. This state-of-the-art elevator whisks people up and down the mountain in less than two minutes, making it the highest and fastest outdoor elevator in the world.

407

Golden Whip Stream

ZHANGJIAJIE NATIONAL PARK

CHINA

Marvel at Zhangjiajie's pinnacles from ground level on this mostly flat 4.5-mile out-and-back path that follows a stream through the forest along the base of the towers. Look for wild monkeys and the critically endangered Chinese giant salamander—some grow up to 6 feet long and weigh 100 pounds. This trail is best hiked in the fall when the leaves are changing colors, but the park is open year-round. Winter can be a magical time to visit, especially if you want to avoid crowds.

408

Leaping Tiger Gorge

JADE DRAGON SNOW MOUNTAIN NATIONAL PARK

CHINA

This astonishing gorge in southwestern China was cut by the Jinsha River as it flows between Jade Dragon Snow Mountain and Haba Snow Mountain, creating a 6,600-foot canyon. At its narrowest point, the gorge is 82 feet wide and the evocative name was inspired by legends of tigers leaping across the gorge. A 14-mile footpath runs along the length of the gorge and is still used by the Naxi people to travel between villages, where you can find simple overnight trekking accommodations.

RIGHT Leaping Tiger Gorge was named for legends of tigers jumping from one side of the gorge to the other.

409

Nine Dragons Waterfall

HUANGSHAN NATIONAL PARK

CHINA

The rugged granite peaks of this national park have inspired Chinese artists and poets for centuries; between the Tang dynasty and the Qing dynasty, more than 20,000 poems were written about Huangshan's distinctive mountains and crooked trees, and the landscape even inspired the Huangshan school of painting. The 2-mile round-trip trail through the forest to Nine Dragons Waterfall is the perfect venue for meeting some of Huangshan's famous trees. The Huangshan pine's gnarled trunk often grows right out of the rocks.

410

Celestial and Lotus Peaks

HUANGSHAN NATIONAL PARK

CHINA

Touch the tops of the Yellow Mountains on this 5-mile round-trip hike to the tops of Celestial Peak and Lotus Peak—the highest point in the park. With any luck, you'll be treated to a bird's-eye view of Huangshan's famous sea of clouds—atmospheric conditions here often result in low-lying cloud banks covering the area. The mountaintops pierce through the clouds and the views are legendary, especially at sunrise and sunset.

BELOW Nine Dragons Waterfall is a series of cascades located near Huangshan Mountain.

411

Thousand Layer Trail

GUILIN AND LIJIANG RIVER NATIONAL PARK

CHINA

This park's surreal landscape of towering pinnacles above a serene river has inspired countless Chinese works of art, including the illustration on the back of the twenty-yuan banknote. The unique terrain is a form of karst topography, where water gradually dissolves limestone bedrock, creating deep canyons and cave systems. The 3.5-mile out-and-back Thousand Layer Trail gains 1,000 feet of elevation to an overlook of geometrically terraced rice fields, against the backdrop of the Pearl River Basin.

412

Reed Flute Cave Trail

GUILIN AND LIJIANG RIVER NATIONAL PARK

CHINA

The wonders of Guilin and Lijiang River National Park don't stop at the surface; the area is also riddled with cave systems. An easy 1.3-mile out-and-back trail leads to the Reed Flute Cave, named for the reeds that grow at the entrance, which can be used to make wind instruments. The interior of the cave is lit by thousands of rainbow-colored lights that accentuate the stalactites, stalagmites, and other cave formations produced by the slow drip of water on limestone over millions of years.

BELOW The scenic setting of the Thousand Layer Trail is amid towering karst pinnacles and terraced rice fields.

413

Mount Qixing

YANGMINGSHAN NATIONAL PARK

TAIWAN

Earn the best view of Taipei from the top of a dormant volcano whose crater has eroded into a ring of seven peaks.

DISTANCE
5 miles round trip, elevation gain 1,020 feet

START
Xiaoyoukeng parking area

DIFFICULTY
Moderate

SEASON
Dry season, September to May; cherry blossoms bloom February and March

RIGHT The trail to Mount Qixing leads to magnificent panoramic views of Taiwan.

Located north of Taipei and New Taipei City, this national park is easily accessed by public transportation. Most people visit in the spring months of February and March, when the cherry trees blossom and rhododendrons bloom in a visual and olfactory feast.

The centerpiece of the park is Mount Qixing, nicknamed Seven Star Mountain. Considered dormant but not extinct, it last erupted around 700,000 years ago—today, you'll see active sulfur deposits, hot springs, and fumaroles, where steam and hot gases escape from deep underground.

A 5-mile round-trip trail ascends to the 3,670-foot summit, where you can enjoy stunning views of Taipei and New Taipei City to the south and southwest, and of the coast of Taiwan to the north.

414

Yangmingshan Trail

YANGMINGSHAN NATIONAL PARK

TAIWAN

The Yangmingshan Trail links several peaks in the park, offering spectacular views—those of Taipei at night are especially magical, hence most people hike the route as an overnight. The strenuous 15-mile one-way trail racks up more than 5,500 feet of elevation along its length. Public transport from Taipei and throughout the park means easy transportation logistics at the start and end of the hike.

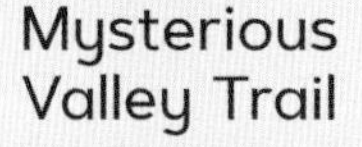

Mysterious Valley Trail

TAROKO NATIONAL PARK
TAIWAN

See one of nature's most exquisite marble sculptures in this stunning valley. Marble is a very hard rock but over geologic time, the Liwu River, flush with water from frequent tropical rainstorms, has carved a deep defile, producing a steep and narrow canyon of shimmering silver-white rock. The Shakadang Trail follows the Shakadang stream through thick, nearly impenetrable jungle into a marble canyon area called the Mysterious Valley, where you'll find a series of bright blue pools perfect for taking a dip.

Zhuilu Old Trail

TAROKO NATIONAL PARK
TAIWAN

This route was originally pioneered by the indigenous Truku people, who used these paths on their wild boar hunts. In the early 1900s, Japanese colonialists forced Truku slaves to widen the path and later used it to transport troops and weaponry during World War II. Rockfall has since closed much of this once multiday backpacking trail, but a 4-mile round-trip section remains. The steep path climbs up through dense jungle and then culminates at the top of a sheer cliff with legendary views of the Taroko Gorge 1,500 feet below.

417

Seoraksan Castle

SEORAKSAN NATIONAL PARK

SOUTH KOREA

Hiking and mountaineering are national pastimes in South Korea, and many of the granite peaks in this park can be accessed by challenging trails. Mere mortals can enjoy the same views by hitching a ride on the cable car to the top of Mount Seoraksan. From the top cable car station, a half-mile out-and-back trail leads you to the summit of neighboring Gwongeumseong Peak, nicknamed the Seoraksan Castle. The view here showcases the craggy mountains, including the striking stegosaurus-like spikes of Dinosaur Ridge.

418

Naejangsan Ridge

NAEJANGSAN NATIONAL PARK

SOUTH KOREA

Naejang means "something hidden in the mountain is infinite" in Korean, perhaps referring to the seemingly infinite number of maple leaves in this heavily forested park. For hundreds of years, people have flocked to Naejangsan in the fall to admire the foliage show. The park offers many trail options, but this 7-mile one-way ridge trail tags all eight summits of Naejangsan Mountain. You can do the trail as a one-way shuttle hike, utilizing park transportation. Fall colors—and crowds—peak in October, but the park is beautiful year-round.

ABOVE Bukhansan Peak overlooks the vast city of Seoul.

LEFT Seoraksan Castle is a popular hiking destination.

419

Bukhansan Peak

BUKHANSAN NATIONAL PARK

SOUTH KOREA

A mere 45-minute subway ride away from Seoul, this park is centered on the Bukhansanseong Fortress, a massive complex built to protect Seoul after the Qing invasion of 1636, although a man-made structure was first built here in 132 CE. Known for its three horns—triple granite peaks that dominate the skyline—Bukhansan offers some of the best rock climbing in Asia. You can bag the highest peak, Baekundae, without roping up on a 17-mile round-trip hike. The route is strenuous and requires some scrambling but no technical climbing.

Mount Fuji

FUJI-HAKONE-IZU NATIONAL PARK

JAPAN

Tag the top of one of the world's most iconic volcanoes, the symmetrical, snowcap-crowned Mount Fuji.

DISTANCE
4.6 miles round trip via Fujinomiya route, elevation gain 4,500 feet

START
Station 5 on Fujinomiya route

DIFFICULTY
Hard due to elevation gain

SEASON
June to August; in winter ice axes, crampons, and mountaineering skills are required

Each summer, around 400,000 people attempt to summit Mount Fuji, with about two-thirds successfully reaching the top, at 12,389 feet. Most Japanese climb the mountain in the dark so they can be on the summit for sunrise and chant the traditional greeting for the new day: *Banzai! Banzai! Banzai!* There's a Japanese word specifically for sunrise on Mount Fuji: *goraiko.*

Four main routes climb to the summit. The most popular ascent route is the Yoshida, on the north side, a 2.8-mile one-way trek. The shortest, at 2.3 miles one way, is on the south side and starts from an elevation of 7,874 feet. Each route has a series of numbered rest stations, all converging at station 10 on the summit.

The routes up Mount Fuji are often loose and rocky, and the climbing can be arduous, inspiring a well-known Japanese saying: A wise person will climb Mount Fuji once in their lifetime, but only a fool would climb it twice.

BELOW Many Japanese climb Mount Fuji in the dark to welcome the new day with a traditional chant.

Akame 48 Waterfalls Trail

MURO-AKAME-AOYAMA QUASI-NATIONAL PARK

JAPAN

Between the fifteenth and eighteenth centuries, Akame Valley was used as a training ground for Iga-ryū ninjas. The area is now a national park most famous for its waterfalls. There aren't actually forty-eight of them on this 5-mile out-and-back trail; the number likely comes from the traditional number of vows taken by bodhisattvas and is sometimes used in Japanese to mean "a lot." You'll actually see around twenty-three waterfalls on this trail. The park also offers a modern ninja training school, where you can sign up for a lesson, and a Salamander Center, where you will see the Japanese giant salamander.

LEFT You can climb Fuji in winter, but you'll need ice axes, crampons, and mountaineering skills.

422

Mount Rausu

SHIRETOKO NATIONAL PARK
JAPAN

The Shiretoko Peninsula, jutting off the island of Hokkaido into the Sea of Okhotsk, is accessible only on foot or by boat. The best views of Shiretoko are from the top of Mount Rausu, a 5,448-foot stratovolcano reached by a 7.5-mile out-and-back trail. Hokkaido is one of the last refuges for the Ezo brown bear, the Japanese relative of the grizzly bear—around 3,000 live here. Hike in groups, make noise, wear a bear bell, and carry bear spray, which can be rented in the park. If you don't use it, you'll be reimbursed. If you do use it, you likely have bigger things to worry about.

RIGHT To reach Mount Mashū, you follow a trail around the translucent Lake Mashū.

423

Lake Mashū and Mount Mashū

AKAN-MASHŪ NATIONAL PARK

JAPAN

Peer into the depths of one the world's clearest lakes, which is filled entirely by rain and snowmelt.

DISTANCE
8.7 miles out and back, elevation gain 1,000 feet

START
Mashū Viewpoint 1

DIFFICULTY
Moderate

SEASON
April to October

BELOW Lake Mashū crater lake is one of the world's most potentially dangerous volcanoes.

This crater lake in northern Japan has visibility down to depths of nearly 100 feet. No streams run into Lake Mashū, which sits inside the walls of a collapsed volcanic crater. It used to be even clearer; the loss of clarity is likely due to the introduction of sockeye salmon and rainbow trout into the lake, as well as landslides from the steep crater walls.

An 8.7-mile out-and-back trail runs around the edge of the crater to the top of 2,812-foot Mount Mashū, providing epic views of the lake. The scene may appear tranquil, but Kamuishu Island in the center of the lake is actually the tip of a still-active volcano. Mashū has a Volcanic Explosivity Index of 6 out of 8, making it one of the most potentially dangerous volcanoes in the world.

424

Valley of the Dragon King

NIKKŌ NATIONAL PARK

JAPAN

A two-hour drive from Tokyo, this popular city escape is widely regarded as Japan's most beloved national park. The sentiment is not new; centuries-old Buddhist temples and shrines are scattered throughout the heavily forested park. Keep an eye out for Asiatic black bears and Japanese sika deer on this easy 3.7-mile out-and-back trail along the Kinu River, through the Valley of the Dragon King. Spring blooms and fall colors light up this picturesque valley in spring and fall.

425

Karikomi Trail

NIKKŌ NATIONAL PARK

JAPAN

Like much of Japan, the landscape of Nikkō National Park was forged by volcanism. The centerpiece of the park is Mount Nikkō-Shirane, an 8,458-foot stratovolcano that last erupted in 1889. Active volcanism still brews beneath the surface, fueling the park's many hot springs. This 6-mile loop trail around the twin lakes Kirikomi and Karikomi is the perfect precursor to a relaxing soak in the nearby Yumoto hot springs, whose minerals are said to be good for the skin.

426

Langtang Valley

LANGTANG NATIONAL PARK

NEPAL

The Himalayan mountains were raised when the Indian tectonic plate collided with the Eurasian plate around 50 million years ago. The Indian plate continues to plow north, subducting under Eurasia, and the Himalayas are still rising at the rate of around an inch per year. In 2015 the magnitude 7.8 Gorkha quake triggered massive avalanches and landslides in the Langtang Valley that killed hundreds of people and destroyed several villages on the popular Langtang trekking route. Many of these villages have since been rebuilt or relocated, and the 48-mile trekking route has reopened.

427

Tengboche

SAGARMATHA NATIONAL PARK

NEPAL

Lay eyes on Mount Everest on this 12-mile out-and-back day hike from Namche Bazaar to the village of Tengboche. One of the first legs of the trail to Everest Base Camp, this ancient route will give you a taste of the rigors of Himalayan hiking. The trail gains 2,880 feet of elevation to top out at 12,687 feet at your destination, where you'll be rewarded with your first glimpse of the mighty Sagarmatha.

RIGHT Catch a glimpse of the mighty Mount Everest on this ancient trail to Tengboche.

428

Gokyo Lakes

SAGARMATHA NATIONAL PARK

NEPAL

Set out on a trek in Mount Everest's neighborhood with views of famous Himalayan peaks.

DISTANCE
57 miles out and back, usually completed over seven days

START
Namche Bazaar

DIFFICULTY
Hard due to high elevation

SEASON
March to May and September to November to avoid summer monsoons and harsh winters

Crowned by 29,032-foot Sagarmatha—also known as Mount Everest—this is the highest national park on Earth. More than 70 percent of the 443-square-mile park is in the alpine, where few plants can survive the harsh conditions.

The animals and people who live in the Himalayas are adapted to cope with the decreased availability of oxygen. The Nepalese Sherpa who have lived at high elevations for many generations have dozens of markers for genetic adaptations to altitude, including a gene that upregulates the production of hemoglobin, the protein that transports oxygen in red blood cells.

If you're visiting Sagarmatha, plan on a few low-exertion days at the beginning of your trek to allow your body to begin acclimating. Within one to three days, hemoglobin will start carrying oxygen more efficiently, helping to reduce the possibility of serious altitude sickness—the most effective treatment is to descend to lower elevations.

The 57-mile round-trip trek from Namche Bazaar to Gokyo Lakes shares part of the route with the footpath to Everest Base Camp. The high point of the spectacularly scenic high alpine trail is on the summit of 17,575-foot Gokyo Ri, with views of Mount Everest, Lhotse, Makalu, and Cho Oyu.

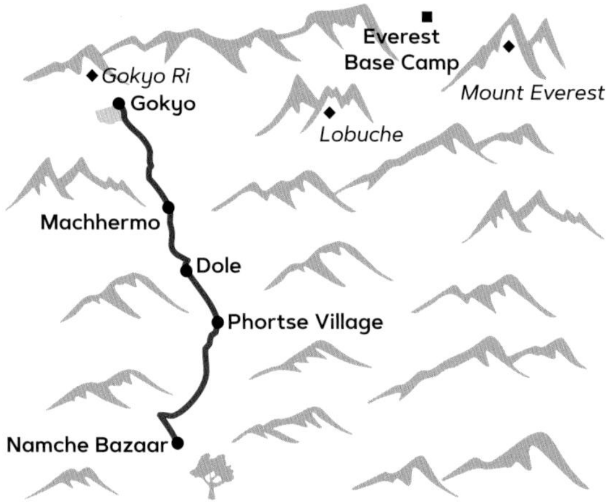

ABOVE The Himalayas loom large behind Nepal's Gokyo Lakes.

Chitwan Safari Loop

CHITWAN NATIONAL PARK

NEPAL

For centuries, Nepal's first national park was a favored hunting ground for the Nepali ruling class seeking tiger, rhino, and elephant trophies. By the time the Chitwan Valley was declared a national park in 1973, the area had been largely deforested and many of its animals were on the verge of extinction. Since then, both the jungle and wildlife have made valiant comebacks—the largest Indian rhino population in Nepal now lives here. Your best bet for seeing a rhino, Bengal tiger, or gharial is by signing up for a walking safari with guides who know where to find them and how to observe them safely. The length of these trips varies from short outings like the 3.5-mile Chitwan Safari Loop to all-day expeditions.

430

Markha Valley Trek

HEMIS NATIONAL PARK

INDIA

Your best bet for seeing a snow leopard, the elusive apex predator of the Himalayas, may be in Hemis National Park, which boasts the highest population density of the endangered big cat in the world. The park is also home to the Tibetan wolf and Eurasian brown bear. The 69-mile Markha Valley Trek runs along the Markha River, through the heart of the park, and connects many small villages between Zanskar and Ladakh, where you can stay and eat meals with local families. Because this area lies in the rain shadow of the Himalayas, summer monsoons are less of a threat here and treks run between June and mid-October.

BELOW A langur monkey watches over Ranthambore Fort in India's Ranthambore National Park.

431

Corbett Waterfall

JIM CORBETT NATIONAL PARK

INDIA

India's oldest national park, named after a British hunter and naturalist, was established in 1936 to protect the Bengal tiger. Today, the park is home to more than 230 of these tigers and 700-plus Indian elephants. You're unlikely to see either species on this easy 1.8-mile out-and-back trail through the jungle to Corbett Waterfall, but that's probably a good thing, given that Jim Corbett made a career out of hunting man-eating tigers. To have a chance of seeing a tiger, sign up for a guided safari.

432

Ranthambore Fort

RANTHAMBHORE NATIONAL PARK

INDIA

You'll be fairly safe from tigers inside Ranthambore Fort, a walled fortress that dates to the tenth century, but the resident langur monkeys are notorious troublemakers. A 1.8-mile walking tour loops through the fort, exploring the extensive ruins. You'll see Hindu temples and other buildings that are constructed out of blocks of red Karauli—a soft sandstone plentiful in this region of northern India.

433

The Valley of Flowers

VALLEY OF FLOWERS NATIONAL PARK

INDIA

Follow a rainbow-colored carpet of wildflowers where botanists have identified 498 species of flowering plants.

DISTANCE
25 miles round trip from Govindghat, elevation gain 8,000 feet

START
Govindghat

DIFFICULTY
Hard due to elevation gain

SEASON
July to September; wildflowers peak in August

The Pushpawati Valley was carved by a glacier, which has now retreated into the mountains. During the summer, a kaleidoscope of flowers blooms here, including orchids, poppies, marigolds, anemones, and daisies.

The Valley of Flowers has been a Hindu pilgrimage site for centuries, but it was only discovered by the Western world in 1931, when a team of wayward British mountaineers stumbled into the valley and bestowed its name. No roads run into it, so you must start from the town of Govindghat and first hike 8.7 miles to the small village of Ghangaria, 2 miles from the park. No overnight trekking or camping is allowed in the valley, so you'll need to stay in Ghangaria and day hike into the park.

One challenging option is to hike to Hemkund Sahib, at an elevation of 13,650 feet. This 7.4-mile round-trip hike from Ghangaria climbs a series of switchbacks uphill 4,000 feet, offering a quite literally breathtaking view of the valley.

ABOVE You can choose a day hike of any length in the Valley of Flowers.

LEFT The switchback trail to Hemkund Sahib with its stunning views of the valley below.

World's End

HORTON PLAINS NATIONAL PARK

SRI LANKA

The Horton Plains unfurl across the top of a high-elevation plateau in the central highlands of Sri Lanka. The 6-mile loop to the World's End cliff starts in the grassland plains and runs uphill into the often misty cloud forest. Partway through the hike, you'll reach Little World's End, a cliff with an 880-foot drop that serves as a rest point. When you get to the actual World's End, you'll peer over the edge of a cliff with a spine-tingling 2,885-foot drop! To make a loop, follow the trail to the northwest, where it meets up with the Belihul Oya stream, which pours over the 66-foot Baker's Falls.

435

Ton Kiol Waterfall

KHAO SOK NATIONAL PARK

THAILAND

This lushly forested park protects the largest swath of virgin forest in Thailand, a surviving remnant of an ancient rainforest that is older than the Amazon. The 8-mile round-trip hike to Ton Kiol Waterfall tunnels through thick jungle, following the Sok River. If you catch a whiff of rotten meat on your hike, look for a reddish-orange flower. *Rafflesia kerrii* blooms grow 2–3 feet across—making this one of the largest flowers in the world—and emit an awful odor to attract flies, which they trap and digest. The noxious but striking flowers bloom between January and March.

436

Buddha's Footprint Trail

DOI SUTHEP-PUI NATIONAL PARK

THAILAND

Located just 9 miles outside the northern city of Chiang Mai, this park serves as the winter residence for Thailand's royal family and is also the home of the Doi Suthep Temple, a sacred Theravada Buddhist site. The Buddha's Footprint Trail is an 8-mile loop that starts at Doi Pui Hmong Tribal Village, near the middle of the park. Best hiked clockwise, the trail ascends more than 2,400 feet, following a mountaintop ridge with glorious views of the park. Bring binoculars for the more than 300 bird species that live here, including Siamese fireback pheasants and crested serpent eagles.

ABOVE Seek out the giant *Rafflesia kerrii* flower on a hike to Ton Kiol Waterfall.

437

Little White Sandy Beach

KHAO LAK-LAM RU NATIONAL PARK

THAILAND

On December 26, 2004, a monstrous tsunami triggered by an offshore earthquake decimated coastlines in the Indian Ocean, killing hundreds of thousands of people. One of the hardest-hit places was Khao Lak, a stretch of beaches on the Andaman Sea, where villages and resorts were ransacked by the 100-foot wave. Marvel at the resilience of nature and the Thai people as you stroll along this mile-long stretch of white sand beach near Khao Lak, where the crystal-clear blue waters beg for a dip. Thailand now boasts one of the most advanced tsunami early warning systems in the world.

438

Erawan Falls

ERAWAN NATIONAL PARK

THAILAND

Erawan Falls is named for its resemblance to the three-headed, five-trunked, ten-tusked pure-white elephant that carries the deity Indra in Hindu mythology. As the shimmering emerald-green water pours over the top of the falls, the water turns white and splits into Erawan's many trunks. The striking hue of the water, as well as the waterfall's many stair-stepped tiers, are formed by travertine, a mineral sourced from the region's limestone. A 3-mile out-and-back trail runs upstream to the falls, offering many striking views of the waterfall, with steps built in a few steep sections. You can swim in some of the deeper pools, but you'll have to share the water with the many fish and frogs that thrive in this river.

BELOW You can swim in the pools beneath the shimmering, scenic Erawan Falls.

Kbal Spean

PHNOM KULEN NATIONAL PARK
CAMBODIA

The Stung Kbal Spean River flows over small waterfalls through the thick jungles of northern Cambodia. After the summer monsoon season passes and water levels drop, the river reveals its hidden splendor—the sandstone riverbanks are covered in intricate carvings.

The repeated geometric patterns represent the lingam and yoni symbols of the Hindu god Shiva and goddess Shakti. Other carvings depict the gods Vishnu, Brahma, Lakshmi, and Rama, as well as some animals. Known as the "Valley of a Thousand Lingas," the carvings are thought to date from the eleventh and twelfth centuries and serve to sanctify the river as it flows over the symbols. A 2-mile round-trip trail runs upstream from a parking area to the site. The carvings are located along a 500-foot stretch of the riverbank. Visit in the dry season from October to April.

RIGHT After squeezing through its tiny entrance, Paradise Cave opens into a large cavern.

440

Paradise, Dark, and Hang Én Caves

PHONG NHA-KẺ BÀNG NATIONAL PARK

VIETNAM

Pitch a tent inside one of the world's largest caves before exploring a vast network of underground caverns.

- **DISTANCE**
  Varies
- **START**
  Village of Phong Nha
- **DIFFICULTY**
  Easy to moderate
- **SEASON**
  Dry season, December to August; avoid the rainy season, when caves are often closed due to flooding

The largest cave systems in the world underlie this park in central Vietnam, including Sơn Đoòng—the world's largest cave. The extensive networks of caverns and passageways are tunneled into a vast region of limestone known as the Annamese Mountains, which supports a thriving ecosystem of tropical evergreen forest.

Of the more than 500 caves in the park, thirty are open to visitors. Paradise and Dark are accessible to most people without prior caving experience. Paradise only requires a short, tight squeeze through its tiny entrance, but then opens into a massive dry cavern festooned with stalactites and stalagmites. Getting into Dark Cave is a bit more of an adventure involving a zip line, a muddy scramble, a short but cold swim, and a kayak.

For a truly unique backpacking trip, sign up for the overnight guided expedition to Hang Én, the world's third-largest cave. The trip begins with an 8-mile trek through the jungle to the entrance of the cave. After setting up tents on a sandy beach just inside the cave's entrance, you'll don helmets and headlamps to be guided deeper into the cave system, which opens into a series of massive rooms.

BELOW Tents pitched in the entrance to Hang Én Cave, lit by natural light.

441

Crocodile Lake

CÁT TIÊN NATIONAL PARK

VIETNAM

Hike to a lagoon where you can kayak with crocs—or view them from a safer distance on raised platforms.

DISTANCE
5.5 miles round trip, elevation gain 350 feet

START
Park headquarters

DIFFICULTY
Easy

SEASON
Dry season, November to April

ABOVE RIGHT Yellow-cheeked gibbons in Cát Tiên National Park.

RIGHT Don't get too close to the crocs when you rent a boat on Crocodile Lake.

Cát Tiên National Park protects one of Vietnam's largest areas of lowland tropical rainforest. The forest is on the road to recovery after being sprayed with defoliant herbicides during the Vietnam War and then logged into the 1990s. There are thriving populations of gibbons, langurs, Asian elephants, clouded leopards, and sun bears. More than 1,600 plant species have been documented here, making it one of the most botanically biodiverse regions in Southeast Asia.

Sadly, the last remaining Vietnamese herd of Javan rhinos, only discovered in the park in 1992, were declared extinct in 2011. The freshwater Siamese crocodile nearly went the way of the rhino due to overhunting, but a captive breeding and release program has boosted its numbers.

See the wild population of 200-plus crocodiles at Crocodile Lake, the largest freshwater lagoon in the park. A 5.5-mile out-and-back trail runs to the lake, where viewing platforms allow you to safely observe the crocs in their natural habitat. You can rent kayaks—but keep your distance, as the crocs can be aggressive. Plan to safely observe the reptiles in the morning or evening, when they are most active. Overnight accommodations are available at the lakeshore station, but make your reservation before you leave park headquarters.

442

Mount Fansipan

HOÀNG LIÊN NATIONAL PARK
VIETNAM

Test your legs and lungs on this strenuous hike to the top of the highest mountain on the Indochinese Peninsula. A steep, 6-mile one-way trail gains over 4,300 feet of elevation on its way to the 10,326-foot summit of the Hoàng Liên Sơn range. From there, you can return the way you came or hitch a ride down in an enclosed gondola, which carries passengers up and down the mountain from Mường Hoa Valley, near the village of Sa Pa.

443

Kim Gaio

CÁT BÀ NATIONAL PARK
VIETNAM

This national park covers nearly the entirety of Cát Bà Island, the largest of the 367 islands in the Cat Bà Archipelago. The park is most famous for Hạ Long Bay—a limestone karst landscape dotted with thousands of tiny islands. One of the best views of the park is from the top of 1,705-foot Ngự Lâm Peak. A steep, 1.8-mile round-trip trail runs through dense jungle to the summit. Keep your eyes open for wildlife—only the luckiest will spot the white-headed langur, one of the rarest primates in the world.

444

Canopy Walk

PENANG NATIONAL PARK

MALAYSIA

For a truly unique hike in this heavily forested island park, sign up for a Canopy Walk. This "trail" is only 820 feet long, but it's suspended 50 feet above the ground, in the midst of the rainforest's lush tree canopy. To protect the vegetation, the route was built using only soft ropes and no nails, bolts, or screws. You will follow a series of suspended planks, which are enclosed by ropes and netting. This adventure is suitable for children and adults, but if you are afraid of heights, you will probably want to keep your feet on the ground.

445

Monkey Beach Lighthouse

PENANG NATIONAL PARK

MALAYSIA

Malaysia's smallest national park packs a lot of unique attractions into less than 10 square miles. At the northwest tip of Penang Island, you'll find beautiful beaches and old-growth rainforest renowned for biodiversity. A 6-mile round-trip hike follows the coast from the Teluk Bahang park entrance to Teluk Duyung, nicknamed Monkey Beach. Crab-eating macaques live here, alongside majestic white-bellied sea eagles and green sea turtles, which lay their eggs on nearby Kerachut Beach. Monkey Beach's calm bay is perfect for swimming, especially since it is free of the stinging jellyfish that plague other beaches on the island. After a dip, head uphill for another half mile to Muka Head Lighthouse. The historic structure is no longer in service but the catwalk around the light provides excellent views of the coastline.

BELOW Walk up to Muka Head Lighthouse at Monkey Beach for views of the Penang coastline.

446

Bukit Teresek

TAMAN NEGARA NATIONAL PARK

MALAYSIA

Malaysia's first official national park protects one of the planet's oldest surviving deciduous rainforests. A lush tropical rainforest has existed here for more than 130 million years, dating back to the Cretaceous period, when dinosaurs ruled this jungle. Climb above the thick canopy of trees for a pterodactyl's view of this lost world from the top of 1,096-foot Bukit Teresek. A 2-mile round-trip hike leads from the park's headquarters to the summit. On a clear day, you'll be able to see Gunung Tahan—the highest peak on the Malay Peninsula.

BELOW The panoramic view from Teresek Hill in Taman Negara National Park.

447

Kepayang Besar Caves

TAMAN NEGARA NATIONAL PARK

MALAYSIA

For a unique backpacking experience, pack a tent and spend a night camping inside a limestone cave.

DISTANCE
11 miles round trip, usually done as an overnight backpack

START
Kuala Tahan

DIFFICULTY
Moderate

SEASON
March to September

LEFT Setting up camp in Malaysia's Kepayang Besar Caves.

BELOW The critically endangered Malayan tiger lives in the Taman Negara National Park jungle.

The Malay Peninsula is underlain by water-soluble limestone that erodes into cave systems. From park headquarters at Kuala Tahan, head to Kepayang Besar Caves, reached by an 11-mile round-trip trek through the dense and muddy jungle. A small population of the critically endangered Malayan tiger survives in this jungle, but the big cats are well fed on deer and wild boar, and are generally not considered a threat to people.

The entrance of the Big Kepayang Cave is deceptively small, but the main interior chamber is huge. You can camp on the flat, sandy floor inside the cave, but bring a tent—rodents, bats, and snakes all call this cave home too. Nearby, you'll find the smaller Kepayang Kecil Cave.

As you explore the caves by headlamp, look up for cave racers—these small, skinny snakes climb cave walls to hunt mice and bats, sometimes catching the flying mammals out of the air. The snakes aren't aggressive toward people and are commonly kept as pets.

448

Camp Leakey Orangutan Trek

TANJUNG PUTING NATIONAL PARK

INDONESIA

Located on the island of Borneo, the Camp Leakey research station was established in Tanjung Puting National Park in 1971 for the study and conservation of orangutans, proboscis monkeys, and other primates. Getting to Camp Leakey—named after the famed paleoanthropologist Louis Leakey—is an adventure in itself, requiring a two-hour boat ride up the Kumai and Sekonyer rivers. No overnight stays are allowed, but a few tour companies offer boat-based accommodations.

The primary goal of the research station is to rehabilitate orangutans rescued from the illegal pet trade and from devastating habitat loss as Borneo's native forests are cleared to make way for palm oil plantations. You'll be able to observe orangutans at feeding stations, as well as sign up for an orangutan trek into the forest. These guided treks of up to 4 miles take you to known observation points where you can see orangutans. Other wildlife, such as sun bears, wild boars, and porcupines, may also make an appearance. Clouded leopards also live here but are rarely seen.

LEFT An orangutan and her baby at the Camp Leakey research station in Indonesia.

RIGHT You won't find any komodo dragons on Padar Island.

449

Mount Semeru

BROMO TENGGER SEMERU NATIONAL PARK

INDONESIA

Hike to the highest point on the island of Java on the summit of 12,060-foot Mount Semeru. This volcano has been almost continuously active since 1967, with small eruptions every few months; a puff of gray smoke can often be seen hovering above the summit.

Check current eruption conditions at park headquarters before you set off on this hike, as the trail is frequently closed due to eruptive activity. Most hikers summit Semeru as a two- or three-day hike, starting from the village of Ranu Pani and climbing up the north face. The 20-mile round-trip trail gains over 8,000 feet of elevation via a series of steep switchbacks, but you'll be rewarded with spectacular views at the top.

450

Pulau Padar

KOMODO NATIONAL PARK

INDONESIA

Komodo dragons, also known as the Komodo monitor lizard, are the world's largest lizard. An apex predator with a fearsome reputation, fully grown 10-foot lizards are capable of taking down large prey like deer—and even humans. Around 1,700 of these beasts live on Komodo Island, the largest island in the national park, with several thousand more scattered around the other twenty-nine islands in the park. You may be relieved to hear that the best hiking in the park is on Padar Island—the one major island that doesn't host Komodo dragons. This short but steep 2-mile round-trip trek leads to an epic viewpoint of the island's three turquoise bays, each lined by a different color of sand: white, pink, and black.

451

Mount Kelimutu

KELIMUTU NATIONAL PARK

INDONESIA

Get up early to visit an active volcano's color-changing lakes on Flores Island before the fog rolls in.

DISTANCE
1.5 miles round trip, elevation gain 300 feet

START
Kelimutu parking area

DIFFICULTY
Easy but some stairs

SEASON
Dry season, May to October

The colors of these three crater lakes change hues, depending on how the volcanic activity affects the chemistry of the water. They each have their own separate groundwater plumbing systems and can change colors independently of one another.

The westernmost lake, Tiwu Ata Bupu, meaning the Lake of Old People, is often some shade of blue. The other two lakes, Tiwu Ko'o Fai Nuwa Muri, which translates to the Lake of Young Men and Maidens, and Tiwu Ata Polo (Bewitched or Enchanted Lake), are typically green and red, respectively. The names come from the Lio people, who believe the souls of the dead come here to rest. Ceremonial offerings of food and tokens can often be seen on rocks around the lakes.

To visit, you'll need to arrange a ride from the village of Moni to the park. From the Kelimutu parking area, an easy trail less than a mile long with a staircase takes you to Inspiration Point, with views of all three lakes. Hiking to the viewpoint for sunrise is popular, but stay until the sunlight hits the lakes, revealing their brightest colors.

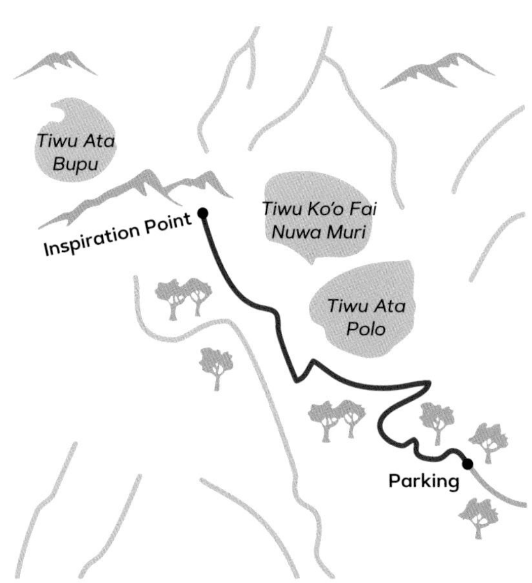

ABOVE The changing colors of Mount Kelimutu's crater lakes.

Underground River

PUERTO PRINCESA SUBTERRANEAN RIVER NATIONAL PARK

THE PHILIPPINES

Hike to the opening of the world's second-largest underground river. An easy 2-mile out-and-back trail runs through the jungle from the town of Sabang to the cave's entrance, on the north central coast. Keep your eyes and ears tuned for wildlife—the jungle is home to more than 250 species of birds, as well as a diversity of mammals like the long-tailed macaque, Palawan bearded pig, and Palawan porcupine.

To explore the subterranean river itself, you'll need to sign up for a boat tour. Cut into the island's layers of limestone by the Cabayugan River, the Saint Paul's Underground River Cave is more than 5 miles long, and contains multiple levels where the river flows over underground waterfalls. Boat tours begin at the river's mouth and motor upstream for 2.7 miles, through several large caverns spangled with stalactites and stalagmites.

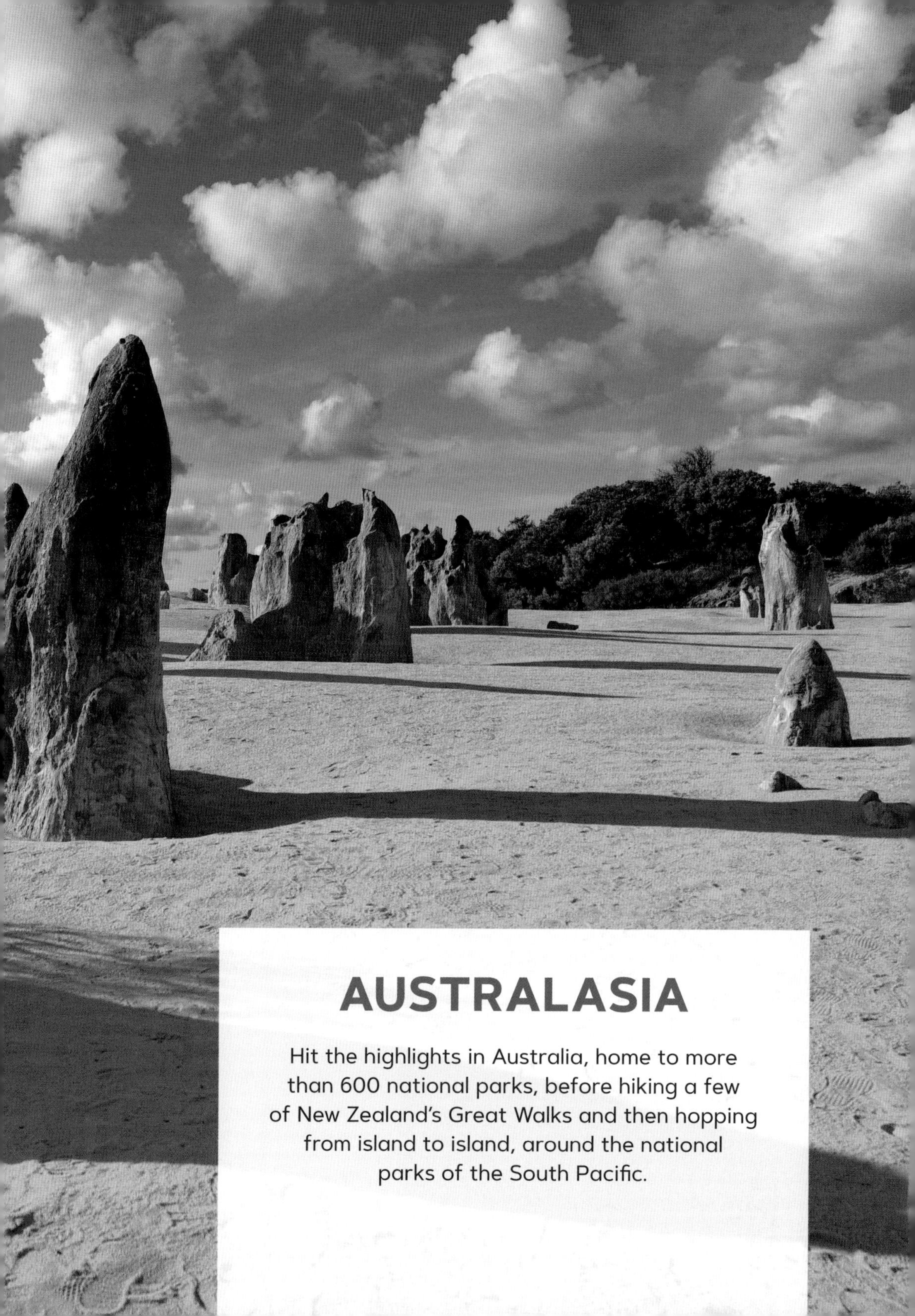

AUSTRALASIA

Hit the highlights in Australia, home to more than 600 national parks, before hiking a few of New Zealand's Great Walks and then hopping from island to island, around the national parks of the South Pacific.

453

Ubirr Aboriginal Art Gallery

KAKADU NATIONAL PARK

AUSTRALIA

Stroll through an ancient art gallery of people, animals, geometric shapes, and abstract designs.

DISTANCE
1.2-mile loop, elevation gain to overlook 820 feet

START
Trailhead on Ubirr Road

DIFFICULTY
Easy; loop is partially wheelchair accessible

SEASON
Year-round

BELOW Take a side trail to reach spectacular viewpoints above the Nadab wetlands.

For at least 20,000 years, people have been overnighting in rock shelters in what is now Kakadu National Park. The artists among them painted the walls and ceilings of these shelters—the act of painting was considered more sacred than the painting itself, so older paintings were frequently painted over, creating a many-layered canvas. Ubirr rock art is considered one of the oldest and most extensive records of indigenous artwork in the world.

A 1.2-mile partially paved trail loops through three main galleries, where you'll find the densest concentration of paintings. A steeper side trail also leads to an overlook of the surrounding Nadab wetlands, with views of the park's famous long escarpments. Most of the paintings are red—iron oxide pigments made from crushed hematite last longer than the fainter orange, yellow, and white pigments.

Approximately half of the land in Kakadu is Aboriginal land under the Aboriginal Land Rights Act of 1976, and the park is jointly managed by Aboriginal traditional owners and the Director of National Parks with assistance from Parks Australia. Look closely but never touch rock art—oils from your hands are very damaging to the paintings.

Jim Jim Falls Plunge Pool

KAKADU NATIONAL PARK
AUSTRALIA

At Jim Jim Falls, Jim Jim Creek plunges over the edge of a 656-foot sandstone escarpment, creating the largest waterfall in the park. The trail to the plunge pool is only a 1.2-mile round trip, requiring some scrambling over boulders. To see the falls, you'll have to use your imagination. By the time the roads have dried up enough to get into this part of the park, the waterfall will probably have dried up too. The scene is still stunning and you wouldn't want to swim here anyway—this is crocodile country! Kakadu is famous for its freshwater and saltwater crocodiles. Salties are the largest living reptile and can grow up to 20 feet long, with a fearsome man-eating reputation to match.

LEFT Aboriginal rock art in Kakadu National Park.

455

Cathedral Gorge Trail

PURNULULU NATIONAL PARK

AUSTRALIA

The curiously named Bungle Bungle Range is the only place in the world you'll find Bungle Bungles—striped beehive-shaped sandstone domes. The banding on the rocks is due to the differences in clay content and porosity of the layers. The orange bands contain oxidized iron compounds that do not support cyanobacteria, whereas the darker gray bands are colored by mats of cyanobacteria growing on layers where moisture can seep through the rock. Over time, the plateau has eroded into deep gorges, chasms, and slot canyons. The 2.5-mile out-and-back Cathedral Gorge Trail follows a canyon into a red amphitheater of rock. The acoustics are so stellar that professional musicians have played concerts here.

BELOW Follow the Cathedral Gorge Trail to a massive amphitheater with great acoustics.

456

Mossman Gorge Rainforest Circuit

DAINTREE NATIONAL PARK

AUSTRALIA

Located on the far northeastern coast, this national park is split into two distinct areas: the dense rainforest and mountain woodlands of Mossman Gorge, and the coastal beaches and lowland rainforest of Cape Tribulation. The gorge is home to the Daintree Rainforest—the largest continuous tropical rainforest in Australia. An easy 2-mile loop explores an old-growth forest at the confluence of Rex Creek and the Mossman River.

Keep an eye out for the endangered, flightless cassowary bird, which can grow up to 6 feet tall. It can be aggressive if threatened, but it is generally a very shy species.

457

Devils Thumb

DAINTREE NATIONAL PARK

AUSTRALIA

This granite dome has long been sacred to the indigenous Eastern Kuku Yalanji people, who call it Manjal Jimalji and believe it marks the spot where their ancestors were given the sacred knowledge of making fire by rubbing two sticks together. Hiking to the top is challenging, involving route finding through thick vegetation, some scrambling, and climbing along downed tree trunks and up roots embedded in steep hillsides. The 8.5-mile out-and-back route gains 4,000 feet to the summit, where you'll be rewarded with outstanding views. Don't attempt this steep and slippery route in the rain; it's also notorious for mostly harmless leeches.

458

Jatbula Trail

NITMILUK NATIONAL PARK

AUSTRALIA

Follow in the footsteps of the Jawoyn Aboriginal people as you retrace this ancient route from Nitmiluk Gorge to Leliyn Falls. The 39-mile route crosses a sandstone plateau and weaves through woodlands and monsoon forests, passing several waterfalls. The trail is usually hiked over five to six days, moving between campsites located near swimming holes, springs, and waterfalls—each are sacred to the Jawoyn as a place their ancestors have visited for thousands of years. You may also find rock art along the route.

459

Thorsborne Trail

HINCHINBROOK ISLAND NATIONAL PARK

AUSTRALIA

Hike across the largest island in the Great Barrier Reef—the world's largest coral reef system.

DISTANCE
20 miles, usually completed over three to four days

START
Ramsay Bay

END
George Point

DIFFICULTY
Moderate

SEASON
Year-round; May to October is cool and dry but water may be harder to find; November to April is hotter and wetter

FAR RIGHT Hinchinbrook Island is made up of mountains, rivers, and beaches.

RIGHT The Thorsborne Trail follows the rugged coastline, skirting beaches and headlands.

Most people visit the Great Barrier Reef to go snorkeling and scuba diving, but while you're there you might as well go for a hike too. The 20-mile Thorsborne Trail runs across the east coast of Hinchinbrook Island, just off the east coast of Queensland.

It usually takes three to four days to complete the one-way trek from north to south, by setting up a ferry shuttle in Ramsay Bay or from George Point. There are seven campsites along the route, with composting toilets, hooks to hang food to keep it safe from rodents, and freshwater creeks for drinking water (always bring a filter). Check the status of these creeks when you pick up your permit, as some dry up between May and October.

Along the trail you'll find a few beaches and creeks suitable for swimming, but be alert for logs with teeth in the water—Hinchinbrook Island is known to host crocodiles.

Whitehaven Beach

WHITSUNDAY ISLANDS NATIONAL PARK
AUSTRALIA

Whitehaven Beach is famous for its finely powdered white sand, made up of 98 percent pure silica. Legend has it that the sand is so pure, it was used to make the glass for the Hubble Telescope, but NASA has neither confirmed nor denied the claim. The tiny grains are also notorious for getting into smartphones, watches, and every nook and cranny of everything! The white sands do not retain much heat, and the clean beach is a prime spot for a shoeless stroll. However, you'll probably want shoes for the 2-mile loop from Hill Inlet Lookout to the tip of Champagne Beach. The partially wooded trail is the perfect complement to a walk along the beach itself, which runs for 4.5 miles along the coast.

461

Passage Peak

WHITSUNDAY ISLANDS NATIONAL PARK

AUSTRALIA

Arrive on top of this mountain before dawn and you'll be rewarded with a spectacular sunrise. You won't have to set off too early—most people can reach the top in under an hour. The 3.2-mile round-trip trail gains 880 feet to the summit of Passage Peak, the highest point in the Whitsunday Islands. From there, you'll have great views of these islands off the northeast coast of Australia, bordered by the Great Barrier Reef and surrounded by the Coral Sea. The peaceful waters here serve as a nursery for humpback whales—between May and September, the behemoths gather here to give birth and raise their young.

462

Pinnacles Outlook Track

NAMBUNG NATIONAL PARK

AUSTRALIA

In southwestern Australia, the Nambung River pulls an incredible vanishing act, disappearing underground into a limestone cavern and leaving a parched desert landscape in its wake. The unusual combination of limestone in an arid coastal environment is punctuated by thousands of tombstone-like limestone pinnacles. A 3.3-mile loop trail wanders through this surreal alien landscape.

BELOW Pinnacles Outlook Track weaves through pinnacles of all shapes and sizes.

ABOVE Cape Leeuwin Lighthouse sits at one end of the Cape to Cape Track.

463

Cape to Cape Track

LEEUWIN-NATURALISTE NATIONAL PARK

AUSTRALIA

The Cape to Cape Track is a 76-mile route that runs the entire length of the Leeuwin-Naturaliste Ridge, a limestone ridge that forms the backbone of this national park that's named for the two lighthouses at either end. Famous for its coastal scenery and beautiful beaches, some sections of sheltered forests and vineyard views add variety to the hike. Several tour companies offer wine-tasting trekking trips that combine the track with detours to the neighboring vineyards.

464

Uluṟu Base Walk

ULUṞU-KATA TJUṮA NATIONAL PARK

AUSTRALIA

Be beckoned by Uluṟu—a 600-million-year-old arkose sandstone monolith in the Australian Outback.

DISTANCE
6.8-mile loop, elevation gain 640 feet

START
Trailhead on west side of formation

DIFFICULTY
Moderate

SEASON
Year-round; cooler weather from May to September

ABOVE RIGHT Walking around the base of the formations is the most considerate way to encounter Uluṟu.

RIGHT Uluṟu is one of the most iconic rocks in the world.

The 1,142-foot Uluṟu appears to stand alone, but the bulk of the formation hides underground, extending 25 miles away to the west, where another outcrop of domed rocks, called Kata Tjuṯa, erupts from the landscape.

Uluṟu and Kata Tjuṯa beckon desert travelers in the vast arid landscape with the promise of shade, springs, water holes, and rock shelters. The formations are sacred to the Aboriginal people, who have lived here for thousands of years—many of their myths and legends revolve around these rocks. Today, 150–450 Aṉangu live in the vicinity, depending on the time of year and cultural activities outside the area. They play an integral role in the management of the park.

Scrambling to the top of Uluṟu was an affront to Aboriginal beliefs and was banned in 2019. The best way to respectfully experience Uluṟu is to hike around its base. A 6.8-mile loop circles the bottom, passing alcoves decorated with rock art paintings, the Mutitjulu Waterhole, and through acacia woodlands. Aṉangu park rangers host guided walks and share the ancient wisdom and creation stories inspired by the formation.

465

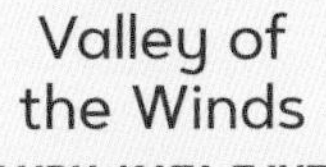

Valley of the Winds

ULUṞU-KATA TJUṮA NATIONAL PARK

AUSTRALIA

Also sacred to the Aṉangu is Uluṟu's lesser-known neighbor, Kata Tjuṯa, a grouping of thirty-six sandstone domes. The highest, Mount Olga, is an impressive 665 feet higher than Uluṟu. A 4.6-mile loop trail explores the northern edge of the domes, climbing to two lookouts and winding through a narrow cleft between domes that gives the trail its name.

466

Alligator Gorge

MOUNT REMARKABLE NATIONAL PARK

AUSTRALIA

Man-eating alligators are a very real threat in some areas of Australia, but not in Alligator Gorge. The largest reptile you're likely to see here is a goanna—a type of monitor lizard that can get quite large but is not a threat to people. Alligator Gorge is a narrow canyon lined by towering red walls of quartzite sandstone. To access the gorge, you'll descend a steep flight of stairs to reach the hiking trail along Alligator Creek. Hiking upstream, the erosional history of this creek unfurls as you cross over terraced ledges and ripple marks carved into the rock by flowing water over millions of years. At the head of the gorge you can follow the marked trail out of the canyon to make a 1.5-mile loop back to the start, or you can return the way you came for a double dose of the fabulously sculpted canyon.

LEFT The walls close in to 6 feet for a few hundred feet in the Narrows section of Alligator Gorge.

467

Mount Remarkable Summit Loop

MOUNT REMARKABLE NATIONAL PARK

AUSTRALIA

Standing on the summit, it's clear that Mount Remarkable was named looking up from the bottom. Views from the summit are limited by eucalyptus trees, but don't let that deter you—wide panoramas open at every turn on your way up. You won't even have to retrace your steps—an 8.6-mile loop trail leads from the town of Melrose to the top, gaining just under 2,000 feet of elevation before looping down another trail. For the best views, hike up the south trail and down the north trail.

BELOW Panoramic views open up along the route to Mount Remarkable's summit.

468

Kangaroo Island

FLINDERS CHASE NATIONAL PARK

AUSTRALIA

See how Kangaroo Island has risen from the ashes, following devastating bushfires.

DISTANCE
38 miles, usually hiked in five days

START
Flinders Chase National Park Visitor Centre

END
Kelly Hill Caves

DIFFICULTY
Moderate

SEASON
March to November

BELOW The inquisitive marsupials that Kangaroo Island is named after.

The devastating bushfires that swept across Australia in 2019 and 2020 razed more than half of Kangaroo Island, the third-largest island in Australia. In the wake of the disaster, the 38-mile Kangaroo Island Wilderness Trail, newly built in 2016, was rebranded as the Kangaroo Island Wilderness Trail—Fire Recovery Experience.

To limit the number of walkers on the fragile landscape, you must book a trip through a licensed tour operator. Most people walk this route in five days, often day hiking sections and staying in nearby hotels. Note: there is no drinking water on the route.

The Kangaroo Island landscape is beautiful and the trek is an opportunity to see how habitats recover from fire. As of 2021, green shoots were already sprouting and seedlings emerging from the blackened soil. The lack of undergrowth makes it easier to spot kangaroos, koalas, wallabies, goannas, and echidnas. The park sponsors a citizen science program, where you can share your wildlife and plant-regrowth observations with scientists who are studying the recovery of the park.

Jack Point Pelican Observatory Walk

COORONG NATIONAL PARK
AUSTRALIA

The Younghusband Peninsula is a long, narrow band of sand dunes that stretches for over 68 miles along the coast south of Adelaide. The dunes separate the brackish waters of the Coorong Lagoon from the salt water of the Southern Ocean. This band of wetlands supports a variety of bird and marine life. Thanks to the powerful flow of the Murray River, this estuary remains wet, even through severe droughts, making it an important refuge for more than 200 species of birds. An out-and-back trail leads through the dunes for less than a mile to an overlook at Jack Point. Bring binoculars to view the small islands offshore that serve as a rookery for the largest breeding colony of pelicans in the country. They typically breed between June and November, laying two eggs in a sandy nest and then raising the stronger chick.

ABOVE LEFT The Remarkable Rocks on Kangaroo Island.

LEFT Raised boardwalks on Kangaroo Island lead to places of interest.

470

Govetts Leap Lookout

BLUE MOUNTAINS NATIONAL PARK

AUSTRALIA

Located west of Sydney, this park is one of the closest places to go outside the city to see wild kangaroos. The park's name comes from the blue haze that often surrounds the plateau, generated by light waves refracting off the oily transpiration of the area's dense eucalyptus tree forests. Four major rivers dissect the high plateau and the park is also famous for dramatic waterfalls. An easy round-trip trail just over a mile long runs to an overlook of the 590-foot Govetts Leap Falls.

471

Blue Fish Trail

SYDNEY HARBOUR NATIONAL PARK

AUSTRALIA

You don't have to leave Sydney to experience one of Australia's 681 national parks. Sydney Harbour National Park protects a 1.5-square-mile zone of the harbor, centered around Port Jackson Bay, with views of the iconic Sydney Opera House and Sydney Harbour Bridge. There's a lot to see here: the architecture; the bustling port; the Aboriginal, colonial, and military history; the coastline; and the wildlife. Savor them all on the 7-mile Blue Fish Trail, which loops between the harborside and oceanside of the Manly peninsula.

ABOVE Govetts Leap is a thin, single drop that flows over the rim of cliffs on the edge of a plateau.

472

Australian Alps Walking Track

KOSCIUSZKO NATIONAL PARK

AUSTRALIA

Check off five national parks—Baw Baw, Alpine, Kosciuszko, Namadgi, and Brindabella—in one epic hike on this 407-mile route through the Australian Alps, the highest mountain range in the country. You'll need to arrange food drops or caches, or have a support crew meet you at designated resupply spots, as the track passes through no towns. Most people hike this route in sections, often tackling one park at a time. At 7,310 feet, Mount Kosciuszko is the highest point on the route—and also the highest point in Australia. It can be reached on an 8-mile round-trip day hike from the top of the Thredbo ski area's Kosciuszko Express chairlift. Kosciuszko is the easiest of the Seven Summits—the mountaineer's checklist of the highest points on each continent that includes Mount Everest and Mount Kilimanjaro.

473

The Great Ocean Walk

GREAT OTWAY NATIONAL PARK

AUSTRALIA

Experience the treacherous Shipwreck Coast of southeastern Australia from the safety of the shore.

DISTANCE
65 miles, usually completed in eight days

START
Apollo Bay

END
Port Campbell

DIFFICULTY
Difficult due to rugged terrain and high tide danger

SEASON
Year-round; summers can be hot; bring a tide chart

ABOVE RIGHT The Great Ocean walk ends near the Twelve Apostles.

RIGHT The London Bridge rock formation is located just beyond Port Campbell.

The Great Ocean Road is a scenic driving route that runs for 151 miles between Torquay and Allansford. One of the most iconic viewpoints on this road is of the Twelve Apostles, a series of limestone sea stacks off the coast, protected by Port Campbell National Park. The section between Cape Otway and Port Fairy is known as the Shipwreck Coast—more than 600 shipwrecks are thought to rest offshore here, felled by strong gales and lurking rocks and reefs.

Explore this rugged coastline safely onshore on the 65-mile hiking trail called the Great Ocean Walk. It runs from Apollo Bay to Glenample Homestead, ending near the Twelve Apostles. Campsites are spaced along the track, with three-sided wind shelters and toilets. The route oscillates between the high clifftops and the sandy beaches. Bring a tide chart to avoid being trapped on the beach at high tide, when the waves come right up to the cliffs.

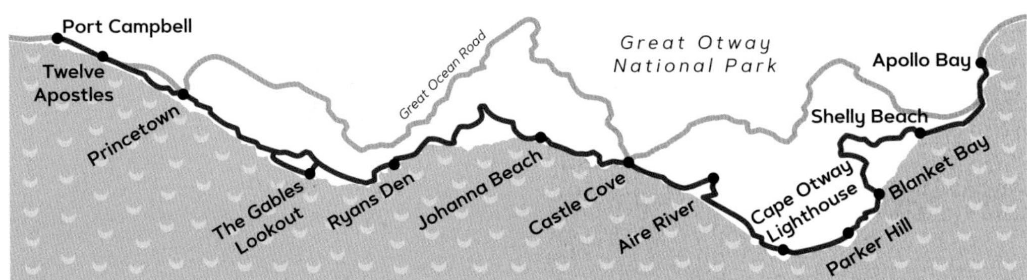

474

Enchanted Forest

CRADLE MOUNTAIN-LAKE ST. CLAIR NATIONAL PARK

AUSTRALIA

Located in the remote central highlands of Tasmania, this national park is rich in species found nowhere else on Earth. You're sure to spot a few exotic plants and maybe even some Tasmanian wildlife on this loop that's less than a mile long through mossy temperate rainforest. Wombats, potoroos, and red-necked wallabies—all different types of marsupial—are commonly spotted here. Kids will especially love investigating the man-made tunnels along the trail that simulate wombat burrows. The first half of the loop is wheelchair accessible.

475

Marion's Lookout

CRADLE MOUNTAIN–LAKE ST. CLAIR NATIONAL PARK
AUSTRALIA

When the British Broadcasting Company went looking for a prehistoric-looking landscape to serve as a backdrop for the documentary *Walking with Dinosaurs*, it found the perfect stand-in for the Mesozoic era in the rugged central highlands of Tasmania. A 5.7-mile loop circles three alpine lakes that sit in the shadow of Cradle Mountain. Hike the route counterclockwise, and you'll climb up to Crater Lake and then to 4,013-foot Marion's Lookout for epic views of the park. You'll then descend past two more lakes before looping back to the start.

476

Overland Track

CRADLE MOUNTAIN–LAKE ST. CLAIR NATIONAL PARK

AUSTRALIA

Follow an ancient Aboriginal path across Cradle Mountain—but be prepared for unpredictable weather.

DISTANCE
40 miles, usually completed in five to seven days

START
Ronny Creek

END
Lake St. Clair

DIFFICULTY
Moderate to hard due to unpredictable weather

SEASON
October to June

ABOVE LEFT The Overland Track follows an ancient Aboriginal path.

LEFT Cradle Mountain and surrounding mountains reflected in Dove Lake.

Connect both of the major highlights of this national park on a 40-mile one-way hike from Cradle Mountain to Lake St. Clair. The route is said to follow an ancient Aboriginal path that runs along the boundary between the Big River and Northern Tasmanian Aboriginal nations, who have lived in these mountains for thousands of years.

During the busy summer season, between October and June, you are required to hike from north to south. There are many variations to the trek, including a 1.7-mile side trip up Cradle Mountain, and an extension along Lake St. Clair that adds 11 miles to the hike. You'll stay in a series of huts along the route or you can camp in a tent, but you must still pay the hut fee.

The most challenging part of this track is the notoriously unpredictable weather. Torrential rainfall is not uncommon in the summer months, and snow can fall on the plateau every month of the year. Bushfires are also a concern in the dry summer months. The route can be completed in winter, when you're permitted to travel in either direction, but be prepared for freezing temperatures and whiteout snowstorms.

477

Hazards Beach and Wineglass Bay

FREYCINET NATIONAL PARK

AUSTRALIA

Tasmania's oldest national park protects most of the Freycinet Peninsula, which hangs off the east coast of the island state. Here, the rugged coastline is composed of pink granite with large, glittering crystals of potassium feldspar. These beautiful rocks are best showcased by the Hazards, a line of mountains between Coles Bay and Wineglass Bay. A 7-mile clockwise loop circles one of the Hazards, Mount Mayson, providing stellar coastal views. The trail also passes through lovely eucalyptus forests and descends to sandy beaches where you can take a cooling dip.

478

Mount Amos

FREYCINET NATIONAL PARK

AUSTRALIA

The most spectacular views of Wineglass Bay are found at the top of Mount Amos, one of the Hazards between Coles Bay and Wineglass Bay. The 2.5-mile out-and-back trail gains 1,300 feet of elevation to the 1,490-foot summit. The route is steep and rocky and requires some scrambling. The big crystals that make up the pink granite rocks can be very sharp, so wear long pants, long sleeves, and gloves. Don't attempt this route in the rain, as the rocks can get very slippery when wet. Fortunately, this park sees 300-plus days of sunshine a year.

BELOW Breathtaking views of Wineglass Bay from the top of Mount Amos.

479

Remarkable Cave Track

TASMAN NATIONAL PARK

AUSTRALIA

Tasman National Park spans the Forestier and Tasman peninsulas and encompasses all of Tasman Island off the east coast of the island state. The park is famous for its towering sea cliffs of columnar dolerite—a volcanic rock that naturally forms columns as it cools. These columns erode into pillars, arches, and sea caves.

This trail of less than half a mile runs along a beach to a cave that has been scooped out of the cliffs by crashing waves. Time your hike for low tide, when you can safely explore inside the cave. Along the way you might see tiny fairy penguins—the smallest species of penguin—as well as Australian fur seals.

RIGHT Look for the Candlestick sea stack on the Remarkable Cave Track.

480

Three Capes Track

TASMAN NATIONAL PARK

AUSTRALIA

Absorb stunning scenery on the spectacular Tasmanian coast where you'll make your way from hut to hut.

DISTANCE
28.5 miles, usually completed in four days

START
Port Arthur

END
Fortescue Bay

DIFFICULTY
Moderate

SEASON
Year-round

This four-day hike takes in almost 30 miles and begins with a boat ride across the bay of Port Arthur to Denmans Cove. From there, you'll make your way through stands of eucalyptus trees to the long, skinny Cape Pillar peninsula, which ends in a narrowing line of dolerite columns that overlook the imposing cliffs of Tasman Island to the south. The trail then runs up and over the high point of the trek on Mount Fortescue and out to the tip of Cape Hauy, before ending at Fortescue Bay, where you can take a celebratory dip before catching the afternoon shuttle bus back to Port Arthur. Three huts spread out along the route offer running water, gas-top cookers, sleeping cots, and toilets. You can also tent camp along the route.

This trail was completed in 2015 and has quickly become one of Australia's most popular multiday hikes. But where's the third cape? Cape Raoul is located west of Port Arthur and can be hiked as a separate day hike. The 8.7-mile out-and-back trail to the tip of the cape makes for an excellent warm-up hike before tackling the Three Capes Track.

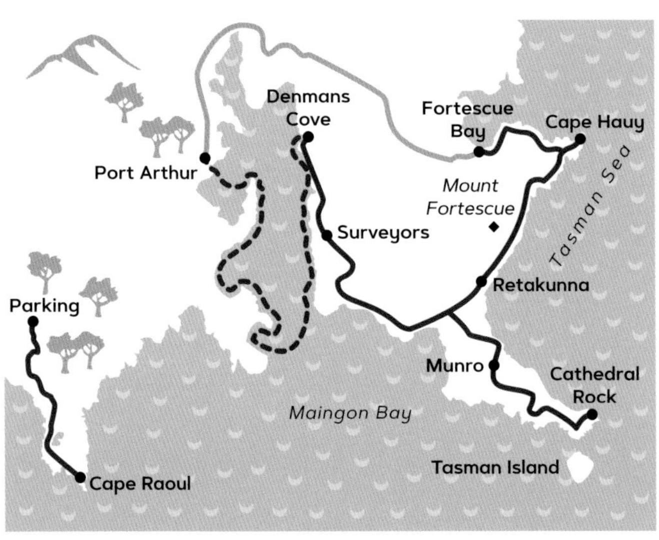

481

Devils Kitchen

TASMAN NATIONAL PARK
AUSTRALIA

This 5.5-mile coastal trail starts at Tasmans Arch—a tall natural bridge eroded into the sea cliffs. The path hugs the coastline, running south to the Devils Kitchen—a narrow cleft cut into the walls—and ends at an overlook of Waterfall Bay, beneath 1,345-foot Clemes Peak. As you gaze out across the Tasman Sea from the top of the sea cliffs, keep an eye out for waterspouts erupting from the blowholes of humpback whales.

ABOVE The picturesque Tasmanian coastline on the Three Capes Track.

LEFT Dolerite columns in Tasman National Park.

482

Tongariro Alpine Crossing

TONGARIRO NATIONAL PARK

NEW ZEALAND

Reenact some of your favorite scenes from *The Lord of the Rings* movies in the locations where they were filmed.

DISTANCE
12 miles one way, elevation gain 2,700 feet

START
Mangatepopo

END
Ketetahi Hot Springs

DIFFICULTY
Moderate

SEASON
Snow-free November to April; winter trips possible with proper snow equipment

Created in 1887, Tongariro, on the North Island, is New Zealand's oldest national park, established after the local Māori tribe campaigned to have the land protected to prevent it from being sold off to European settlers. The park's dramatic volcanic landscapes, which have featured in Māori legends for thousands of years, were the perfect backdrop for director Peter Jackson's re-creation of J. R. R. Tolkien's Middle-earth, with the striking stratovolcano Mount Ngauruhoe starring as Mount Doom.

The best way to see the park is on the Tongariro Alpine Crossing, a 12-mile point-to-point trail that passes through the shadows of the park's three largest mountains: 9,176-foot Ruapehu, 7,516-foot Ngauruhoe, and 6,490-foot Tongariro. It crosses an open alpine landscape of solidified lava flows, active fumaroles, crater lakes, and hot springs. The day hike is part of the Tongariro Northern Circuit, a 31-mile loop that circumnavigates Mount Ngauruhoe and is one of New Zealand's nine Great Walks.

You won't be able to summit "Mount Doom," as the Māori have requested the trail be closed to the public. Don't be too disappointed—its steep slopes are piled with loose ash and the hiking feels more like stumbling uphill through deep sand.

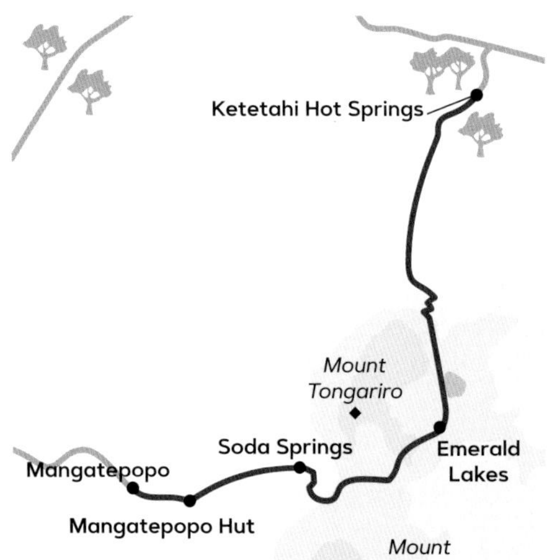

ABOVE RIGHT Hikers make their descent after completing the Tongariro Alpine Crossing.

RIGHT You'll come across the Emerald Lakes just after you've reached the highest point of the trail.

483

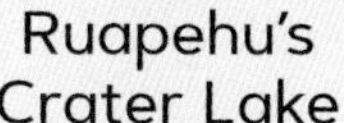

Ruapehu's Crater Lake

TONGARIRO NATIONAL PARK
NEW ZEALAND

Hike to a crater lake near the summit of the North Island's highest mountain, Ruapehu. A challenging 7.3-mile out-and-back trail gains nearly 3,500 feet of elevation on its way up to the crater lake. The route requires some minor scrambling over sharp rocks, so wear sturdy boots and gloves. The word *Ruapehu* means "pit of noise" or "exploding pit" in Māori and indeed there are active volcanic vents under the lake. Eruptions in 1945 and 1995–96 emptied the lake, which has since refilled with rainwater and snowmelt. In 2007, an ash dam broke and released the lake's water, forming a lahar—a moving fluid mass of volcanic debris—that slurried down the mountain, triggering evacuation alarms, but the event caused no injuries and only minor damages.

484

Wainui Falls Track

ABEL TASMAN NATIONAL PARK

NEW ZEALAND

New Zealand's smallest national park is centered on a stretch of pristine beaches between Golden Bay and Tasman Bay on the north tip of the South Island. Up the valley from Wainui Bay, a 2-mile round-trip hike follows the Wainui River upstream through a dense, native fern forest. At Wainui Falls, the river tumbles over the edge of granite blocks and falls 66 feet into a plunge pool. You can swim here, but be ready for a polar plunge—the snowmelt-fed Wainui River is cold year-round. As you hike, look for giant carnivorous *Powelliphanta* snails, which grow to the size of a baseball. Snails sometimes feed on empty shells to recycle the calcium, and collecting the shells is illegal.

485

Abel Tasman Coast Track

ABEL TASMAN NATIONAL PARK

NEW ZEALAND

Of New Zealand's nine Great Walks, the scenic Abel Tasman Coast Track is considered the easiest. The 37-mile route runs from northern Mārahau to Wainui Bay. Most people hike the trail in three to five days, staying in a series of huts along the way. The most challenging part of the trek is timing your pace to match the tides, as some sections can be negotiated only at low tide, so bring a tide chart and plan your route ahead of time.

BELOW Be sure your pace matches the tides when hiking the Abel Tasman Coast Track.

486

Heaphy Track

KAHURANGI NATIONAL PARK

NEW ZEALAND

At almost 50 miles long, the Heaphy Track is the longest of New Zealand's nine Great Walks and is known for crossing the most diverse array of landscapes. The route runs from the upper valley of the Aorere River down to the west coast of the South Island at Kohaihai. The trail begins in a mossy beech forest and gradually descends through tussock moors to an open river valley, with views opening to the Tasman Sea. After crossing the Heaphy River several times on swinging bridges, the last section passes through a nīkau palm forest before emerging at the coast. Most people tackle the track over four to six days, staying in a series of huts spaced one day's walk apart.

487

Mount Robert Circuit

NELSON LAKES NATIONAL PARK

NEW ZEALAND

A favorite among fishermen, this South Island national park is centered on the glacially carved lake of Rotoiti, which is stocked with trout. For epic views of Rotoiti and neighboring Lake Rotoroa, head up 4,662-foot Mount Robert on a 5.6-mile loop trail. Best tackled counterclockwise, the trail climbs 2,000 feet up a steep ridge with excellent views of Rotoiti to the east and the surrounding Saint Arnaud mountain range. The loop can be done as a day hike, or you can plan ahead and spend a night at the Bushline Hut, one of many huts scattered throughout the park.

BELOW Spectacular scenic views of Lake Rotoiti await on the Mount Robert Circuit.

488

Punakaiki Pancake Rocks

PAPAROA NATIONAL PARK

NEW ZEALAND

At Dolomite Point, evenly layered limestone plates have been eroded by wave action, forming surge pools and blowholes. At high tide, water and air trapped in caverns under the rocks burst upward, escaping through the blowhole openings with a whoosh of spray. These are most active at high tide, when there is a southwesterly swell. A wheelchair-accessible loop circles the promontory for less than a mile, offering several overlooks. Don't miss the Devil's Cauldron—a churning surge pool.

489

Devils Punchbowl

ARTHUR'S PASS NATIONAL PARK

NEW ZEALAND

Many rivers and waterfalls on the Australasian continent dry up in the often rainless months between May and September. Devils Punchbowl Creek, however, flows year-round. A 1.5-mile round-trip trail, starting in the village of Arthur's Pass, follows a series of steps to an overlook. The dramatic falls plunge 430 feet down a cliff face and will be at their highest volume in the spring, when snowmelt drains out of the Southern Alps.

LEFT Punakaiki Pancake Rocks are evenly layered limestone plates that look a little like stacks of pancakes.

490

Roberts Point Track

WESTLAND TAI POUTINI NATIONAL PARK

NEW ZEALAND

Oversee the ever-changing Franz Josef Glacier—also known by its Māori name, Kā Roimata o Hine Hukatere.

DISTANCE
6.8 miles, elevation gain 1,800 feet

START
Lake Wombat car park

DIFFICULTY
Moderate

SEASON
Year-round; ice-traction devices or snowshoes may be needed in winter

Westland Tai Poutini National Park is most famous for its glaciers, including the Franz Joseph and Fox Glaciers, which spill out of the Southern Alps and run nearly down to sea level. A 6.8-mile out-and-back trail runs along the former path of the Franz Josef Glacier—now the Waiho Valley—crossing several side creeks on swinging bridges. The trail ends at Roberts Point, which looks directly down on the tip of Franz Josef Glacier.

Most of the world's glaciers have been steadily retreating over the past century, due to global warming and decreasing snowfall. But between 1983 and 2008, several of New Zealand's glaciers, including Franz Josef, actually advanced significantly due to a period of local cooling in the Tasman Sea. Starting in 2008, the trend reversed and the Franz Josef Glacier is now nearly 2 miles shorter than it was in 1920.

ABOVE Franz Josef Glacier is one of the steepest glaciers in New Zealand.

LEFT The mountainous view of Franz Josef Glacier in Westland Tai Poutini National Park.

Welcome Flat Hut

WESTLAND TAI POUTINI NATIONAL PARK
NEW ZEALAND

What's better than a beautiful hike to a cozy mountain hut? Ending your day with a well-earned soak in a natural hot spring, just steps away from camp. The 22-mile round-trip Copland Track runs along the Copland River upstream from the Karangarua River bridge, gaining 2,240 feet on its way up to Welcome Flat Hut, crossing the glacially blue Copland River several times on swinging bridges. The hut has a kitchen, but you'll need to bring your own food, basic cookware, and a sleeping bag—or you can rough it in your own tent on a site around the hut. Hot springs in varying shades of blue and green are a five-minute walk from the hut, where you can enjoy stunning views of the surrounding mountains while you soak. Check the temperature with your hand or foot before immersing yourself in the springs, as some of them can get very hot!

492

Hooker Valley Track

AORAKI MOUNT COOK NATIONAL PARK

NEW ZEALAND

Take a stroll through a spectacularly beautiful landscape among New Zealand's highest peaks and biggest glaciers.

DISTANCE
6.2 miles out and back to Hooker Lake overlook, elevation gain 650 feet

START
White Horse Hill Campground

DIFFICULTY
Easy

SEASON
Year-round; snow-free November to April; in winter, skis or snowshoes may be needed

BELOW Be dazzled by the scenic surroundings of the Southern Alps on this hike.

Aoraki Mount Cook National Park protects a 37-mile stretch of the Southern Alps, and contains most of the country's highest mountains. More than 40 percent of the park is covered by seventy-two glaciers—Tasman Glacier is New Zealand's largest. You can see these on an easy stroll on the Hooker Valley Track, a 6.2-mile out-and-back trail that begins near the Alpine Memorial—a sobering reminder of the toll exacted by the stunning but unforgiving landscape.

As you cross the open grassy meadows and gently rolling alpine tussocks, you'll be treated to unfolding views of the Southern Alps and the glaciers that spill out of the mountains. The trail curls around the shore of Mueller Lake and then climbs up to Hooker Lake, where you'll have unobstructed views of New Zealand's highest mountain: 12,218-foot Aoraki/Mount Cook, with Tasman Glacier on its southern flank.

Mount Ollivier

AORAKI MOUNT COOK NATIONAL PARK
NEW ZEALAND

The summit of Aoraki is best left to experienced mountaineers; the route is highly technical, with a great risk of ice and rockfall, avalanches, and yawning crevasses, not to mention extremely volatile weather. For a more attainable summit, set your sights on Mount Ollivier. This 6,342-foot peak overlooks the Hooker Valley, with scenic views stretching all the way to Aoraki/Mount Cook. The 7.2-mile out-and-back route gains 3,800 feet and can be done in a long day hike, or you can make reservations and spend a night at the Mueller Hut, at just under 6,000 feet.

LEFT The Hooker Valley Track is widely considered one of the best day hikes in New Zealand.

494

Blue Pools Track

MOUNT ASPIRING NATIONAL PARK

NEW ZEALAND

At the confluence of the Blue and Makarora Rivers are a series of bright blue pools. The otherworldly color comes from fine silt in the glacially fed rivers that reflects the sunlight, creating a shimmering blue hue. An easy mile-long out-and-back trail runs through a mature beech forest to two swinging bridges over the Makarora River. Daredevils jump off the second bridge into the water, but more sensible people enjoy the views of the pools and the upstream gorge from the bridge and then ease into the clear blue water from the bank for a cool dip.

BELOW You can swim in the pristine Blue Pools, but the glacier-fed water is very cold.

495

Diamond Lake and Rocky Mountain

MOUNT ASPIRING NATIONAL PARK

NEW ZEALAND

Mount Aspiring's 9,951-foot summit pyramid is well guarded by many grueling miles of rocky terrain. For a more accessible but still spectacular summit, set your sights on 2,543-foot Rocky Mountain. The top can be reached via a 4.4-mile round-trip loop hike that also circles around Diamond Lake. The park recommends taking the east route up, gaining 1,600 feet to the top, and the west route back down. On top, you'll be rewarded with awe-inspiring views of Lake Wānaka and Lake Hawea to the east, Mount Aspiring to the north, and the fjords of Fiordland National Park to the west and south.

496

Milford Track

FIORDLAND NATIONAL PARK

NEW ZEALAND

New Zealand's largest national park sprawls across 12,600 square miles on the southern tip of the South Island. During the last Ice Age, glaciers descending from the 8,000-foot peaks of the inland Darran Mountains to the coast scooped fourteen deep fjords into the landscape. When these glaciers retreated, they left behind the fjords as well as dramatic U-shaped valleys lined by sheer cliffs.

Three of New Zealand's Great Walks run through this park: the Milford, Kepler, and Routeburn Tracks, with the 33-mile Milford Track being the most famous. The four-day route starts at Lake Te Anau and finishes at Milford Sound, passing through rainforests and wetlands, and over the high-alpine Mackinnon Pass before descending to the deep and narrow Milford Sound.

497

Milford Foreshore Walk

FIORDLAND NATIONAL PARK

NEW ZEALAND

Known to the Māori as Piopiotahi in honor of a now-extinct bird, Milford Sound is famous for being New Zealand's most popular tourist attraction. This easy loop is less than a mile long and explores the southeast shoreline of the fjord, where the mouth of the Cleddau River empties into the sound. The fjord supports a variety of marine life, including seals, dolphins, and penguins; humpback and southern right whales are also occasionally seen swimming here.

BELOW Make sure you book months in advance to walk the popular Milford Track.

498

Tavoro Waterfalls

BOUMA NATIONAL PARK

FIJI

The third-largest island in Fiji, Taveuni Island is actually an extinct shield volcano topped by dozens of volcanic cones, including the 4,072-foot Uluigalau, Fiji's second-highest peak. Nearly 80 percent of the island is protected by Bouma National Park, where the rich volcanic soils and steep elevation profile have given rise to tremendous biodiversity. A 3.7-mile trail leads past the three Tavoro waterfalls; the first is the tallest and can be seen after just ten minutes of walking.

ABOVE Lower Tavoro Waterfalls is the tallest of the three, at 78 feet.

499

Sand Dunes Hike

SIGATOKA SAND DUNES NATIONAL PARK

FIJI

Covering less than a square mile, this is one of the smallest national parks in the world. The Sigatoka Sand Dunes are parabolic sand dunes nearly 200 feet high that have formed at the mouth of the Sigatoka River. People have been visiting these dunes for thousands of years—pottery dating back 2,600 years has been uncovered here, along with ancient human burials. The sand is always shifting, but you can follow the crest of the dunes to the river for an out-and-back hike less than a mile long.

Mount Alava Adventure Trail

NATIONAL PARK OF AMERICAN SAMOA

UNITED STATES

Located in the South Pacific more than 6,000 miles from the U.S. mainland, the National Park of American Samoa can be reached with flights from Hawaii, Tonga, Fiji, Australia, and New Zealand. If you've taken the trouble to get to the islands, you might as well hike to the top on the 5.6-mile Mount Alava Adventure Trail—a steep trail that includes fifty-six ladders and 783 steps. From the summit, on the island of Tutuila, you can see Pago Pago Harbor and the rest of the Samoan Islands.

Index

A

Albania
- Balkans Peace Park 238–239
- **Butrint National Park 239**
- Cape of Stillo 239
- Valbona Pass 238–239
- **Valbona Valley National Park 238–239**

Algeria
- **Gouraya National Park 272**
- Oued Djerat Gorge 272–273
- **Tassili n'Ajjer National Park 272–273**
- Yemma Gouraya 272

American Samoa
- Mount Alava Adventure Trail 393
- **National Park of American Samoa 393**

Angola
- Beach Walk 290
- **Kissama National Park 290**

Argentina
- Cerro Guanaco Summit Trail 146
- Costera Trail 147
- Fitz Roy Trail 149
- **Los Glaciares National Park 148–149**
- **Nahuel Huapi National Park 146**
- Perito Moreno Glacier Trail 148
- Refugio Frey 146
- **Tierra del Fuego National Park 146–147**

Aruba
- **Arikok National Park 107**
- Rooi Tambu 107

Australia
- Alligator Gorge 366
- Australian Alps Walking Track 371
- Blue Fish Trail 370
- **Blue Mountains National Park 370**
- Cape to Cape Track 363
- Cathedral Gorge Trail 358
- **Coorong National Park 369**
- **Cradle Mountain-Lake St. Clair National Park 373–375**
- **Daintree National Park 359**
- Devils Kitchen 379
- Devils Thumb 359
- Enchanted Forest 373
- **Flinders Chase National Park 368–369**
- **Freycinet National Park 376**
- Govetts Leap Lookout 370
- Great Ocean Walk 372–373
- Great Otway Walk 372–373
- Hazards Beach and Wineglass Bay 376
- **Hinchinbrook Island National Park 360–361**
- Jack Point Pelican Observatory Walk 369
- Jatbula Trail 359
- Jim Jim Falls Plunge Pool 357
- **Kakadu National Park 356–357**
- Kangaroo Island 368–369
- **Kosciuszko National Park 371**
- **Leeuwin-Naturaliste National Park 363**
- Marion's Lookout 374
- Mossman Gorge Rainforest Circuit 359
- Mount Amos 376
- **Mount Remarkable National Park 366–367**
- Mount Remarkable Summit Loop 367
- **Nambung National Park 362**
- **Nitmiluk National Park 359**
- Overland Track 374–375
- Passage Peak 362
- Pinnacles Outlook Track 362
- **Purnululu National Park 358**
- Remarkable Cave Track 377
- **Sydney Harbour National Park 370**
- **Tasman National Park 377–379**
- Thorsborne Trail 360–361
- Three Capes Track 378
- Ubirr Aboriginal Art Gallery 356–357
- Uluṟu Base Walk 364–365
- **Uluṟu-Kata Tjuṯa National Park 364–365**
- Valley of the Winds 365
- Whitehaven Beach 361
- **Whitsunday Islands National Park 361–362**

Austria
- Celts, Sumpters, and Romans Path 226–227
- Grossglockner Peak 228
- **High Tauern National Park 226–228**
- **Kalkalpen National Park 229**
- Krimml Waterfalls and Old Tauern Trail 228
- Merkersdorf and Umlaufberg 229
- **Thayatal National Park 229**
- Wurbauerkogel Loops 229

B

Bolivia
- **Cotopata National Park 140–141**
- El Choro Trek 140–141
- Pomerape Volcano 140
- **Sajama National Park 140**
- Torotoro Canyon 141
- **Torotoro National Park 141**

Bosnia and Herzegovina
- Štrbaćki Buk 236
- **Sutjeska National Park 236**
- **Una National Park 236**
- Via Dinarica 236

Botswana
- **Chobe National Park 292**
- San Walking Safari 292

Brazil
- **Aparados da Serra National Park 138–139**
- Black Needles 136–137
- Boi River Trail 139
- Cachoeira da Fumaça 137
- **Chapada Diamantina National Park 136–137**
- Cotovelo Trail 138
- Dolphin Bay 135
- Dunes Trek 134–135
- **Fernando de Noronha National Marine Park 135**
- Gruta do Lapão 136
- Iguazú Falls 138
- **Iguazú National Park 138**
- **Itatiaia National Park 136–137**
- **Jericoacoara National Park 134**
- **Lençóis Maranhenses National Park 134–135**
- Lighthouse Trail 135
- Pedra Furada Trail 134

Bulgaria
- **Central Balkan National Park 252**
- Musala Peak 252
- Raiskoto Praskalo Waterfall 252
- **Rila National Park 252, 253**
- Seven Rila Lakes 253

C

Cambodia
- Kbal Spean 342
- **Phnom Kulen National Park 342**

Canada
- Alberta
  - Astotin Lakeview Trail 13
  - **Banff National Park 16–17**
  - Bear's Hump Trail 18–19
  - Continental Divide Trail 20–21
  - **Elk Island National Park 13**
  - **Jasper National Park 14–15**
  - Lake Louise Lakefront Trail 17
  - Salt Pan Lake Trail 18
  - Skyline Trail 14
  - Tunnel Mountain Trail 17
  - Valley of the Five Lakes Loop 14
  - **Waterton Lakes National Park 18–21**
  - **Wood Buffalo National Park 18**
- British Colombia
  - Iceline Trail 11

Pacific Rim National Park and Reserve 10–11
Rainforest Figure Eight 10
Walcott Quarry 12–13
Yoho National Park 11–12
New Brunswick
Fundy Footpath 24–25
Fundy National Park 24–25
Newfoundland
Green Gardens Trail 26
Gros Morne National Park 26–27
Long Range Traverse 26–27
Terra Nova Coastal Trail 27
Terra Nova National Park 27
Nova Scotia
Acadian Trail 26
Cape Breton Highlands National Park 26
Kejimkujik National Park 25
Merrymakedge Beach 25
Ontario
Beausoleil Island Trail 21
Bruce Peninsula National Park 21
Georgian Bay Islands National Park 21
Georgian Bay Marr Lake Trail 21
Québec
Coastal Trail, Fundy National Park 24–25
Forillon National Park 22–23
Gaspé Point Trail 22
International Appalachian Trail 22–23
Yukon
King's Throne Peak Trail 10
Kluane National Park and Reserve 10
Canary Islands
Caldera de Taburiente National Park 266
Chinyero Volcano Loop 264
El Golfo 266
Mirador de los Brecitos a Barranco 266
Mount Teide 264–265
Teide National Park 264–265
Timanfaya National Park 266
Chile
Desolation Pass 144–145
Lauca National Park 140
Monte Terevaka Volcano 142
Petrohué Waterfalls 143
Pomerape Volcano 140
Rano Raraku via Aro o Te Moai 142
Rapa Nui National Park 142
Torres del Paine National Park 145
Vicente Pérez Rosales National Park 143–145
W, O, and Q Circuits 145
China
Badaling National Park 316
Celestial and Lotus Peaks 322
Five-Color Pond 317
Golden Whip Stream 320
Great Wall 316
Guilin and Lijiang River National Park 323
Huangshan National Park 322
Jade Dragon Snow Mountain National Park 320–321
Jiuzhaigou Valley National Park 317–318
Leaping Tiger Gorge 320–321
Nine Dragons Waterfall 322
Pearl Shoal Waterfall 318
Rainbow Rocks 316
Reed Flute Cave Trail 323
Thousand Layer Trail 323
Yuanjiajie Mountain 319
Zhangjiajie National Forest Park 319–320
Zhangye Danxia National Geopark 316
Colombia
Cabo San Juan 124
El Cocuy National Park 125
Nine Stones Trail 124
Ritacuba 125
Tayrona National Park 124
Costa Rica
Arenal 1968 Volcano Trail 114–115
Arenal Volcano National Park 114–115
Corcovado National Park 113
La Leona Madrigal Trail 113
La Trampa 113
Manuel Antonio National Park 113
Poás Volcano National Park 114
Poás Volcano Trail 114
Río Celeste Trail 113
Tenorio Volcano National Park 113
Croatia
Krka National Park 233
Plitvice Lakes Loop 234–235
Plitvice Lakes National Park 234–235
Risnjak National Park 232
Roški Waterfall 233
Trail A, Plitvice Lakes 235
Veliki Risnjak 232
Czech Republic
Bohemian Switzerland National Park 224–225
Cave of Fairies 224
Plechý 224
Prebisch Gate 225
Šumava National Park 224

D

Democratic Republic of the Congo
Bekalikali 275
Gorilla Trek 277
Mount Nyiragongo 276
Nyiragongo National Park 276–277
Salonga National Park 275
Denmark
Kirkeby Forest 188
North Sea Trail 188–189
Thy National Park 188–189
Wadden Sea National Park 188
Dominica
Boiling Lake 104–105
Cabrits National Park 105–107
Douglas Bay Battery Trail 105
Morne Trois Pitons National Park 104–105
Waitukubuli Trail 106–107

E

Ecuador
Cotopaxi National Park 128–129
Darwin Bay 130–131
Galápagos National Park 130–131
Limpiopungo Lagoon 129
Refugio Route 128–129
Sierra Negra Volcano Trail 131
Egypt
Chicken and Mushroom Trail 274
Sahara Desert Hike 274
White Desert National Park 274
England
Catbells, Maiden Moor, and High Spy 169
Coast to Coast Trail 169
Dartmoor National Park 172–173
Lake District National Park 168–169
Long Man of Wilmington 172
Mallyan Spout 170
Mam Tor 171
North York Moors National Park 169–170
Peak District National Park 171
Roseberry Topping 170
Saddle Tor to Hound Tor 173
Scafell Pike 168
South Downs National Park 172
South Downs Way 172
Wistman's Wood 172
Yorkshire Dales National Park 169
Estonia
Karula National Park 240
Rebäse Landscape Trail 240
Ethiopia
Geech Camp to Chenek 275
Simien Mountains National Park 275

F

Fiji
Bouma National Park 392
Sand Dunes Hike 392
Sigatoka Sand Dunes National Park 392
Tavoro Waterfalls 392
Finland
Iisakkipää Fell 187
Little Bear's Ring 186
Oulanka National Park 186
Rautalampi Hiking Trail 186
Urho Kekkonen National Park 186–187
France
Black and White Glaciers 204–205
Calanques de Port-Miou, Port-Pin, and d'En-Vau 202

Calanques de Sugiton and Morgiou 202
Calanques National Park 202
Cascades du Pont d'Espagne Trail 200
Écrins National Park 204–205
Grand Tour, Vanoise National Park 203
Lac du Saut to Lac de la Sassière 203
Lacs des Millefonts Trail 205
Lauvitel Lake 204
Mercantour National Park 205
Pyrénéan Way Trail 200–201
Pyrénées National Park 200–201
Vanoise National Park 203

G

Germany
Bastei Bridge 208–209
Berchtesgaden National Park 210–212
Black Forest National Park 206–207
Elbe River Canyon 207
Königssee to Kärlingerhaus am Funtensee 212
Lothar Path 206
Malerwinkel 212
Saxon Switzerland National Park 207–209
Schrammsteine 209
Watzmann Peak 210–211
Westweg 206
Greece
Mount Olympus 256
Mount Olympus National Park 255–256
Orlias Waterfalls 255
Oxya Viewpoint 255
Pindus Horseshoe 257
Pindus National Park 257
Samariá Gorge National Park 254
Samariá Gorge Trail 254
Vikos-Aoös National Park 254–255
Vikos Gorge Trail 254
Guatemala
Causeways 110
Pacaya Volcano 111
Pacaya Volcano National Park 111
Tikal National Park 110
Guyana
Kaieteur Falls 127
Kaieteur National Park 127

H

Honduras
Jeannette Kawas National Park 111
Jeannette Kawas Trail 111
Pico Bonito National Park 111
Unbelievable Falls 111
Hungary
Aggtelek National Park 250–251
Baradla Cave 250–251
Bükk National Park 250
Bükk Plateau 250
Fertö-Hanság National Park 250
Hany Istók Nature Trail 250
Hortobágy National Park 250
Lake Tisza 250

I

Iceland
Falljökull Glacier 157
Jökulsárlón Glacier Lagoon 158
Kirkjufellsfoss 153
Laugavegur Trail 159
Nautastígur Trail 152–153
Öxarárfoss Waterfall 154–155
Snæfellsjökull National Park 152–153
Svartifoss Waterfall 156–157
Thingvellir National Park 154–155
Vatnajökull National Park 156–159
Vatnshellir Cave 153
India
Corbett Waterfall 337
Hemis National Park 336
Horton Plains National Park 339
Jim Corbett National Park 337
Markha Valley Trek 336
Ranthambore Fort 336–337
Ranthambore National Park 336–337
Valley of Flowers 338–339
Valley of Flowers National Park 338–339
World's End 339
Indonesia
Bromo Tengger Semeru National Park 351
Camp Leakey Orangutan Trek 350
Kelimutu National Park 352
Komodo National Park 351
Mount Kelimutu 352
Mount Semeru 351
Pulau Padar 351
Tanjung Puting National Park 350
Ireland
Burren National Park 160–161
Cliffs of Moher Coastal Walk 160–161
Connemara National Park 161
Devil's Ladder 162
Diamond Hill Loop 161
Killarney National Park 162–163
Lough Ouler Loop 163
Torc Waterfall Walk 163
Wicklow Mountains National Park 163
Israel
Beach Trail 302–303
Caesarea National Park 302–303
Masada National Park 302
Snake Path 302
Wadi Wurayah National Park 302
Wadi Wurayah Trail 302
Italy
Abruzzo, Lazio, and Molise National Park 220–221
Alta Via Dei Monzoni 216
Arcipelago di la Maddalena National Park 223
Aspromonte National Park 222–223
Blue Trail 218–219
Cala Napoletana 223
Cinque Terre National Park 218–219
Dolomites Bellunesi National Park 216–217
Gran Paradiso National Park 214–215
High Paths of the Dolomites 216
Jorio Refuge 220–221
Montalto Mountain 222
Mount Lagazuoi 216
Pietra Cappa to Saint Peter's Rocks 223
Riomaggiore Ring Trail 219
Valnontey River Trail 214–215
Vittorio Sella Refuge 214

J

Japan
Akame 48 Waterfalls Trail 329
Akan-Mashū National Park 331
Fuji-Hakone-Izu National Park 328–329
Karikomi Trail 332
Lake Mashū and Mount Mashū 331
Mount Fuji 328–329
Mount Rausu 330
Muro-Akame-Aoyama Quasi-National Park 329
Nikkō National Park 332
Shiretoko National Park 330
Valley of the Dragon King 332

K

Kazakhstan
Altyn-Emel National Park 310–311
Singing Dunes 310–311
Kenya
Central Tower Trail 282
Hell's Gate National Park 282
Maasai Mara National Park 283
Maasai Mara Walking Safari 283
Mount Kenya National Park 284
Mount Kenya via Sirimon Route 284
Mount Longonot 284
Mount Longonot National Park 284
Nairobi National Park 285
Nairobi Safari Walk 285
Ol Njorowa Gorge 282

L

Latvia
Gauja National Park 240
Great Ķemeri Bog Boardwalk 241
Ķemeri National Park 241
Turaida Castle Museum Reserve Loop 240

M

Madagascar
Andasibe-Mantadia National Park 299
Andringitra National Park 300
Isalo National Park 300
Pic Boby 300

Piscine Naturelle 300
Sacred Waterfall Circuit 299
Malaysia
Bukit Teresek 347
Canopy Walk 346
Kepayang Besar Caves 348–349
Monkey Beach Lighthouse 346
Penang National Park 346
Taman Negara National Park 347–349
Mexico
Basaseachic Falls 109
Basaseachic Falls National Park 109
Tulum National Park 108
Walled City 108
Mongolia
Eagle Valley 314
Gobi Gurvan Saikhan National Park 314–315
Khongoryn Els Singing Dunes 315
Khövsgöl Nuur National Park 312–313
Mother Sea 312–313
Montenegro
Bobotov Kuk 237
Durmitor Ice Cave 237
Durmitor National Park 237
Morocco
Akchour Cascades and Bridge of God 271
Forgotten Forest Loop 267
Haut Atlas Oriental National Park 268–269
Ifrane National Park 267
Kasbah du Toubkal 270
Monkey Trail 267
Mount Lakraa 268
Talassemtane National Park 268, 271
Tislit and Isli Lakes 268–269
Toubkal Circuit 270
Toubkal National Park 270

N

Namibia
Namib-Naukluft National Park 290–291
Olive Trail 290
Waterkloof Trail 291
Nepal
Chitwan National Park 335
Chitwan Safari Loop 335
Gokyo Lakes 334–335
Langtang National Park 332
Langtang Valley 332
Sagarmatha National Park 332–335
Tengboche 332–333
Netherlands
Drentsche AA National Park 190
Hoge Veluwe National Park 191
Hoge Veluwe Rondje Bezoekerscentrum Trail 191
Meinweg National Park 190
Pieterpad 190
Waalsberg-Meinvennen 190
New Zealand
Abel Tasman Coast Track 382
Abel Tasman National Park 382
Aoraki Mount Cook National Park 388–389
Arthur's Pass National Park 384–385
Blue Pools Track 390
Devils Punchbowl 385
Diamond Lake and Rocky Mountain 390
Fiordland National Park 391
Heaphy Track 383
Hooker Valley Track 388–389
Kahurangi National Park 383
Milford Foreshore Walk 391
Milford Track 391
Mount Aspiring National Park 390
Mount Ollivier 389
Mount Robert Circuit 383
Nelson Lakes National Park 383
Paparoa National Park 385
Punakaiki Pancake Rocks 384–385
Roberts Point Track 386–387
Ruapehu's Crater Lake 381
Tongariro Alpine Crossing 380–381
Tongariro National Park 380–381
Wainui Falls Track 382
Welcome Flat Hut 387
Westland Tai Poutini National Park 386–387
Nicaragua
Crater Hike 112
Masaya Volcano National Park 112
Norway
Besseggen Ridge 181
Hardangervidda and Mannevasstoppen 182
Hardangervidda National Park 182
Husedalen Waterfalls 182
Jostedalsbreen National Park 180–181
Mount Skåla 180
Nigardsbreen Glacier 180

P

Panama
Bastimentos Island National Park 116–117
Darién National Park 120–121
Pirre Mountain Trail 120–121
Quetzal Trail 118–119
Volcán Barú 117
Volcán Barú National Park 117–119
Wizard Beach 116–117
Peru
Huascarán National Park 131
Laguna 69 131
Lake Otorongo 132–133
Manú National Park 132–133
Santa Cruz Trek 131
Philippines
Puerto Princesa Subterranean River National Park 353
Underground River 353
Poland
Białowieża Forest National Park 242
Kościeliska Valley 244
Morskie Oko 245
Obszar Ochrony Ścisłej 242
Pieniny National Park 243
Priečne Sedlo Loop 244
Słowiński National Park 242–243
Tatra National Park 244–245
Three Crowns 243
Wydma Łacka 242–243
Portugal
Geira Roman Road 199
Pedra Bela Trail 198–199
Peneda-Gerês National Park 198–199

R

Réunion Island
Cap Noir and Roche Verre Bouteille Circuit 301
Peak of the Furnace 301
Réunion National Park 301
Romania
Cheile Nerei-Beuşniţa National Park 252
Ochiul Beiului 252
Russia
Alpine Meadows and Medvezhiy Waterfall 306
Great Baikal Trail 310
Land of the Leopard National Park 310
Losiny Ostrov National Park 306
Mount Markova 308–309
Mount Zyuratkul 307
Pribaikalsky National Park 310
Semivyorstka Trail 310
Sochi National Park 306–307
White Rocks Canyon 307
Yauza River 306
Zabaikalsky National Park 308–309
Zyuratkul National Park 307

S

Scotland
Ben Macdui 165
Bracklinn Falls Circuit 166
Cairngorms National Park 164–165
Glen Clova Mayar and Driesh 165
Lairig Ghru 164
Loch Lomond & the Trossachs National Park 166–167
Ptarmigan Ridge Path 166
West Highland Way 166–167
Senegal
Gandiol Lighthouse 271
Langue de Barbarie National Park 271
Slovakia
Dry White Gorge 246
Ďumbier and Chopok Peaks Loop 249
Green Lake 247
High Tatras National Park 246–247
Low Tatras National Park 249
Slovak Karst National Park 248–249

Slovak Paradise National Park 246
Štrbské Lake to Popradské Lake 246–247
Tatranská Magistrála 247
Zádielska Valley 248–249
Slovenia
Mostnica Gorge 230–231
Mount Triglav 232
Triglavski National Park 230–232
Valley of the Seven Lakes 232
Vintgar Gorge Loop 230
South Africa
Addo Elephant National Park 294–295
Alexandria Hiking Trail 294–295
Garden Route National Park 296–297
Kruger National Park 299
Olifants Wilderness Trail 299
Otter Trail 296
Skeleton Gorge Trail 298–299
Table Mountain National Park 298–299
Woody Cape Nature Reserve 294
Zuurberg Trail 295
South Korea
Bukhansan National Park 327
Bukhansan Peak 327
Naejangsan National Park 326
Naejangsan Ridge 326
Seoraksan Castle 326
Seoraksan National Park 326
Spain
Atlantic Islands of Galicia National Park 194–195
Cahorros de Monachil 196–197
Castle of Monfragüe 196–197
Covadonga Lakes Trail 192–193
Faja de las Flores 195
Hunter's Trail 194
Monfragüe National Park 196–197
Mulhacén 197
Ons Island Lighthouse and Castle Route 194
Ordesa y Monte Perdido National Park 194–195
Picos de Europa National Park 192–193
Sierra Nevada National Park 196–197
Sweden
Abisko National Park 182–185
Aurora Sky Station Loop 182–183
King's Trail 184–185
Sarek Circular Trail 184
Sarek National Park 184
Switzerland
Swiss National Park 213
Val Trupchun 213

T

Taiwan
Mount Qixing 324–325
Mysterious Valley Trail 325
Taroko National Park 325
Yangmingshan National Park 324–325
Yangmingshan Trail 324
Zhuilu Old Trail 325
Tanzania
Arusha National Park 287–289
Kilimanjaro National Park 286–287
Lake Tanganyika 285
Lumemo Trail 289
Mahale Mountains National Park 285
Mount Kilimanjaro 286–287
Mount Meru 288–289
Mount Meru Waterfall Loop 287
Sanje Waterfall 288
Serengeti National Park 287
Udzungwa Mountains National Park 288–289
Walking Safari 287
Thailand
Buddha's Footprint Trail 340
Doi Suthep-Pui National Park 340
Erawan Falls 341
Erawan National Park 341
Khao Lak-Lam Ru National Park 341
Khao Sok National Park 340
Little White Sandy Beach 341
Ton Kiol Waterfall 340
Tunisia
Ichkeul National Park 271
Lake Ichkeul 271
Turkey
Beydağlari Coastal National Park 260
Göreme National Park 258–259
Köprülü Canyon 261
Köprülü Canyon National Park 261
Lycian Way 260
Mount Nemrut 260
Nemrut Daği National Park 260
Rose and Red Valleys 259
Zemi Valley Loop 258–259

U

Uganda
Bwindi Impenetrable National Park 277
Chimpanzee Trek 278
Ivy River Trail 277
Kibale National Park 278
Kitum Cave 281
Mount Elgon National Park 280–281
Murchison Falls 279
Murchison Falls National Park 279
Rwenzori National Park 277
Sipi Falls 280–281
Weissman's Peak 277
United Kingdom
see England; Scotland; Wales
United States
Alaska
Bartlett Cove to Point Gustavus Beach Trail 35
Brooks Fall 32
Denali National Park and Preserve 30–31
Gates of the Arctic National Park and Preserve 28–29
Glacier Bay National Park and Preserve 35
Harding Ice Field Trail 34–35
Horseshoe Lake Trail 30
Katmai National Park 32–33
Kenai Fjords National Park 34–35
Koyukuk River Route 28–29
Mount Healy Overlook Trail 31
Savage Alpine Trail 30–31
Seven Pass Route 35
Valley of Ten Thousand Smokes 33
Wrangell-Saint Elias National Park and Preserve 35
Arizona
Arizona National Scenic Trail 77
Boucher Trail to Hermit Trail Loop 76
Bright Angel Point Trail 77
Bright Angel Trail to Three-Mile Resthouse 75, 76
Grand Canyon National Park 74–77
King Canyon Wash Trail 78–79
Long Logs Trail and Agate House Trail Loop 79
Petrified Forest National Park 79
Rim Trail 74–75
Saguaro National Park 78–79
Wasson Peak 79
Arkansas
Grand Promenade 93
Hot Springs National Park 92–93
Sunset to Hot Springs Mountain Loop 92–93
California
Badwater Basin Salt Flats Trail 56
Bumpass Hell Trail 46
Cathedral Lakes Trail 50
Cavern Point Loop Trail 56–57
Channel Islands National Park 56–57
Clouds Rest 48–49
Condor Gulch Trail to High Peaks Trail Loop 47
Congress Trail 52
Death Valley National Park 54–56
49 Palms Oasis Trail 58–59
Hidden Valley Nature Trail 58–59
High Sierra Trail 52
John Muir Trail 51
Joshua Tree National Park 58–59
Kings Canyon National Park 52–53
Lady Bird Johnson Grove Trail 44–45
Lassen Peak Trail 46
Lassen Volcanic National Park 46
Lower Yosemite Falls Trail 50
Mist Falls 52–53
Pinnacles National Park 47
Redwood Creek Trail 45
Redwood National Park 44–45
Sequoia National Park 52
Telescope Peak Trail 54–55
Yosemite National Park 48–51
Zabriskie Point 54–55

Colorado
Black Canyon of the Gunnison National Park 82–83
Chasm Lake 80–81
Great Sand Dunes National Park and Preserve 83
Longs Peak via the Keyhole 80
Mesa Verde National Park 81
North Vista Trail to Exclamation Point 82
Petroglyph Point Trail 81
Rocky Mountains National Park 80–81
Star Dune 83
Florida
Anhinga Trail 100–101
Biscayne National Park 102–103
Dry Tortugas National Park 103
Everglades National Park 100–101
Fort Jefferson Loop 103
Shark Valley Trail 100–101
Spite Highway and Maritime Heritage Trail 102–103
Hawai'i
Haleakalā National Park 37
Hawai'i Volcanoes National Park 36–37
Observatory Trail to Mauna Loa 36–37
Pipiwai Trail 37
Pu'u Loa Petroglyphs 37
Indiana
Cowles Bog Trail 95
Indiana Dunes National Park 95
Kentucky
Beneath Your Feet Tour and Sinkhole Trail 96
Mammoth Cave National Park 95–96
Violet City Lantern Tour 95
Maine
Acadia National Park 98
Cadillac Mountain South Ridge Trail Loop 98
Michigan
Greenstone Ridge Trail 94
Isle Royale National Park 94
Scoville Point Loop 94
Minnesota
Blind Ash Bay Trail 91
Voyageurs National Park 91
Montana
Glacier National Park 61
Highline Trail 61
Trail of the Cedars 61
Nevada
Bristlecone Pine Glacier Trail 60–61
Grand Palace Tour of Lehman Caves 61
Great Basin National Park 60–61
New Mexico
Alkali Flat Trail 84
Big Room Trail 85
Carlsbad Caverns National Park 85
Natural Entrance Trail 85
White Sands National Park 84
North Carolina
Great Smoky Mountains National Park 100
Ramsey Cascades Trail 100
North Dakota
Caprock Coulee Loop 88–89
Maah Daah Hey Trail 88–89
Theodore Roosevelt National Park 88–89
Ohio
Brandywine Gorge Trail 97
Buckeye Trail 97
Cuyahoga Valley National Park 97
Oregon
Cleetwood Cove Trail 42–43
Crater Lake National Park 42–43
Garfield Peak Trail 42
South Carolina
Boardwalk Loop Trail 100
Congaree National Park 100
South Dakota
Badlands National Park 90
Notch Trail 90
Wind Cave National Park 90
Wind Cave Tour 90
Tennessee
Great Smoky Mountains National Park 100
Texas
Big Bend National Park 86–87
Guadalupe Mountains National Park 86
Guadalupe Peak Trail 86
Lost Mine Trail 87
McKittrick Canyon Trail 86
Santa Elena Canyon Trail 86–87
Utah
Angel's Landing 67
Arches National Park 72–73
Bryce Canyon National Park 68
Canyonlands National Park 68–69
Capitol Reef National Park 70–71
Cassidy Arch Trail 70
Chesler Park Loop Trail 69
Delicate Arch Trail 73
Devils Garden Loop Trail 72–73
Fairyland Loop Trail 68
Grand View Point Trail 69
Halls Creek Narrows 70–71
Narrows 66
Observation Point 66
Subway 67
Sunset Point to Sunrise Point 68
Zion National Park 66–67
Virginia
Appalachian Trail 98
Old Rag Mountain Loop 99
Rose River Trail 99
Shenandoah National Park 98–99
Washington
Blue Lake Trail 39
Cascade Pass Trail 39
Hoh River Trail to Blue Glacier 38–39
Mount Rainier National Park 39–41
North Cascades National Park 39
Olympic National Park 38–39
Panorama Point 39
Wonderland Trail 40–41
West Virginia
Long Point 98
New River Gorge National Park 98
Wyoming
Bechler Canyon 64
Cascade Canyon Trail 64
Grand Teton National Park 64–65
Mammoth Hot Springs Trail 63
String Lake Trail 64
Teton Crest Trail 64–65
West Thumb Geyser Basin Trail 62–63
Yellowstone National Park 62–64

V

Venezuela
Angel Falls 126–127
Canaima National Park 125–127
Mount Roraima 125
Vietnam
Cát Bà National Park 345
Cát Tiên National Park 344–345
Crocodile Lake 344–345
Hoàng Liên National Park 345
Kim Gaio 345
Mount Fansipan 345
Paradise, Dark, and Hang Én Caves 342–343
Phong Nha-Kẻ Bàng National Park 342–343
Virgin Islands
Honeymoon Beach 105
Petroglyph Trail 105
Virgin Islands National Park 105

W

Wales
Aberglaslyn Gorge 178–179
Llyn Idwal Trail 178
Pembrokeshire Coast National Park 174–175
Pembrokeshire Coast Path 174
St. David's Peninsula Circular Walk 175
Snowdonia National Park 176–179
Snowdon via Watkin Path 176–177
Welsh 3000s 178

Z

Zimbabwe
Boiling Point 293
Victoria Falls National Park 293
Zambezi River Walk 293

Image credits

t = top, b = bottom, l = left, r = right

Alamy: GERAULT Gregory / Hemis 10; Mari Omori / All Canada Photos 12; John Sylvester 18–9; Andreas Prott 22; Dan Leeth 23; Mike Grandmaison / All Canada Photos 26–7; Carl Johnson / Design Pics Inc 28–9; Joe Eldridge 52–3; darekm101 / RooM the Agency 81; Jim Brandenburg / Minden Pictures 94; BRUSINI Aurélien / Hemis 104; RIEGER Bertrand / Hemis *t* 107; Dipak Pankhania 111; Ida Pap 116; Panama Landscapes by Oyvind Martinsen 120; Michael Nolan / robertharding 130; Pulsar Imagens 136; Christian Kapteyn / imageBROKER 147; Realimage 177; PearlBucknall 178–9; Markus Thomenius 187; Willi Rolfes / Premium Stock Photography GmbH 191; Andrés Benitez / Westend61 GmbH 194; Dolores Giraldez Alonso *t* 196–7; Ken Welsh 214–5; Random Lights Photography *b* 219; Martin Siepmann / imageBROKER 229; Katerina Parahina 241; Sergey Dzyuba 244; Richard Nebesky / robertharding 247; Zadielska dolina, Slovakia 248; Hercules Milas 254; Ioannis Mantas 257; David Keith Jones / Images of Africa Photobank 275; Bella Falk 276; MikeAlpha01 280; RZAF_Images 282; Konrad Wothe / Image Professionals GmbH 285; Andreas Strauss / Image Professionals GmbH 290; Bert de Ruiter 291; Michael Valigore 300; Sergey Fomin / Russian Look Ltd. 306; DPK-Photo 307; John White Photos 312; Paul Quayle 325; travel Photo/a.collectionRF / amana images inc. 330; Graham Prentice 336–7; HIRA PUNJABI 339; H-AB 347; Subodh Agnihotri 351; Frommenwiler Fredy / Prisma by Dukas Presseagentur GmbH 358; Andrew Watson *b* 369; Andrew Bain 371; Ray Wilson 377; janetteasche / RooM the Agency *t* 379; Matthew Williams-Ellis / robertharding *t* 381; Jon Sparks 383

Getty: James Gabbert *t* 13; Anna Gorin 21; Blue Barron Photo 91; John Coletti 141; Delpixart 173; Jedsada Puangsaichai 180; AGF 205; 360cities.net 237; Barcroft Media *t* 279, 343

Mary Caperton Morton: 4–5, *b* 7, 11, *b* 13, 25, 38, 42, 43, 46, *t* 49, *b* 49, 50, 51, *t* 54, *b* 54, *t* 58–9, *b* 58–9, 59, 65, 66, 67, 68, 69, *t* 73, *b* 73, *t* 75, *b* 75, 76, 77, 78–9, 82, 83, 84, 85, 86–7, 90, 98, 99, 101, 128, 152–3, 158, *t* 165, *b* 165

NPS: NPS Photo *b* 32, 44, 95, *b* 97; Jim Pfeiffenberger 34–5; Kurt Moses 47; Laura Thomas *t* 89; Geoscientists-in-the-Parks *t* 97; Shaun Wolfe 103

Shutterstock: f9project 3, 261; Pete Stuart 6–7, 203; Roman Khomlyak 8–9, 41; GUDKOV ANDREY *t* 32; MN Studio 37; Kris Wiktor 45; Bram Reusen *t* 56, 93; Kyle T Perry *b* 56; Sandra Foyt 60; LOUIS-MICHEL DESERT 63; The Steve 71; Sean Xu 80; drew the hobbit *b* 89; Kelly vanDellen 92; Tadas_Jucys *b* 107; Alexander Sviridov 108; Aleksandar Todorovic *t* 110; Diego Grandi *b* 110; Esdelval 115; Einer Garcia 118; Milan Zygmunt 119; makinajp 122–3, 138; Douglas Olivares 126; Vadim Petrakov 127; RPBaiao 132; Jeff Cremer 133; Mapu Fotografia 143; Sabine Hortebusch 144; viktorio 155; Dawid K Photography 162; zkbld 163; Nadine Karel *b* 166; Michael Hilton 168; Muessig 171; Charlesy *b* 174; Travellor70 188–9; Alxcrs 195; pcruciatti 202; Aliaksandr Antanovich *t* 219; ValerioMei 220; Liudmila Parova 221; Marco Barone 223; Nadezda Murmakova 224; Josef Skacel 225; Andrea Cimini 231; DaLiu 233; ollirg 238; EvijaF 240; Majonit 242; Milosz Maslanka 243; Anna Szella 245; Robi-Robertos *t* 251; Tainar *b* 251; MNStudio 255; dinosmichail 256; aquatarkus 258; kataleewan intarachote 260; marketa1982 269; Dmitry Pichugin *t* 273, *b* 273; Oleg Znamenskiy 274; Martin Mecnarowski 278; Cheryl Ramalho *b* 279; Pixeljoy 283; Jake Keeton 294; Noradoa *b* 295; Max Allen *t* 297; Great Stock *b* 297; aphotostory 304–5, 323; Nikitin Victor *t* 309; Katvic *b* 309; Piu_Piu 311; otorongo 314; Kevin Tsang 315; Efired 317; OLOS 319; martinho Smart 320–1; Macro-Man 322; Guitar Photographer 328; CHEN FANGXIANG 331; Daniel Prudek 333; Olga Danylenko 335; riddhi varsani 338; Nattakritta Phromnate 340; SUWIT NGAOKAEW 341; DAIKI.I 342; JamesEHunt *t* 345; Nella *b* 345; Ilya Sviridenko 346; Julian Peters Photography 348; Felineus 349; Christopher Mazmanian 353; Aaron Zimmermann 356; Robirensi 357; Thomas Rattenberger 360; Coral Brunner 361; Matt Deakin 363; Donna Latour 366; mastersky 367; Andrea Izzotti 368; Uwe Bergwitz *t* 369; irisphoto1 370; Olga Kashubin *b* 374; crbellette 376; Blue Planet Studio *b* 379, 391; Maridav *b* 381; Chingfoto 386; Puripat Lertpunyaroj 387; Daniel Huebner 388; Lin4pic 390; Don Mammoser 392; emperorcosar 393

Unsplash: Pavel Brodsky 15; Zak Jones 16; Joris Beugels 31; Suresh Ramamoorthy 102; Etienne Delorieux 113; Nate Landy 124; David Emrich 135; Sam Power 142; Sean Wang 156; Michael Hacker 159; Connor Misset 160; Mick Haupt 161; Ilya Ilford *t* 166; Matthew Waring 169; Trevor Pye 170; Matt Gibson 172; Red Hat Factory 181; Dylan Shaw 182–3; Oscar Ekholm Grahn 185; Miriam Eh 186; Ben Berwers 190; Quick PS 193; Sven Vee 206–7; Cezar Sampaio 208; Colin Moldenhauer 211; Joshua Earle *b* 217; Karsten Würth 226; Marek Lehák 246; Ralf 262–3, 270; Michal Mrozek 265; Thibault Mokuenko 266; Random Institute 277; Kristoffer Darj 287; Luke Tanis 292; ROMAIN TERPREAU *t* 295; Tom Podmore 298; Jim Molloy 303; Vista Wei 316; Mirko Blicke 326; Karl JK Hedin 327; Tomáš Malík 329; Dimitry B 350; Mohamad Ibrahim *t* 374; Will Turner 389

Wiki Commons: Saraedum 112; Yosemite *t* 125; M M from Switzerland *b* 125; Portal dos Canyons 139; Macidiano 146; Dreamy Pixel 150–1, 228; Bryan Ledgard 154; Dave Croker *t* 174; Por los caminos de Málaga *b* 196–7; Razevedo172010 198–9; Jean-Christophe BENOIST 200; Krzysztof Golik 201; Myo at wts Wikivoyage 212; WillYs Fotowerkstatt 213; Terensky 222; Dreamy Pixel 228; Se90 232; Nacionalni park Una 236; Tobias Klenze 239; Giuseppe Milo 252; Anthony Ganev 252–3; Noumenon 259; Reda Abouakil 267; Nicholas Gosse 271; Jyotkanwal S. Bhambra 284; Ferdinand Reus 293; Sylvain JORIS 301; Jakub Michankow 354–5, 362; Hector Garcia 382; Christian Michel 384–5

Also: Adam Lint 4; Rica Dearman 109, *t* 235, *b* 235; Daniel Rainwater 149; c Kiki Deere *t* 217, 289; Jeremy Scott @jeremyscott007 318, *b* 365, *t* 373, *b* 373; Michael Nelson, Parks Australia *t* 365